A History of Poland

PALGRAVE ESSENTIAL HISTORIES
General Editor: Jeremy Black

This series of compact, readable and informative national histories is designed to appeal to anyone wishing to gain a broad understanding of a country's history.

Published

A History of Spain   *Simon Barton*
A History of the British Isles (2nd edn)   *Jeremy Black*
A History of Israel   *Ahron Bregman*
A History of Ireland   *Mike Cronin*
A History of the Pacific Islands   *Steven Roger Fischer*
A History of the United States (2nd edn)   *Philip Jenkins*
A History of Denmark   *Knud J.V. Jespersen*
A History of Poland   *Anita J. Prażmowska*
A History of India   *Peter Robb*
A History of China   *J.A.G. Roberts*

Further titles are in preparation

A History of Poland

Anita J. Prażmowska

palgrave
macmillan

First published 2004 by
PALGRAVE MACMILLAN
Houndmills, Basingstoke, Hampshire RG21 6XS and
175 Fifth Avenue, New York, N.Y. 10010
Companies and representatives throughout the world

PALGRAVE MACMILLAN is the global academic imprint of the Palgrave Macmillan division of St. Martin's Press, LLC and of Palgrave Macmillan Ltd. Macmillan® is a registered trademark in the United States, United Kingdom and other countries. Palgrave is a registered trademark in the European Union and other countries.

ISBN-13: 978-0-3339-7253-3   hardback
ISBN-10: 0333-972538   hardback
ISBN-13: 978-0-3339-7254-0   paperback
ISBN-10: 0333-972546   paperback

This book is printed on paper suitable for recycling and made from fully managed and sustained forest sources. Logging, pulping and manufacturing processes are expected to conform to the environmental regulations of the country of origin.

A catalogue record for this book is available from the British Library.

Library of Congress Cataloging-in-Publication Data
Prazmowska, Anita.
    A history of Poland/Anita J. Prazmowska.
        p. cm.—(Palgrave essential histories)
    Includes bibliographical references and index.
    ISBN 0-333-97253-8 (cloth)—ISBN 0-333-97254-6 (pbk)
        1. Poland—History. I. Title. II. Series.
DK4140.P73 2004
943.8—dc22
                                        2003070197

Printed and bound in Great Britain by
4edge Ltd, Hockley. www.4edge.co.uk

Contents

List of Maps

All the maps are taken from Dennis P. Hupchick and Harold E. Cox, *The Palgrave Concise Historical Atlas of Eastern Europe* (Basingstoke and New York: Palgrave Macmillan, 2001). Copyright © Dennis P. Hupchick and Harold E. Cox. Reprinted with permission of Palgrave Macmillan.

Preface

If we view history as a discipline the role of which is to explain the present, we run the risk of being selective in what we consider relevant historic information. We might well miss or leave out what was important at the time, but which has no relevance to today's developments. We are likely to overlook trends, developments, movements and facts that were not part of the determinist progression through centuries. But most importantly we are likely to end up neither studying, nor explaining, history.

The twentieth century's preoccupation with nation states made it difficult to conceive that the right of nations to rule themselves was not the driving force in developments of the past. Even less are we willing to accept, without some hesitation, that this is not the ultimate right of each nation. Where a national group experienced persecution, mistreatment or oppression in recent history, the desire for independence and the right to self-determination was strengthened. A present-day historian and his audience might only too easily slip into an analysis of only those factors which led to that manifold destiny of national independence.

'The Polish Question' had dominated contemporary debates on the rights of national groups to independence in Europe. Until recently, when asked to make any comment on Poland and Poles, outsiders would refer to the nation's suffering and pain, betrayal and denial of rights. That is because they usually refer to the fate of the Polish kingdom during the partitions and the long fight for independence. But Polish history consists of more than just suffering. Nor is the history of Polish people that of victims, suffering because they had no say over their fate. It has been my attempt to move beyond issues which contributed directly to Poland's place in present-day Europe. I was not inclined to view Poles as passive in the face of events unfolding around them. The aim of the present volume of *The History of Poland* is to probe into the history of Poland, beyond the facts which determined the character of present-day Poland. Indeed, the history of Poland would be so much poorer, were its parameters to be defined by what we know to be present-day Poland. This volume attempts to look at the history of people who inhabited the territory of what came to be known as the Kingdom of Poland, at its rulers and their objectives and finally at the factors which moulded and buffeted the region.

When I was asked by Palgrave to write this volume, I accepted the commission with excitement. I knew that in the process of writing the present volume, my understanding of past events would be extended. I also expected that many issues, which until now I took as said, would never again seem either obvious or simple. I admit to having found this commission intellectually challenging. Looking at the history of one's people was bound to be a test of historic skills. My failures and successes can ultimately be judged by the readers.

Many people had influenced me in my attempt to understand my past and that of Poland. Franciszka and Stefan Themerson had always encouraged me to be sceptical of received wisdoms. Tamara Deuscher encouraged me to probe further and not to be constrained by reactions to my findings. I remain indebted to them for pushing me to be bolder in my conclusions. But my biggest debt of gratitude is to Jan Toporowski, without whose help and companionship my life would have been incomplete. To Miriam and her English Babcia I dedicate this book.

Poland under Mieszko I, 970
Additions to Poland under Bolesław I, 1018
- - - - Border of the Kingdom of Bohemia

0   100   200   300 miles
0   100 200 300 400 kilometres

Map 1 Poland, late 10th–13th Centuries.

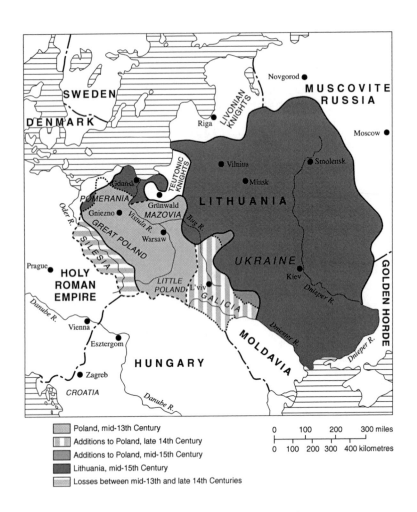

Map 2 Poland, 14th–15th Centuries.

Border of Poland in 1771
Border of Poland following the First Partition, 1772
Border of Poland following the Second Partition, 1793
Central European Borders after the Third Partition, 1795
Polish Lands taken by Russia
Polish Lands taken by Prussia
Polish Lands taken by the Habsburg Empire

| 0 | 50 | 100 | 150 | 200 miles |

| 0 | 100 | 200 | 300 kilometres |

Map 3 Poland, 1772–95.

— — — Border of Polish Nationalist Claims, Versailles, 1919
------ Proposed Curzon Line
············ Limit of Polish Army Advance, June 1920
- - - - - Limit of Soviet Red Army Advance, August 1920
▓ Poland after the Treaty of Riga, March 1921

Map 4 Poland, 1920–22.

1

. . . .

The People of Central Europe

History has never been free from the politics of today. Only too frequently it has been a tool in the hands of those who use the past in order to justify present-day attitudes and actions. It has been suggested that Central Europeans are particularly adept at using remote historical events to justify the present. Thus in their claim to justify Germany's right of expansion eastwards some historians have suggested that the catalyst for the creation of the first Slav states had not emerged from within the local tribes, but was the result of German influence and organisation. By the same token Polish historians have defined as 'Polish' prehistoric archaeological evidence which in reality could at best only be evidence of tribal or regional developments, since the Polish state did not exist at the time. Any claim that evidence reflects some early 'Polish' national consciousness would be pure invention. The nineteenth century, preoccupied with the rise and fall of nation states, has created a particularly fertile ground for the proliferation of such spurious historic debates, aimed at suggesting that from their earlier days people wished to be ruled by 'their own people'. Since the creation of ethnically homogenous states is nearly entirely confined to the twentieth century, we should be careful in ascribing to any earlier development significance which was not present at the time.

During the inter-war period historians seeking to justify Poland's extended boundaries to the east suggested that the area which should be considered as the cradle of the Polish nation is that defined by the rivers Vistula, Dnieper, San and Dniester. After the Second World War when Poland's frontiers were shifted westwards a new historic interpretation was put forward. Since Poland lost over one-third of its inter-war territories to the Soviet Union, but gained undeniably German areas of East and West Prussia together with a western border on the river Oder, the politically correct view changed accordingly. During the Communist period the cradle of Polish nationhood was redefined as being between the Vistula and the Oder rivers, which flow from the south to the Baltic Sea in the north. The political stability achieved at the end of the twentieth century and the acceptance by Poland's neighbours that the present borders are here to stay, have created preconditions for a less impassioned and more academic debate. The history of the present-day Polish state can be hopefully freed from the duty it had of supporting the reasons of state and concentrate on presenting the historic developments that resulted in the creation of the present-day Polish state. In Poland's case, the past is sufficiently turbulent and interesting not to need further embellishment.

Geography has played an important role in defining the boundaries within which human settlements developed in northern Europe. In the areas where the first Polish kingdom was to emerge at the beginning of the tenth century, the geographical features were sufficiently prominent to have made a marked impact on the evolution of human settlements. These determined movement across the region, contact between people, trade, but also the exchange and spread of ideas. In the north the Baltic Sea encouraged coastal trade, which in turn facilitated coastal settlement, but also enabled invasions. South of the coast, the terrain is flat, but the predominance of great primeval forests and marshes in the east was always a constraint on movement. Not until these forests and marshes were depleted did contact between scattered tribes take place. Thus the river valleys, which in the future Polish territories invariably start in high terrain in the south and then meander to the Baltic, have acted as communication routes. In the south the generally impassable Tatra and Carpathian mountain ranges formed a natural barrier between tribes north of the mountains and those south of them. One mountain pass between the Sudeten and Tatra Mountains, the Moravian Gate, allowed communication with areas south. It has also been possible to skirt the Carpathians by going south-east and along the valley of the river Dniester. These geographical features explain population movements and trading patterns.

North and north-eastern Europe had also been directly affected by the ice ages. The glaciers, which covered territories of future Poland, changed its geography and directly affected the pace of future human settlement. During the Palaeolithic period, approximately 40,000 years ago, mammoths were hunted in north-eastern Europe. There is some, though scant, evidence of human settlement, whose temporary nature points to a nomadic lifestyle. The glacial period which followed destroyed most archaeological evidence. The ice cover tended to alter but most of northern Europe continued to be covered by glaciers. Between 12,000 and 8000 years BC the glaciers receded first to the Baltic and then further north freeing the seas. By then tribes which led a migratory lifestyle, based on limited agriculture and on following reindeer herds, lived in the region. It is estimated that by that time the climate had stabilised and became like the climate we know in what would later become Poland. As the glaciers receded, mixed forest grew and covered most of the area. Because of the density of growth it inhibited population movement. Pockets of human settlements established themselves in clearings and in areas where the forest cover was not too dense, but it is assumed that the pattern of forest cover limited contacts between groups and facilitated the emergence of strong tribal consciousness. Limited archaeological evidence suggests that it also encouraged economic self-sufficiency.

Opinions differ on what caused a change in this pattern of life. The key question is what led tribes to break out of the isolation imposed by geography and the topography of the region? Historians of this early period seem have put forward various interpretations. Some subscribe to the theory that what happened was no less than a revolutionary change, one which forced communities to change drastically the way in which they had hitherto obtained food and shelter. These are clearly theories influenced by the Marxist interpretation of historic evolution. This presupposes that the driving force behind all social changes is economic, usually accompanied by violent breakdown of the old order, which is in turn replaced by one more appropriate to new forms of production. Since there is little evidence of such a trauma before the Roman period, it might be wiser to assume that the population of north-eastern Europe was affected by a variety of influences, none necessarily violent nor sudden. In the south new agricultural methods absorbed from contacts with more advanced cultures might have encouraged further inter-tribal contacts. In the north, where trade in amber had always created preconditions for contact between the local population and traders from the outside, there is evidence of more exchange of commodities but also of use of hitherto unknown metals. In the interior, communities might have continued undisturbed, pursuing traditional methods of agriculture which in most cases amounted to the slash and burn method, followed by a few years of cultivation and then a temporary abandonment of the cleared field until nutrients in the soil had been replenished. Whether one does or does not subscribe to the theory of a 'Neolithic revolution' resulting in a sudden and possibly rapid rate of change, there is agreement that by the end of this period, approximately between 5200 and 3700 BC, a more settled agriculture and animal husbandry became the norm. Communities ceased being nomadic and obtained most food from cultivation rather than hunting.

At this stage it is still not possible to speak of any specific ethnic groups inhabiting the territory of present-day Poland, though already during the Bronze Age communities emerged which appeared to share common cultural traits, such as similar styles of pottery, burial patterns and common agricultural methods. And although initially these groups would have consisted of no more than a few related families sharing common fields and herds, in due course some form of social stratification took place. Some burials are more elaborate and endowed with symbols of authority, such as arms, decorations and occasionally human and animal sacrifice, suggesting that a group of tribal elders and possibly also a priestly caste were emerging within the communities. The inclusion of horse bridles and decorations in some graves is evidence that a caste of warriors defined by their use of horses in fighting was also present in the Bronze Age. During the Roman period rich burials bear witness to substantial differentiation within local communities. By then a ruling or leadership group, possibly hereditary, had become defined. The reasons for these differences are not always easy to identify. Families breaking away from communities and successfully pursuing agriculture might offer one explanation. Other sources of wealth might have been booty and slaves obtained by the warriors during attacks on other communities.

During the early Bronze Age (1300–400 BC) a distinct local culture emerged around the river Bug. Historians have called it the Łużyce (Lusatian) culture. This was an economically stable community, associated with successful cultivation of a variety of grains and produce. During this period family groups combined into tribal groups, which united for the purpose of defence. Metallurgy and blacksmithing were known to the Lusatians. As the Łużyce culture declined, Scythian invasions left a mark on the region. The Celts were another distinct outside group which left a strong mark on the region. During the Roman period for the first time certain population groups were defined as Slav. During the fourth century they inhabited the areas of present-day Czech and Slovak lands and some parts of south-eastern Germany.

At the time of the great migration of peoples during the first half of the first millennium, territories around the Vistula and Oder rivers were temporarily inhabited by a number of tribes about which we have more information. During the years AD 45 and 53 Attila, the leader of the barbarian tribe of the Huns, ravaged areas of present-day Poland. By the fifth century AD, as the Germanic tribes moved on, the Slavs came to occupy most of the regions between the Carpathian Mountains and the Baltic Sea. In common with other parts of Europe, the region appears to have suffered from the cessation of the little trade that had taken place with the Roman Empire. Rapid movements of whole tribes, the reasons for which remain not entirely clear, ravaged the land. Grave discoveries suggest that standards of cultivation and levels of wealth fell and that tribes withdrew into isolation, making very little contact with the outside world and maintaining only limited economic exchanges across the region.

There is archaeological evidence that, during the ninth and tenth centuries AD, tribes combined to organise themselves, mainly for defence purposes. There is conclusive evidence of quite sophisticated building of fortified settlements, called *grodziska*. These were usually on raised terrain, sometimes where a river or lake provided some added security. Additionally, raised earth and stone structures surrounded the *grodziska*; sometimes a moat was dug around it. These settlements were not isolated. The fact that they usually appeared to be linked, either surrounding an area or providing defence against attack from one direction, suggests that inhabitants of the region had purposefully combined to form an alliance. Inhabitants would flock to the *grodziska* during time of danger, though at times of peace they most probably were the focal point of local economic and political life. Local tribal leaders with their warriors were most probably based in the fortified settlement. It would be expected that they would also have acted as religious centres. In most cases after the introduction of Christianity to Poland, the first bishoprics were established in pre-existing *grodziska*. The largest number of such settlements existed in the Wielkopolska region near the rivers of Warta and Wełna. At the same time there is evidence that, by means of tribal alliances or possible conquest, tribal leaders from within the Wielkopolska region extended their influence beyond their own areas, exacting some form of tribute. Trade between the centralised region and the periphery flourished, suggesting that Wielkopolska was becoming a centre of economic activity and trade for the whole area. Within Wielkopolska human settlements were denser and exploitation of land more intense than outside the region. Evidence suggests that barter and sometimes cash trade using silver coins were also taking place between the centre and periphery areas.

The absence of an advanced literary culture means that it is not possible to be precise about how and when this process, whereby tribal leaders combined into defensive alliances, became a self-conscious desire to centralise and develop a more permanent political structure. Existing evidence gives only a fragmentary picture of the origins of the emergence of the state structure. We will probably never know who initiated the process of centralisation, which then was followed by state building. Nevertheless some intelligent speculation, based on the little that is known, is permissible. The existence of a number of powerful tribes dominating territories east of the Oder River had been recorded during the second half of the ninth century by a chronicler known as The Geographer of Bavaria. This source states that among a number of approximately 50 tribes, some became dominant. The Wiślanie and Lędzianie inhabited Małopolska, the Mazowszanie the Masovia area, the Polanie were in Wielkopolska, Goplanie in Kujawy, the Ślęzanie in Silesia and finally the Pomorzanie in Pomerania. Initially these tribes existed independently. The reason why it became necessary to unite or bring together these tribes is not obvious. Military threat and the need to consolidate forces had in some circumstances acted as a catalyst towards state formation. But since the areas, which subsequently came to be known as the territory of the Polish kingdom, were not under threat of invasion, the incentive to centralise remains obscured by history.

By the eighth century the Polanie seem to have taken the lead in establishing control over neighbouring tribes. Their power might be explained by their strong economic position based mainly on the control of the salt trade. The centre of the Polanie's territory was the fortified stronghold of Gniezno, which in AD 850 was, by the standards of the time, a substantial town with fortifications, markets and settlement of craftsmen. The establishment of the first Polish dynasty came as a result of an internal coup during which the then ruler Popiel was removed and replaced by Ziemovit. Again the precise details are vague, but it would appear that through a process of conquests Ziemovit and his successors Leszek and then Ziemomysł incorporated the districts of Masovia, Małopolska and possible also Pomerania into the emerging state of Gniezno. The final stages of the consolidation of the state took place during the rule of Mieszko I (960–92) who assumed leadership in approximately AD 960. Mieszko is the first ruler about whom we have some knowledge. This was mainly because the increasing power of the new state attracted the attention of the Christian German lords and the German Emperor who at that time bore the title of the Holy Roman Emperor. The Moravians and the Papacy, for different reasons, also paid attention to political developments around the Vistula River. The state of Gniezno, which increasingly was referred to as Poland, even at this early stage became a player in European politics.

The 180 years which started with Mieszko I and ended with the death of Bolesław Krzywousty (Boleslaus Wrymouth, 1102–38) was a time of the consolidation of Poland's new frontiers, the establishment of Christianity, the end of pagan faiths and, finally, the creation of permanent state structures. The transition from tribal rule to a hereditary monarchy was inevitably complex. This was a time of turbulence, strife and bloodletting. But at the end of Bolesław Krzywousty's reign Poland was considered to be a Christian state, with an established monarchy and a centralised administrative structure. It had won the recognition of the two European arbiters of power, the Holy Roman Empire and the Papacy.

In present-day thinking Poland's faith is inextricably linked to that of the Catholic Church, or as it was then referred to, the Church of Rome. History textbooks would like to present the Christianisation of Poland in mystical and possibly determinist terms. Thus the image of Poland as the frontier between the Western Christian world, on the one hand, and the Russian Orthodox Church, which derived from the Byzantine Church, on the other, rather conveniently symbolises a present Polish preference to be considered as belonging to the West European cultural traditions. The fact that first lasting contacts with Christianity came from Bohemia, rather than Germany, is also presented as a stroke of fate, even as an act of defiance. Since Germany has traditionally been Poland's key enemy, Poles fondly point out that conversion to Christianity came about not through the efforts of the German bishops but though contacts with Bohemia, making this in some way a voluntary act, rather than that of submission. History reveals a more complex and not so obvious a picture.

Although the eastern territories has been of some interest to the Papacy for some time, it was not until the tenth century that Christian missionaries made any impact on the region. Tribes east of Germany had been exposed to some Christian influence even before Mieszko's reign. There are suggestions that cremation of bodies had ceased as a traditional way of disposing of the dead, possibly as a result of changing burial practices in Christian Western Europe. Christian symbols were known in the east. Missionaries had travelled eastwards, even though we know of no lasting consequences of their efforts before AD 966. The breakthrough was made when the ruler and his entourage converted and made the Christian faith the one official faith of the ruling family and their subjects. This act pitched the Christian faith in direct confrontation with pagan beliefs. In reality it would still be a long time before the Polish state would be truly rid of pagan religions, their symbols and centres of practice. For the newly emerging Polish state the critical moment occurred when Mieszko I married a Bohemian princess who was herself a convert to Christianity. With her entourage a Benedictine missionary of the name Jordan arrived in Poland. The fact that he was a missionary priest was important as it meant that he owed loyalty not to a bishop but directly to the Papacy. Mieszko appears to have made a political decision to convert and to be accepted into the Christian faith. On the eastern border of the German Holy Roman Empire the establishment of the so-called marches, dedicated to the conquest of the eastern territories, was a particular threat to the newly emerging state. By converting, Mieszko denied the Holy Roman Empire an excuse for conquest, since the right to military subjugation of pagans in order to convert them to Christianity would no longer be valid. By the same token Mieszko could now justify his military conquest against the still pagan Pomerania and territories to the east by claiming that this was an attempt to introduce Christianity. Mieszko's immediate successors, mindful of the ongoing conflict between the Papacy and the Holy Roman Empire, frequently took the Papacy's side in order to weaken the Emperor's authority, and simply to destabilise their strong neighbour. On several occasions Polish kings accepted the tutelage of the Emperor, but at the same time appealed to the Pope to insure against inconvenient tutelage. The acceptance of the Christian faith was at the time a political decision, not a spiritual journey.

From the outset the Papacy saw advantages in encouraging Mieszko's independence. By receiving baptism from a Papal missionary, the newly emerging state had become a Papal protectorate. In its conflict with the Holy Roman Empire the Papacy was on the lookout for ways of controlling the spread of German influence eastwards. For the time being Poland was not drawn into the German sphere.

Conversion to Christianity brought with it numerous international benefits. These were possibly confined to the ruling groups. It brought Poland into the community of developed, well-organised and economically advanced West European states. The arrival of foreign priests and monks, skilled and willing to act as scribes and administrators, was a further advantage. Monks brought with them new skills, unknown implements and advanced cultivation methods. But to Mieszko the Church's direct links with the centres of power were just as important. The Church upheld the monarch's authority, now seen not merely as a tribal leader, but in accordance with the new faith, chosen by God himself to rule his people. We have to presume that Mieszko had still to contend with challenges to his own personal authority, but also that his and his predecessor's policy of centralisation had caused disquiet among the leaders of other tribes and the nobility. His acceptance of Christianity united the main tribes in a common faith, imposing a unifying set of beliefs and codes. The Church's commitment to the support of the ruler was particularly important to Mieszko. His international standing was enhanced, but the Church supported his temporal authority by defining the monarch's rule as a sign of divine will. In return the Church and its priests benefited from the ruler's patronage and support.

We can safely presume that initially the extent of Christian influence was minimal; possibly it was only confined to the court, the top nobility and to Mieszko's immediate entourage. The fact that the first church was not built in Gniezno, but in Poznań, suggests an anxiety about a pagan backlash. This did emerge in coming years when the Christian Church decided to exact a tithe from all the people. The efficient taxation system introduced and operated by the clergy, while giving Mieszko and his successors a guaranteed source of income, was deeply resented by the population. There must also still have been strong attachment to local religions and beliefs. The Christian Church's uncompromising hostility to them was bound to cause a reaction. Polygamy was still generally practised and the ownership of slaves was the norm among the wealthy. The Church's attempts to combat these practices and efforts to persuade the princes and nobility to respect Christian marriage vows brought them into conflict with long-standing practices. At times of political instability the Christian Church was attacked and its organisation was on more than one occasion virtually wiped out. This was the case during the period immediately after Mieszko's death, when the state structure, still so tenuous, atomised. Several times the Church presence had to be re-established. During the reign of Bolesław Chrobry (Boleslaus the Valiant, 992–1025), the authority of the Church was only with the greatest difficulty reaffirmed after the civil war. The weakening of the Church inside Poland had its dangerous implications in foreign relations as successive rulers became anxious lest the German rulers succeed in their claim that the areas to the east were pagan. This would have legitimised their conquests. After a period of internal turbulence, Bolesław Chrobry anxiously sought to reaffirm Poland's commitment to the Church of Rome. An opportune murder of the missionary Vojtěch who had earlier been Bishop of Prague, by a pagan tribe in Prussia, allowed the Polish king to obtain the Papacy's full recognition of the independent status of the Polish Church. The King retrieved the martyr's body and, due to the fact that Vojtěch was well connected with the European ruling houses, his death attracted the Papacy's attention. His body was brought to Gniezno and when canonised the Poles appropriated him as St Wojciech. The Poles, on whose territories he had undertaken his missionary activities, were able to present themselves as defenders of the faith. As a result the Pope looked upon the Poles sympathetically and agreed to publicly reaffirm the Polish Christian Church's independence of the German hierarchy. Within the next few years in addition to the already existing Gniezno bishopric, three more were established, in Kraków, Wrocław and Kołobrzeg. All came under the jurisdiction of the Archbishop of Gniezno and thus the unity of the Church underpinned the unity of the state.

The process of state building did not proceed smoothly. After Mieszko's death, internal rebellions and military confrontations with neighbours on several occasions threatened to undermine what degree of centralisation had been achieved. It is possible to identify several stages whereby the process of state building progressed, faltered and was again continued under the leadership of a strong ruler. Mieszko's son Bolesław Chrobry marks a key stage in Poland's progression towards the creation of a Polish kingdom. His rule is characterised by nearly continuous struggles with the Holy Roman Empire to consolidate the international authority of the newly emerging state and the conquest of new territories. In 1000 Bolesław Chrobry appeared to have secured a major coup. By then the Papacy and the Emperor had agreed on a formal process whereby both would agree to the coronation of a new king. Otto III, the young Emperor swayed by deep mystical and religious emotions, visited the grave of St Wojciech in

Gniezno. Bolesław Chrobry appears to have impressed him enough during the course of the visit to obtain his consent to becoming King of Poland. He nevertheless still needed the Pope's agreement to being crowned. The Papal consent to the 'anointing' of a king, was in effect a process whereby the head of the Christian Church identified the chosen ruler and granted him God's authority. Chrobry's misfortune was that, while Otto was inclined to crown him, the then Pope Benedict VIII maintained the policy of opposition to the spread of German influence east. As the Polish ruler dispatched his emissaries to Rome to plead his case, Otto III died and was succeeded by Henry II who was determined to destroy the growing power of the Poles. The conflict between the two related to the extension of Polish influence over Łużyce and the region of Miśnia. In 1003 Bolesław Chrobry intervened in the Czech state, at that time torn by fratricidal conflicts between the ruler Boleslaus the Red and his brothers. In February 1003 Bolesław Chrobry assumed direct control over Bohemia and his troops occupied Prague. Henry II, hostile to the growth of Polish power, sided with Chrobry's opponents in the Bohemian and Moravian territories and forced the Poles to abandon Prague. Nevertheless conflicts continued with the Emperor until 1018. The outcome was advantageous to the Poles who defended their control of Łużyce and effectively stemmed German aspirations to eastern territories. Territories east of Poland also attracted Bolesław Chrobry's attention. The reason for this was that he still needed to consolidate the boundaries of the newly emerging state. Tactical considerations also played a role, as the Polish ruler needed to ensure that Henry II did not gain the allegiance of the rulers of Kiev. But in spite of marrying his daughter to the ruler of Kiev, Bolesław was not successful in his eastern policies. His son-in-law Svetopluk was first overthrown and, when reinstated, turned against Bolesław. The Principality of Kiev would henceforth mark the boundaries of Poland's eastern expansion.

In 1024 Bolesław was finally crowned King of Poland. This was achieved in the brief time between the death of Henry II and that of the Pope Benedict VIII. The latter's successor John XIX gave his consent to the Polish ruler being anointed. This made the earlier coronation by Otto III fully valid and the two requirements of the process were completed. Bolesław Chrobry had secured temporal and spiritual authority to become the King of Poland. Although purely symbolic, the implications of this act were immense. In the first place, Poland had achieved full recognition of its status of a European state by being accepted into the Christian community. In the second place it was a confirmation of Bolesław's authority within his own community and the state which had by then emerged. The Church's full support for his authority strengthened his and his son's claim to rule.

But the process of centralisation, which was reflected in the strengthening of the authority of the King, met with opposition from the nobility. They took advantage of frequent crises which occurred when the issue of succession was either unclear or under attack, to try to destroy or weaken the power of the Crown. The nobility traditionally resented the strength of the Crown, which limited their power and reduced their role from that of being the ruler's companions to being his servants. The creation of the state bureaucracy also likewise met with resentment. It further diminished the ruler's dependence on the warrior nobility, thus robbing them of an opportunity to gain privileges. Henceforth the nobility would have to pledge its resources to the King and through supporting his policies and wars would obtain rewards either in the form of plunder or grants of estates.

But by the beginning of the new millennium the process of Christianisation, which had initially been confined to the court and the rulers' immediate entourage, became more aggressive and caused a reaction leading to revolts. Poland's neighbours who were on the look-out for an opportunity to interfere in Poland's internal affairs encouraged and facilitated these conflicts. Thus the German Emperor and the rulers of Bohemia, Moravia and Kiev all at one time or another supported pretenders to the Polish Crown and conspired to undermine internal stability. But there were limits to the likely cooperation between Poland's neighbours. The weakening of the Polish state was seen as desirable. Its destruction was not. Neighbouring rulers realised that a political vacuum would bring them into conflict with each other and would possibly result in disorder, which could eventually spill over into their own states. As none could destroy the Polish kingdom outright, a state of simmering internal instability was preferred. This consideration always acted as a moderating factor on the extent of interference in the internal affairs of the Polish kingdom.

Bolesław Chrobry's death in 1025 was followed by an extended period of conflict between his successors. Although the principle that the oldest son should succeed his father was generally accepted and was in particular upheld by the Church, the rulers' successive marriages, freely repudiating and discarding wives whose political usefulness had ended, made that principle unclear in its application.

The Christian Church had tried to oppose what it viewed as the rulers' lax attitudes towards marriage, but clergymen found it difficult to persuade the new Christians to abandon their traditional ways. In any case marriage remained a strong bond between allies. Its political usefulness could not be overlooked. When new alliances were consolidated, so new marriages were contracted. The result was that a successor to the throne had to contend with numerous and in many cases older half-brothers. These frequently lurked in the distant monasteries to which they had been banished by their father, or in the courts of neighbouring rulers, to which they had fled in fear of their life. These pretenders gave a veneer of legitimacy to any internal opposition or outside interference. Poland's descent into chaos between 1025, when Bolesław Chrobry died, and 1122 when Bolesław Krzywousty managed to re-establish the Crown's authority, was a time of internal conflict, foreign intervention and loss of territories conquered earlier.

Bolesław's son Mieszko II started his reign by undertaking an unfortunate, as it turned out, military incursion west. His allies were the pagan Łużyce and a number of Saxon noblemen who had fallen out with Emperor Conrad II. His initial military victories were cut short when Bezprym, his older half-brother from his father's earlier marriage, and his younger brother Otto fled east and sought the help of the Rus princes. Internal opposition emerged in the form of an anti-Christian backlash. Faced with military action in the east and west and rebellion in his own lands Mieszko was forced to negotiate with Conrad. Bezprym in the mean time gained the support of Mieszko's wife who was aggrieved by her husband's decision to deprive their son Kazimierz of the succession by placing him in a monastery. Mieszko was forced to accept Conrad's fairly harsh conditions. He renounced the title of king and agreed to carve out principalities for his brother Otto and an opportunistic uncle, who at this stage also appeared to challenge the King's authority. Nevertheless within two years Mieszko II managed to get rid of both and re-establish some authority over his territories. He then died violently, possibly assassinated. Mieszko's oldest son succeeded as ruler but soon died violently. This left only one legitimate male of the Piast dynasty. Kazimierz Odnowiciel (Casimir the Restorer, 1034–58), was Mieszko's son who had earlier been incarcerated by his father in a monastery. His reign was brief, as he too faced rebellion and was forced to flee to the court of Conrad II. In 1037 the Emperor, fearful of the consequences of the collapse of the Polish kingdom, restored him to power. Kazimierz had to overcome years of lawlessness and internal strife. Without strong central authority whole areas had fallen under the control of tribal warlords. Historians have concluded that in effect two overlapping revolutions had taken place simultaneously; a political and a pagan revolution. The strongest reaction against the Church manifested itself close to the three bishoprics and the seat of the archbishopric. This would suggest that the proximity of the Church had been particularly oppressive to the local population. Kazimierz had to move the capital from Gniezno to Kraków and rebuild the Polish Church. Gniezno had been sacked by a Czech invasion and the relics of St Wojciech had been taken to Prague. The issue of the restoration of ecclesiastical authority had to be addressed urgently, in particular if the Polish state was to retain its independence and not allow itself to be dominated by its powerful German neighbour.

The restoration process had been temporarily successful and Kazimierz's son Bolesław Śmiały (Boleslaus the Bold, 1058–79) was able to build on his father's achievements. He also took advantage of the breach between the German Emperor Henry IV and Pope Gregory VII. By siding with Gregory's policies of freeing the Papacy from its dependence on the Emperor, the Polish prince was able to obtain Papal concessions in particular for the establishment of a Papal legate in Poland and the appointment of a fourth bishop. In the conflict between the two giants of the Christian world, Bolesław had backed the winning side. As a result, as Henry had to make his humiliating pilgrimage to Canossa to beg Papal forgiveness, Bolesław was crowned King of Poland.

Stability thus restored in Poland was only brief. For reasons that remain unclear, a new rebellion broke out. A number of noblemen sided with the King's younger brother and the Bishop of Kraków supported them. The King's decision to have the Bishop of Kraków executed for treason then led to a conflict between the state and Church. In the disorder that followed, the King had to flee the country. In 1079 Władysław Herman (Ladislaus Herman, 1079–1102), the deposed king's younger brother, took power in particularly difficult circumstances. Internal rebellion continued. Although he appears to have disposed of the exiled brother's eldest son, thus reducing the likelihood of rebellion coalescing around him, his own sons proved to be a source of difficulty. Władysław Herman had two sons, the first-born, Zbigniew, by his first wife who was a noblewoman. That marriage had not been sanctioned by the Church. But by the standards of the time, it was still considered to have been a valid marriage and the son was treated as legitimate. His second son, Bolesław, was from his second marriage to the daughter of the Czech king. But Władysław Herman's third wife Judith, the sister of the German Emperor Henry IV, caused discord. Under his third wife's influence, the King despatched his first-born to a distant monastery and agreed with Judith that he should be declared illegitimate. Judith in the mean time formed an alliance with a powerful nobleman Sieciech and gave her support to the younger stepson.

The conflicts within the King's household allowed the opposition to crystallise around various factions. When the older son Zbigniew escaped from his monastery his cause was taken up by the Pomeranians on whose conquest the King had concentrated throughout his reign. The neighbouring Kujawy region also sided with the Pomeranians. Although both were finally defeated militarily, the King had to accept the son's claim to legitimacy. The Church threw in its lot with the oldest son and declared him to be legitimate and thus a rightful heir. In 1079 in an attempt to conciliate his sons Władysław Herman, by all accounts a weak and irresolute man, gave his two sons their own principalities. On receiving their own domains they proceeded to jointly wage war against their father and his supporters. When in 1102 the King died, his sons inherited a divided kingdom. It was inevitable that they would fall out and, in due course, the younger Bolesław Krzywousty forced his older brother into exile. When subsequently Zbigniew, enticed by false promises, returned to Poland, Bolesław had him first blinded and then killed. This was a common way of dealing with any likelihood of a challenge from male relatives. Bolesław Krzywousty's rule, until 1138, marked the last stage of stability before the next conflagration.

On his deathbed Bolesław Krzywousty decided that the kingdom should be divided between his sons. Some historians have seen in this decision the malign influence of a second wife, desperate to secure an inheritance for her sons. But the royal ordinance, defining precisely the rights and entitlements as well as duties of each son, was an attempt to deal with the inevitable conflicts which would follow his death. Thus far from being the King's weak response to a bullying wife, desperate to limit the authority of her stepson, the ordinance was a document aimed at consolidating the oldest son's authority, while recognising the rights of the younger siblings. It was the King's intention that his ordinance should be the guarantee of future stability, regulating inheritance matters and securing both frontiers and power within the Polish state. To strengthen the impact of his ordinance Bolesław Krzywousty secured the approval of the Church, lay leaders and even of the Pope, thus committing them to upholding his decisions.

The ordinance stipulated that the oldest son was to be the absolute ruler of Poland. Each of the younger brothers received a clearly defined principality, the boundaries of which overlapped with tribal boundaries, thus making them more stable. Their right to each principality was to be hereditary. But only the oldest brother, the Senior, would have absolute control over Polish sovereignty. To him was assigned the main principality, which was the central area. This was meant to allow the Senior to exercise some control over his brothers' principalities. The Senior was to make all decisions concerning foreign relations and military affairs. The town of Kraków was designated as the capital of the kingdom. Unfortunately, soon after Bolesław's death his last wife Salomea, acting in defence of her sons' interests, conspired to undermine the authority of her stepsons and the Senior of the dynasty. What followed was the break-up of the state into self-governing principalities with each brother making extensive use of Poland's neighbours' willingness to assist them in the fratricidal conflicts which followed. For the next 200 years the territory of Poland was a battleground. Notwithstanding the state of anarchy into which Bolesław Krzywousty's successors plunged the Polish kingdom, it is worth noting that at the time of his death in 1138 the basic territorial unity of the state had been defined. It is also possible to speak of economic and social development, which paralleled those taking place in other European regions.

Bolesław Krzywousty's foreign policy was focused principally on the Pomeranian district. Its conquest served two purposes. Strategically it seemed a good idea to secure the region for Poland, thus stemming the growth of German influence in the region. The waging of a constant war against Pomerania also gave the Polish nobility a purpose and opportunity for enrichment through the acquisition of booty and slaves. This was likely to reduce their desire to challenge the power of the Crown and to decrease internal intrigues. The development of a community of knights, dedicated to the waging of war, made wars a necessary aspect of medieval life. Bolesław, in any case, did not seek the outright incorporation of the Pomeranian region into Poland, being satisfied with the incorporation of the Gdańsk district and the securing of areas up to the river Noteć. Western

Pomerania was subordinated to Poland without outright incorporation. Military conquest was accompanied by missionary activities and the Polish ruler paid a lot of attention to the Christianisation of conquered territories. Polish priests were sent to Pomerania and money was made available to build churches and to support the newly emerging ecclesiastical structure, which still had to contend with a very strong pagan presence. Bolesław's reasons were primarily political. He was determined that Pomerania should not become part of the German Church, but should be incorporated into the Polish Church, thus creating a barrier to the spread of German influence east. But the issue of the independence of the Polish and Pomeranian Christian churches briefly became an issue in the conflicts which were being played out in Rome. The Poles had backed Anaklet, the candidate of the Council of Florence, in his claim to the Papacy. When Pope Innocent II was able to defeat the so-called 'anti-Pope', the Poles found themselves on the wrong side of the complicated contest and the German bishops were able to persuade Innocent to subordinate the Polish Church to the authority of the German hierarchy. Only in 1135, after Emperor Lothar's death, did the Polish Church reverse this ruling, thus once more confirming the independence of the Polish Christian Church.

Bolesław's interference in the Hungarian battle of succession had resulted in disaster. It would seem that the Polish ruler had the knack of more than once backing the wrong man. Over the years the Poles realised that successive Czech Bohemian rulers and German emperors shared the same objective of weakening Poland. Thus while the Poles could only try and counteract Germany's power, in the Czech regions they were able to make their decisions effective. They were determined to make sure that the Bohemian Principality was weak. In that endeavour Hungary was Poland's natural ally. In 1131 during the battle of succession between two pretenders to the Hungarian throne, the Poles militarily backed Borys against Bela II. When Bela managed to gain the support of most of the Hungarian nobility Polish troops had to flee. But while they had been pursuing a war of intervention in Hungary, the Czechs occupied Silesia, a contested region between the two countries. The only way out for Bolesław Krzywousty was to accept the adjudication of the German Emperor Lothar II. Lothar forced him to accept Bela's claim to the Hungarian throne. In relation to Pomerania Lothar's decision was more complicated, as Bolesław was made to pay homage to the Emperor as the feudal lord of Pomerania. The Polish ruler's situation was undeniably very humiliating, nevertheless the independence of the Polish lands had been retained. Even though the German emperors had successfully prevented any Polish ruler being crowned they were not able to subordinate Poland to the German Empire.

By the end of the twelfth century Poland had established the basic framework of state structure. However, as has been noted, the rulers' authority was never absolute. The nobility fought against the ruler gathering all authority in his hands. By the eleventh century tribal gatherings, which had still been called on special occasions, had become less relevant and infrequent. The nobility, the knights and the high clergy had through their contact with rulers and because of the rulers' dependence on them been able to have a say in matters relating to the waging of wars, conquests and distribution of lands. They were also in a position to extract from the ruler the rights to certain privileges, such as exemption from taxes and laws. The relationship between the rulers, who sought to strengthen their own position, and the nobility was inevitably antagonistic. During disturbances and rebellions which followed the death of Mieszko and Bolesław Chrobry, the nobility's rights and privileges were increased at the expense of the powers of the ruler. The twelfth century witnessed the establishment of a principle that only the nobility had the right to hold royal office, this being a guarantee of access to the ruler and a means of securing further privileges.

The peasantry, which in principle retained the right to petition rulers, in effect was removed from all forms of decision making deriving from tribal practice. The transformation of the structure of society and political turbulence, which affected the country, had its consequences upon the village communities. Peasants gradually lost the right to the land which they had cultivated. The beginning of the millennium was a time when the state encroached upon the peasants' personal liberties. The peasant communities became more differentiated. Thus in addition to free peasants there were those who together with landed estates had been handed over to the nobility or the Church by the Crown. They were tied to that land which they were not free to leave. After wars of conquest slaves were settled in villages, creating communities whose members had no personal rights.

As is only to be expected, life was short and difficult for those at the bottom of the social pyramid. Average life expectancy of women was not much more than 20 and for men 30. Political instability, wars and rebellions contributed to short life expectancy. But grave excavations suggest that tuberculosis was rife and deaths in childbirth were common. At the same time there is little evidence of hunger and short-age. At the beginning of the eleventh century the previously noted practice of wives being either killed or committing suicide on their husbands' death, was abandoned. There had never been any evidence of husbands having a reciprocal obligation to die with their wives. Infanticide was practised in particular during time of hunger. Although some chroniclers have suggested that Slav communities traditionally killed older people, this is not confirmed by archaeological excava-tions. On the contrary, it would seem that Slav communities held their elders in very high esteem. Graves, which previously contained ashes, were increasingly replaced with graves containing bodies. This change of burial practice is evidence of the spread of Christianity, since the Church disapproved of all forms of cremation.

In spite of a relatively low level of agriculture, enough progress had been made in cultivation techniques to provide sufficient food for the community. Although ploughs had been introduced by foreign monks in their estates, most of the land was still cultivated by more primitive methods which meant that the soil was broken with digging imple-ments or primitive ploughs but not turned over. The most commonly cultivated grain was millet, but wheat, barley and for the first time rye were also grown. Apple, pear and even peach trees became common-place. A variety of beans and pulses were grown. Cucumbers, still not known in Germany, were cultivated in Polish lands as were garlic and poppy flowers. Flax and linen were the most common forms of cloth, since sheep rearing was not the norm in the lowlands occupied by the Slav people. Average peasant farmyards would have contained long-horn cows, pigs, sheep, goats and horses. Foreign travellers had noted that the eating of horsemeat was associated with Russian tribes and not with Slav people, who kept horses for work only. Hunting of wild animals became increasingly a royal monopoly, and excavations suggest that most meat consumed was from cultivated animals, which indicates that animal husbandry had become the norm.

There is extensive evidence of local and regional trade. In addition to regular local markets, where produce would have been sold and purchased, goods were carried over distances. Certain districts and villages developed specialist production of goods. In some cases this had happened because the ruler wanted to encourage production of goods such as weapons, iron implements and pottery. In other cases this would be a spontaneous development caused by the availability of raw materials, or ready markets. Thus production for wider markets was already taking place.

During the tenth and eleventh centuries patterns of human habitation changed dramatically. Earlier, people lived either in small settlements or in villages. The beginning of the new millennium witnessed the emergence of towns. By the twelfth century several towns containing up to several thousands of permanent inhabitants were well established. Kraków, Gniezno, Kruszwica, Opole, Szczecin and Gdańsk all contained closely crammed buildings, usually still dugouts, which were entirely or partly sunk in the earth. Although the first stone buildings made their appearance around that time, they were usually church buildings constructed by foreign craftsmen. Bricks were not used until the thirteenth century. The origin of towns continues to be the source of historic controversies, but it is possible that several parallel economic and political processes had been taking place, which resulted in the emergence of larger population centres. In some cases the volume of local trade might have stimulated the formation of larger trading centres. In other instances, a convenient geographic situation might have been the catalyst for tradesmen and merchants to settle. Military centres and religious foundations were just as important in creating preconditions for larger volumes of trade, production and the dense settlements that these entailed. The process of centralisation of authority appears to have simulated further the growth of towns. On the Baltic coast towns sprang up purely in response to trade which took place in that region.

International trade, which virtually ceased during the turbulent times of the migration of the barbarian tribes, resumed during times of political stability. Though it was always limited by the fact that the Slav territories provided few commodities which were valued on international markets, the exception was amber, which was found on the coast of the Baltic Sea. This tended to be purchased by foreign traders who then transported it either along the northern route to Western Europe or along the southern route to the Danube and the Black Sea.

By the end of the twelfth century the country was divided into seven provinces which were administered by appointed administrators. These were Silesia, Kraków and its district, Sandomierz, Masovia, Kujavy with Łęczyca and Gdańsk Pomerania. Although Kraków came to be seen as the seat of the capital this was only nominally the town where the rulers resided. In reality they continued to tour the provinces, making themselves available to their subjects, but no doubt also to enforce discipline and to maintain authority. The ruler's entourage usually consisted of members of the immediate family and those whose duty it was to see to all their personal needs. But by the twelfth century the court came also to include some form of administrative offices, usually staffed by clerics or monks, retained on account of their knowledge of writing and Latin. They had the task of maintaining records, including taxation and financial records. The Christian high clergy were valued intermediaries with the outside world. Through their contacts they were better informed than anyone else of what was happening in Rome, in other major centres and in the courts of other rulers. Thus we see the development of a mutually advantageous relationship between the rulers and the Church hierarchy, who were not only committed to upholding the authority of the ruler, but also were able to direct him in finer points of foreign affairs.

By the twelfth century Polish rulers had already established the basis of state financial systems. Taxation was levied on behalf of the ruler and the Church. This must have been oppressive, as we know of rebellions which had occurred because of the excessive burden of fiscal demands. The rulers also established monopolies over certain economic activities. The minting of coins was traditionally a royal monopoly, but extraction and trade in salt, a scarce and vital commodity, was likewise a royal prerogative. The existence of a taxation system suggests that money transactions had become the norm in Polish lands. Silver coins were preferred to gold on account of the low value of trade taking place. Silver coins were also broken up to make small change. At the same time other commodities continued to be used as a form of mutually acceptable payment. In Poland's case lengths of linen were traditionally used, the value of which both transacting sides agreed on.

Thus by 1138 Poland was economically, socially and politically at the same level of development as the other countries of the region. On account of the growing influence of the Christian Church culturally, Poland turned west towards the Latin culture, which divided it from the areas dominated by the Byzantine Church and culture. But through intermarriage with other ruling dynasties in the region, the Polish rulers and the nobility retained just as strong contacts with the Russian princes as with the Czech, Hungarian and German nobility.

2

. . . .

Poland in the Middle Ages

After the establishment of a Polish polity according to the standards of the time, the twelfth and thirteenth centuries witnessed a process of progressive, though on no account inevitable, disintegration of the state into principalities. Bolesław Krzywousty had anticipated conflicts between his sons, and tried to pre-empt their desire for independence, while also attempting to forestall the weakening of central authority. Both as a father and a legislator he failed. His sons, and subsequently their successors, refused to grasp the basic principle of strength through unity. They not only destroyed the existing state but also lost control of territories. Bolesław had decreed that the oldest of his sons and after him the oldest successor, should discharge overall authority over the country. Thus the Senior, in addition to holding his own principality, would have full authority over the central province with its capital in Kraków. But Bolesław's sons and his widow fell out with each other. As his sons died their heirs challenged the principle of succession and fought for control of Kraków and the central principality. The political power of the Kraków nobility, the wealthy burghers and the Church grew in proportion to the weakening of central authority. It would be 200 years before any attempts to reunify Polish lands would be successful.

Bolesław's sons fell out with each other immediately after their father's death. Initially the sons from the second marriage turned against their older half-brother Władysław, who then allied himself with the Rus prince. They combined forces and successfully fought against the half-brothers. On the death of Bolesław's widow the issue of tenancy of her principality exacerbated the already tense family relations. In the course of the conflict Władysław tried to oust his half-brothers, but ended fleeing to Germany where Emperor Conrad III intermittently championed his cause. Conrad's participation in the Second Crusade to the Holy Lands distracted him from European matters. Only after his death in 1157 did his successor Frederick Barbarossa concentrate once more on Germany's eastern border. The crusading enterprises of Conrad and his successor reflected a dilemma between the conquest of the heathen Slavs of Pomerania and Brandenburg, which were of immediate concern to Germany, and the desire to play a role in international affairs, in which case action in the Holy Lands was more important. For the Polish princes who tried to benefit from German support there was a price to be paid. In the years to come, as each Piast prince, on various occasions, appealed to the Emperor for assistance in rivalries with the other princes, German authority over Silesia and Pomerania increased.

A serious, though ultimately unsuccessful, attempt to consolidate authority over the principalities was made in 1173 by Mieszko Stary (Mieszko the Old, 1173–1202). But by the time Mieszko became the Senior Prince, the Kraków nobility and burghers had enjoyed the benefits of a degree of independence which they were not going to give up easily. Mieszko's attempt to increase state revenue by reclaiming lapsed fiscal privileges raised strong opposition. In 1177 the nobility, supported by the Bishop of Kraków, forced Mieszko to flee. His place was taken by Kazimierz Sprawiedliwy (Casimir the Just, 1177–1227), who, though lacking legitimate grounds to Seniority, resorted to the use of force to gain control of the Senior's principality and then claimed authority over the Kraków district. The principle of the oldest of the dynasty acting as Senior Prince was thus abandoned. The question of succession would henceforth be increasingly decided on the basis of concessions which pretenders to Seniority would be willing to make to the nobility and wealthy burghers of Kraków. The Church took an active role in that process by also bidding for concessions and further privileges. At the same time all attempts to reunify lands held by the Piast dynasty, or at least to hold them together, were abandoned. Rulers of each principality came to be preoccupied with local problems and lost interest in the increasingly distant concept of unity. Henceforth the Piast dynasty split into regional ruling houses associated with a given area: Małopolska, Wielkopolska, Pomerania, Silesia and Masovia.

The weakening, and ultimate collapse, of central authority in Poland coincided with the Papacy's increased determination to strengthen its spiritual role in society through direct involvement in temporal matters. The Papacy, never timorous in its desire for power, now became an aggressive champion of bishops' involvement in politics. Opportunities for this arose as secular rulers sought Papal and Church support for the policies which, as both sides knew, were unrelated to spiritual matters. In 1180 in order to obtain secular and ecclesiastical approval for usurping the position of Senior, Kazimierz Sprawiedliwy called a meeting of the nobility in Łęczyca. The Church hierarchy, which turned out in force, made sure that Kazimierz paid an appropriately high price for their support. This took the form of the Church being granted exemption from certain obligations to the Crown. This was the first recorded case of a section of the community, which enjoyed the benefits of Crown lands, being freed from its duties to the ruler. By the Łęczyca convention the Church was released from the duty to supply provisions and means of transport as requested by the prince or his agents. The second critical concession stated that henceforth the ruler could not make a claim to movable property of a deceased bishop. In return for these privileges the Polish Church hierarchy used its influence in Rome to secure the Pope's agreement to set aside rules governing succession to the district of Kraków. This further destroyed the principle of the Senior's automatic right to the district and the capital and through that made all further efforts for unity less likely to succeed.

When the rightful Senior tried to gain Frederick Barbarossa's support, the fact that Pope Alexander III supported the usurper Kazimierz's claim, weakened the German Emperor's inclination to meddle in Polish affairs. The new situation was advantageous to the German Emperor because, henceforth, with the principle of succession muddied further, the Piast princelings concentrated on fighting each other. That in consequence reduced the likelihood of a threat from the east. Critically, the collapse of even the pretence of central authority weakened ties between the Pomeranian princes and the Piast dynasty. Both Denmark and Germany had an interest in those regions and by 1181 Western Pomerania accepted the suzerainty of the German Empire. Eastern Pomerania together with the Gdańsk area continued to be loyal to the Piast princes, though these ties continued to diminish in importance. In effect by the beginning of the twelfth century the extension of Polish influence into Pomerania had stalled and in some cases was reversed. In retrospect Kazimierz is seen as having turned the direction of Poland's expansion from the west and in consolidating influence in the east. Pomeranian and Silesian areas increasingly came under German influence, absorbing German cultural and economic examples. German Church missionaries completed the task of introducing Christianity to the region.

During this period the Piast princes, although frequently preoccupied with internal conflicts, looked east. Dynastic ties strengthened this eastern orientation with the Rus princes. Kazimierz extended his influence over the Ruthenian, Kiev and Halicz areas, conflicting with and forestalling Hungarian aspirations in the same regions. The consolidation of Polish influence over the areas of the Rus principalities and the conquest of the still pagan Jadźwigs in the north-east allowed for the expansion of Polish settlements. These in turn further justified and stimulated continuing Polish involvement in the area.

Kazimierz Sprawiedliwy died in 1194. With his death all attempts to maintain central authority also came to an end. Five distinct principalities emerged but these continued to divide further. While the rulers retained an awareness of having a common heritage and of being part of Poland, they concentrated on pursuing their own interests, in the course of which they sometimes cooperated. Where a common threat brought them together they combined to take joint action. At the same time they continued to use outside support to resolve fratricidal conflicts. Not surprisingly, in the circumstances, the fate of Polish lands was affected by incidental events. One such was a decision made at the beginning of the thirteenth century by the Prince of Masovia to invite the religious military of the Teutonic Order of the Holy Virgin, better known as the Teutonic Knights, to settle on the borders of Masovia which was threatened by attacks from Prussia. At the time, this attempt to strengthen the borders of this principality was not unusual. Unfortunately the Teutonic Knights' power and aspirations grew rapidly and the Prince of Masovia was unable to control or limit their aggressive policies. The decision to invite the Teutonic Knights had momentous implications on the future course of East European history. The pace of future developments has to be viewed in the context in the growing belligerence of the Christian Church and the ideology of Crusades, which appeared to legitimate conquest of territories deemed to be pagan.

Behind the new militarism of the Catholic Church was the determination of Pope Innocent III (1198–1216) to reform the Christian Church. This had profound international and internal implications. Innocent III's reforms inevitably affected relations between rulers and the Church hierarchy. The aim was to make the Church independent of secular authority and to protect its spiritual role and its considerable economic position. By enforcing, much more thoroughly than any of his predecessors had done, the celibacy requirement, the Church was protecting its property. Sons of priests who laid claim to their father's wealth effectively weakened the Church's authority and depleted its resources. Innocent was determined to regularise a practice which had always been difficult to enforce. By banning the sale of ecclesiastical offices and the appointment of bishops by the sovereign, temporal interference in Church affairs was reduced. Within the Polish principalities Archbishop Kietlicz took up the reforms with fervour. Initially these were difficult to implement, as clergy marriages in spite of the Church's basic commitment to celibacy, were common in twelfth-century Poland and in no way cast doubts upon the validity of either the marriage or the priest's commitment to his Church. The reform of Church appointments was made easier by the local rulers' need for Church support when fighting each other. Innocent's aim was no less than the Church's absolute control over secular life. This led the Pope to claim for the Papacy the role of the feudal lord of the Christian world. The Polish princes rightly perceived that, if they submitted themselves and their principalities to the Pope's authority, they would receive his protection and support in internal conflicts. By this process of submission at least three principalities became Papal fiefdoms. The power of the Church within the Polish territories continued to grow unopposed.

But the reforms of Innocent III also stimulated and legitimised armed attack on the remaining pagan territories. This was the time of the great Crusades to the Holy Land where the conquest of Jerusalem was marked by the massacre of infidels. In Eastern Europe the idea that territories inhabited by pagan tribes could be conquered, and then legitimately claimed by the conqueror on grounds of the need to convert the inhabitants, was an attractive proposition. The subjugation of Prussia, from which the pagan tribes menaced the Polish principalities of Masovia and Kujavy, was an obvious attraction to those who were moved by the Crusading spirit but did not want to go to the Middle East. Before his death in 1216 Innocent III called for a Crusade in Prussia. The Polish princes and bishops had a vested interest in Prussia, but so did Denmark and Germany, both of whom were keen to establish control over the Baltic coast.

In 1226 conflicts between the Polish princes coincided with the Crusading ventures in Prussia. Conrad of Masovia sought ways of defeating the Prussians. He needed respite from the threat to his principality so that he could concentrate on laying claim to the principality of Kraków. As a result Conrad invited the Teutonic Knights to settle on the border of Masovia and Prussia hoping that they would quell the Prussians. In due course the Knights extracted further grants of land and an assurance that they would be allowed to retain absolute control over all Prussian territories which they captured. The Polish princes were inexperienced and naive in their dealings with the Knights. They had thought that they would thus gain the military services of the crusading knights. What they had not realised was that they were dealing with a politically experienced and aggressive militaristic community, an arm of the growing power of a Church fighting for political expression of its spiritual role. Once they had become established in Prussia the Teutonic Knights showed no intention of subordinating themselves to the Polish Church. Nor were they willing to accept the authority of petty Piast princelings. Claiming that they had been promised Chełmno and all conquests in Prussia, they succeeded in obtaining the Pope's support for their claim to the region. In effect, areas claimed by the Teutonic Knights became a Papal fief, which was then granted to the Knights. They found willing allies in the German military order of the Knights of the Sword who established themselves further north in territories around the river Dźwina. By 1283 the conquest of Prussia was completed and the new state, held by the Knights as a fiefdom from the Pope and the German Emperor, was fully consolidated in the region. Inevitably, because of the German character of both orders and close relations between their Grand Masters and the German nobility, Prussia became closely allied to the German Empire. In conflicts with the Polish rulers, the Teutonic Knights could count on German support. Conversely, when jostling with Germany for control over Western Pomerania, successive Polish rulers had to keep a wary eye on the Teutonic Knights who, with German approval, were always on the lookout to extend their territories at Poland's expense.

In the mean time, a new force appeared from the east. Since the beginning of the thirteenth century rumours suggested that nomadic Mongol tribes, organised under a new and inspired elected leader, the Genghis Khan, were moving west. By 1223 the force which came to be known as the Golden Horde had scored a military victory against Ruthenia. In 1240 the city of Kiev was sacked and the Horde moved to conquer Hungary. In April 1241 a confrontation between the Prince of Małopolska Henryk Pobożny (Henry the Pious, 1238–41), and the Mongol Horde took place near Legnice. While some historians were in the past only too willing to portray the confrontation as a major battle, more recent research has suggested that Henry and the flower of Western knighthood, together with the Knights of the Cross and the Knights Templars, faced an attack from the flank units of the Horde, the majority of which were advancing towards Hungary, their main objective. Henryk Pobożny together with most of his knights was slaughtered in the battle. Within the year the force of the Mongol invasion was spent. Nevertheless continuing minor attacks from the Balkans and the Black Sea region were a constant reminder of the destructive nature of the earlier attack.

By the time the Mongols had reached southern Polish territories they had acquired a ferocious reputation for military prowess based on the swiftness with which they moved. Popular Polish interpretations of the nature of the conflict have little to do with historic truth. One of those enduring and romantic myths relates the story of the trumpet player in the church tower in Kraków. Legend has it that as he played a signal of warning that the Mongols were approaching the town his playing was cut short by a raider's arrow. Visitors to Poland and in particular to Kraków will hear this simple tune played at noon and transmitted on Polish radio, which is suddenly cut short as a reminder of the fate that befell the original trumpet player.

Reality, predictably is more prosaic, with suggestions that Henry unnecessarily sought a confrontation with the Mongols, who had no intention of moving north and merely took a detour though Polish territories to deter the Piast princes from going to Hungary's aid. The long-term consequences of the attack and the continuing political presence of the Mongols, who increasingly were referred to as the Tatars, on Poland's eastern and south-eastern flank related more to their defeat of their hitherto important Piast allies, the Ruthenian princes. The flourishing city of Kiev had been destroyed and with it the growing political power of that region. In due course the Duchy of Moscow assumed the role of the regional power and extended its influence over regions to the west of Moscow. The Piast princes had hitherto only indirect interaction with Moscow, which in due course would become a major consideration in Poland's eastern policies. Initially the destruction of the political power of the Ruthenian princes and collapse of the local economy created a vacuum into which the Lithuanian rulers, hitherto confined to the north and coastal areas, were now able to spread. This led to the establishment of Lithuanian influence between the rivers Dnieper and Niemen and its spread towards the coast of the Baltic Sea. The Polish princes had the choice of either allying themselves with pagan Lithuania or in fighting it. The course of historic developments led them in due course to take the former option. The reunification of the Piast land was achieved by Władysław Łokietek (Ladislaus the Short, 1306–33). By the time of his death he had re-established the territorial basis of the Polish kingdom. Małopolska with Kraków as its capital was united with Wielkopolska. Outside the boundaries of the restored Polish kingdom were Masovia, Prussia, where the Teutonic Knights ruled, and Silesia. Pomerania had also been lost. Unimpressive though this limited consolidation might seem, it was a critical achievement for it reversed the process of fragmentation which had proceeded relentlessly since Krzywousty's death. Of equal significance was the fact that Łokietek was crowned King of Poland, a sign that he had obtained Papal and Imperial support. In accordance with prevailing values, the coronation was thus recognised as valid by European monarchs and the whole of Christendom.

The idea of unity and centralisation of a Polish state continued to be a goal to which the Piast princes kept returning. Nevertheless, at the end of the thirteenth century, conflicts and rivalries between the various strands of the Piast dynasty continued to stand in the way of these ideas being realised without bloodshed. Poland's powerful neighbours had an interest in maintaining a state of anarchy, either because they hoped to benefit territorially, or because it prevented their enemies from gaining a foothold, and thus building up alliances with the Piasts. The Margrave of Brandenburg had a direct interest in the fate of Pomerania and the Gdańsk region. Venceslas II of Bohemia, having established a powerful monarchy in Prague, developed ambitions which went beyond the control of Silesia and extended to the Polish Crown. The Catholic Church, itself representing clearer political objectives and driven by the Papacy's aspirations to a dominant role in temporal matters, was in favour of unity and consolidation both of territories and power. The Archbishop of Gniezno and the Bishop of Kraków both took a direct interest in the issue of unity, and on account of their authority, had a say in the matter. The growth of trade and the development of town administrative structures gave the merchants and townspeople power which they used to influence the question of succession, naturally, to their advantage. The wealthy burghers of Kraków played an important role in determining who was to control the city and their choice was based on who was most likely to bring peace, order and clarity into administrative matters. Lawlessness and the collapse of central administration were increasingly viewed by the nobility as unfavourable to their own interests. While generally seeking to retain their privileges, they came to favour strong central authority which would overcome the state of anarchy. Finally, although the Piast princelings fought to retain their principalities, the principle of Seniority had not been entirely abandoned, even though transfer of authority along the legitimate line of succession had been challenged and to all practical purposes was lost.

Although, as all historians stress, the road to unity was complex and full of missed opportunities, distinct stages can nevertheless be identified. At the end of the thirteenth century three Piast princes who had no legitimate successors agreed to will their principalities to each other. These were Mściwoj of Gdańsk, Bogusław IV of Western Pomerania and Przemysł II of Poznań. As a consequence in 1290 Wielkopolska, Małopolska with Kraków and Western Pomerania were brought together as Przemysł's inheritance. In June 1295 Przemysł was crowned King of Poland by the Archbishop of Gniezno Jacób Świnka who was the new king's staunchest ally. By obtaining Pope Boniface VIII's agreement to the coronation, which was in turn motivated by the Pope's desire to block Venceslas of Bohemia's claims to Poland, the Archbishop consolidated Przemysł's authority. Unfortunately his rule was cut short a few months later when he was killed on the order of the Margrave of Brandenburg who sought to block the Polish king's rule over Pomerania and the Baltic coast.

As a result of the earlier agreed succession pact, Przemysł's territories were inherited by his cousin, Władysław Łokietek, ruler of Sieradz, Kujawy and Łęczyca. But because he lacked the support of the clergy and gentry, and most probably mainly because he was not able to show that he was in control of his inheritance, those in favour of centralisation looked elsewhere for leadership. Of critical importance was Kraków's decision to hand over the city to Venceslas. Łokietek's first attempt at ruling the recently united areas broke down when Venceslas laid claim to Małopolska. In 1300 the Church hierarchy decided to support Venceslas' claim to the Polish throne. The Czechs had only a dubious claim to the Polish throne, but the militarily dynamic state could not be opposed. In 1300 Venceslas was crowned King of Poland. In 1305 he died and was succeeded by his son. Within the year Venceslas III was assassinated.

Łokietek's restoration was facilitated by the attitude of the Papacy. In the first place Pope Boniface VII was more inclined to support the Piast claim to the Polish Crown as Poland was viewed favourably in Rome. Poland was a Papal fiefdom and paid an unusual tax called Peter's Pence, which the Papacy both needed and appreciated. The Czech claim on the other hand was unwelcome because the Czech king was the German Emperor's vassal. The Papacy had no interest in aiding the growth of Czech power, which when combined with that of Germany, could pose a formidable challenge to Papal authority. There were also pecuniary considerations. The Papacy preferred to see Peter's Pence going into its own coffers rather than for the Czechs to pay a tithe on the Polish lands to their overlord the German Emperor. Łokietek's efforts to regain control over Polish territories were furthermore made easier by the fact that Hungary was equally threatened by the growth of Czech power. When Venceslas II had tried to interfere in the succession issue in Hungary in 1301, this proved too much even for the German Emperor. By losing international support Venceslas' claim to the Polish Crown was put in doubt. The Czechs were not able to follow through their initial advantage, and by 1305, Łokietek took action against them. During the course of the next few years he was able to bring territories under his direct control. The fact that the Czech rule had been oppressive and financially a drain on Polish territories proved an advantage, since Łokietek benefited from local uprisings. In 1306 he entered Kraków.

In the north the Margrave of Brandenburg fought to prevent Łokietek from consolidating his hold over Gdańsk Pomerania. When in November 1308 Łokietek besieged Gdańsk, the defenders called on the Teutonic Knights to assist them. The Knights first aided the besieged town and then occupied it. The event attracted bitter controversy as the Knights were accused of massacring thousands of the town's inhabitants. It is now accepted that the Knights' occupation of Gdańsk was the subject of a skilful propaganda campaign and counter-campaign. One was to justify holding the strategically important castle and the other to dislodge them by accusing them of having perpetrated the massacre. The Knights in effect took advantage of the complex situation to reinforce their presence in the region. In that they obtained support from the Margrave of Brandenburg. For the Poles this meant that they lost access to the sea.

Unfortunately for the process of reconstructing the state, Łokietek was not the only, or even the obvious, Piast prince with whom hopes for unity were associated. In the early stages of his attempt to consolidate his rule, Łokietek was to face opposition from a variety of groups. Some of his most serious rivals were opponents of Venceslas who supported Henry of Głogów, of the Silesian branch of the Piast dynasty. After Venceslas' death Henry held on to Wielkopolska. Not until 1314 when Henry's sons were defeated was Łokietek able to consolidate his control over Wielkopolska, an area which was seen as the cradle of Polish statehood. From 1314 the future king could also confidently claim that he had defeated internal opposition in the form of revolts in major cities, including Kraków. Nevertheless in spite of having the support of Archbishop Świnka, Muskata the Bishop of Kraków opposed him to the end.

The final Papal decision to grant the Polish prince the right to be crowned took longer than expected because of conflicts between the Papacy and the King of France, as a result of which the seat of the Papacy was removed to Avignon. When the request for the right to be crowned was made to Pope John XXII in 1318 it was supported by two arguments which were carefully calculated to seduce the Pope into granting his approval. The first was that the strengthening of Polish authority by the coronation of its ruler would lead to the conquest of the pagan Lithuanians that would increase missionary activities in the east. The second argument was Poland's commitment to the continuing payment of Peter's Pence and its subordination to the Papacy. Arguments against Łokietek being crowned King of Poland were put forward, not surprisingly, by the Teutonic Knights and John of Bohemia who claimed the right to the Polish Crown. Having taken into account his own complex interests, the Pope resorted to a 'Solomonic' judgement. He neither forbade nor approved the coronation of the Polish king. On that basis the Archbishop of Gniezno and the Polish bishops decided to proceed and on 20 January 1320 Łokietek and his wife Jadwiga were crowned King and Queen of Poland.

It is debatable whether the coronation altered anything on its own account. The newly crowned king still had to resort to diplomacy and military action to maintain his authority. The act of being crowned nevertheless was a tangible proof, however qualified, of support given by the Papacy and its allies to the Poles. It can also be argued that in the days when authority depended largely upon the claimant's ability to discharge power and the mythical concept of divine will, the act of coronation strengthened the former and was a tangible proof of the latter. In any case Łokietek could not rely upon any sense of

'Polishness' or shared heritage to bring into the fold those princes who chose to look elsewhere for support. Thus the process of consolidation of the kingdom's territories went hand in hand with wars and alliances negotiated with Poland's neighbours.

The Teutonic Knights were Łokietek's constant and implacable adversaries in the north-east. They found common cause with the Wittelsbachs who ruled Brandenburg after 1323. John Luxemburg, who established himself in Bavaria after the last Premislid ruler died intestate, laid claim to the Polish Crown. He found unity of purpose with the Teutonic Knights. However, Łokietek could depend on the support of the new Hungarian king, Charles Robert of the Angevin dynasty, who was elected in 1301 after the death of the last Arpad ruler. Since the Polish and Hungarian leaders had a shared anxiety about Bavaria, cooperation was a foregone conclusion. At the same time the rapid emergence of Lithuania onto the international scene encouraged the establishment of an alliance with its tribal leader Gedymin. A need to defeat the Teutonic Knights and a shared desire to keep the Wittelsbachs out of Western Pomerania were an added incentive towards close cooperation notwithstanding the fact that the Lithuanians refused to abandon pagan beliefs and to convert to Christianity.

In foreign and internal policies Łokietek utilised all means at his disposal. Diplomacy and recourse to arbitration were initially employed to try and force the Teutonic Knights out of Eastern Prussia. When this appeared to fail, military confrontation combined with periods of negotiations became the norm. Alliances were a critical means of strengthening his diplomatic position. Dynastic rule in most of the European states created circumstances whereby marriages became a means of consolidating relations between dynasties and thus cementing alliances. For this reason Łokietek's sister was married to the King of Hungary and his son's first wife was the daughter of the pagan Lithuanian ruler.

By the time of Łokietek's death in 1333 the presence of the Polish kingdom on the political map of Eastern Europe was clearly established. Poland also became a player, albeit a minor one, in the ongoing dynastic and political West European balance of power. But for all his successes there were just as many disappointments which in effect marked the limits of the new kingdom's power.

The King's biggest failure was his inability to dislodge the Teutonic Knights from Eastern Prussia. From 1308 until his death Łokietek repeatedly petitioned the Papacy to force the Knights to return Pomerania to the Polish kingdom. And even though in 1321 an ecclesiastical commission found in Poland's favour, the Poles and the Papacy failed to persuade the Knights to relinquish their conquests. An alliance with newly emerging rulers in Lithuania did not help, as the Knights were militarily strong enough to withstand attacks by the combined Polish and Lithuanian forces. Throughout the 1320s Łokietek was involved in successive military conflicts with the Knights, none of which were conclusive. Numerous truces and peace treaties were negotiated, with both sides resorting to warfare as soon as the weather permitted, or the political situation allowed it. The Polish king had to be wary of attacks from Bohemia, as John Luxemburg was only too happy to cooperate with the Knights. Between 1329 and 1343 the Knights, in addition to retaining Pomerania, captured and held Kujawy and Dodrzyn. On 27 September 1331 Łokietek's forces scored a military victory against the Knights in Płowce. But they were unable to follow it up with an attack on their strongholds or to rout the remaining forces. The battle clearly manifested the military stalemate which prevailed between the two. Since neither side was prepared to leave the situation as it was, conflict continued. A further truce confirmed as much without resolving or dispelling either side's hostility.

During the latter part of Łokietek's reign Poland finally lost control of Silesia. The Polish king was unable to secure the allegiance of the Silesian princes. John Luxemburg's military successes and increased German political and economic influence in the region led them to pledge feudal allegiance to the Bohemian king. By 1327 most of Silesia with its major towns of Wrocław, Cieszyn and Opole were lost. On Poland's eastern border the situation remained unclear with the Tatars' continuing menacing presence. The alliance with Lithuania, although sealed by young Kazimierz's marriage to the Lithuanian princess, did not lead to the expulsion of the Knights from Pomerania, although it was important in securing Lithuanian goodwill for the Polish king. In the north-west, although the Pomeranian princes agreed to help Łokietek in his conflict with the Wittelsbachs of Brandenburg, in the end both sides agreed on a truce, which left them free to pursue their primary objectives. In the case of the Polish king this was his battle against the Teutonic Knights, while the Wittelsbachs concentrated on their conflict with Pope John XXII. As a result Western Pomerania remained outside the Polish kingdom.

Łokietek died, exceptionally for the times, at the ripe age of 70 in March 1333. To his 23-year-old son he handed over a kingdom the boundaries of which had been roughly outlined and tested in battles with neighbours. The loss of Pomerania and the King's inability to stem the growth of the power of the Teutonic Knights there can be seen as one of his biggest failings. Against that, nevertheless, has to be balanced the fact that he bequeathed to his son a kingdom, the authority of which was equal to that of other kingdoms in the region. The younger Kazimierz's task would be made easier by the fact that Łokietek had only one surviving son whose legitimacy was not in doubt. The line of succession having thus been secured it was left to the son to continue the task of consolidating the kingdom within its defensible borders and to build up again a state administration.

When Kazimierz was crowned King of Poland in April 1333, the act of coronation was supported by the nobility, the Church and the Pope. His father had already involved him in administrative and military matters and he had been well prepared to assume the responsibility of kingship. In the King of Hungary he had a staunch ally, but John of Bohemia continued to lay claim to the Polish throne. The Teutonic Knights had, in the mean time, tried to undermine him by spreading rumours about his suitability to become king, implying that he was a lightweight, more concerned with sexual pleasure and a coward to boot, who fled from the battlefield. The Knights had mastered the art of negative publicity. While the first accusation was fully justified, the second was of a dubious nature. During the course of his lifetime, Kazimierz contracted two legitimate marriages and two possibly polygamous ones. After the death of his first bride, the Lithuanian Anna, Kazimierz in 1341 married Adelheid of Hesse. The marriage was an unhappy one. In 1356 while visiting Charles IV in Prague Kazimierz met a beautiful widow with whom he unwisely fell in love. In a manner not uncommon in middle-aged men, Kazimierz set aside his barren wife and married the lovely widow Krystyna. The problem was that the marriage ceremony took place even before a Papal annulment of the previous marriage had been secured. In 1363, having bored of Krystyna and troubled by questions of succession, Kazimierz married Jadwiga, daughter of the prince of the Silesian district of Żagań. Adelheid who outlived both later wives and her wayward husband, challenged both later marriages in Papal courts. Kazimierz died without leaving a legitimate male heir, though he did have illegitimate sons.

From the outset Kazimierz recognised that the Knights were his most serious enemies. But as neither side could secure a decisive victory, both were inclined to conclude that a truce was mutually advantageous. Thus Kazimierz took the diplomatic route in dealing with Poland's most serious enemy. In the first place the truce signed by his father was extended, then both sides submitted themselves to the mediation of the kings of Bohemia and Hungary. The new Pope Benedict XII gave his blessing to attempts to resolve the dispute peacefully. The Poles' hand was strengthened by the Bohemians being wary of Kazimierz's rapprochement with the Wittelsbachs. John Luxemburg of Bohemia continued to press his claim to the Polish throne, though his son Charles of Moravia, soon to become the German Emperor Charles IV as well as King of Bohemia, realised the importance of reducing tension with the Poles in order to free himself to continue his conflict with the Wittelsbachs of Brandenburg. Thus in return for the Czechs renouncing their claim to the Polish Crown the Poles accepted Bohemian feudal stewardship over Silesia. This made sure that the Poles remained out of the German conflicts, which is what the Luxemburgs wanted. But for the Poles, their agreement with the Bohemian ruling dynasty guaranteed that they would not have to face a joint threat on two fronts, from Bohemia and the Knights. By 1343 as a result of the treaty of Kalisz, relations between the Teutonic Knights and the Polish king were normalised. The Knights wanted to concentrate on consolidating their hold over the Baltic coast and on defence of their territories from incursions from Lithuania. Kazimierz on the other hand was forced to recognise that it was up to him to resolve his problems with the Teutonic Knights as the Pope, the Bohemians and the Hungarians were preoccupied with their own affairs and would not mediate further. The Poles thus accepted a compromise whereby they renounced Chełmno and the Knights agreed to return Kujawy and Dobrzyń to Poland. Although on no account satisfactory, the treaty freed Kazimierz to concentrate on more pressing matters, namely conflicts in the east.

The earlier Tatar military successes had created a political vacuum in Ruthenia and Halicz. The Rus principalities paid tribute to the Tatars and were fragmented and unstable. Kazimierz decided to invade. Whether this was done to prevent Lithuania and/or Hungary from moving first, or in order to consolidate Polish hold over areas with which there had in the past existed political ties, is not entirely clear. The Polish invasion of Ruthenia in 1340 was precipitated by two factors. Renewed military action by the Tatars meant that once more they were poised to enter Central Europe. The other factor was the poisoning of the Ruthenian ruler by his nobility, the boyars, which in turn signalled the beginning of a period of political instability. In his desire to establish control over Ruthenia and Halicz, Kazimierz faced less of a threat from Hungary, which was most likely only concerned with reducing the Tatar threat. Lithuania had a more direct interest in the region. Gedymin, Kazimierz's one-time father-in-law, died in 1341 leaving seven sons, who fought over the succession. They represented a dynamic and unbridled force in the region. In 1349, having first obtained Papal authority for military action against the pagans in the east, which was a way of confirming future ownership of conquered territories, Kazimierz started a major military campaign. He was successful in capturing Ruthenia. This might not have been entirely due to Polish military prowess and could well have been due to the collapse of the Tatar thrust into Europe, caused by the death of their Khan and ravages by the Black Death which on this occasion had affected the eastern and south-eastern regions of Europe.

The new territories were a mixed blessing to the Polish kingdom as the defence and consolidation of the unexpectedly easy conquest preoccupied Kazimierz until his death. The Tatars periodically were able to mount attacks into Ruthenia, but conflicts with Lithuania were of a more serious nature. Unusually, the Papacy had been unwilling to sanction a Crusade against the Lithuanian rulers, due most likely to fears that such a declaration would push them towards the Orthodox Christian Church. Thus the doors were kept open for the Lithuanians to join the Church of Rome which, perversely, still reigned in Avignon at the time. The Papacy and Kazimierz did declare the Polish attack eastward as a Crusade against the Tatars. It was accepted that the region was a front line and marked the boundary between Christendom and the pagan world. By 1366 the limits of Polish conquests had been defined by a treaty signed with Lithuania. Ruthenia was divided between them, with Poland retaining the southern part with the town of Lvóv. Poland also kept Halicz, though it is still unclear whether Podole went to Poland at that time or was conquered later. Southern sections of Wołyn and the districts of Chełm and Bełż became part of the Polish kingdom. Other areas became fiefdoms, with the lords owing their allegiance to the Polish king. Through his conquest of Ruthenia, Kazimierz incorporated into his kingdom Orthodox and Armenian Christians whose religious rights were nevertheless respected. The area was never fully incorporated into the Polish kingdom, always retaining its distinctiveness. Although through a process of settlement and royal grants the Polish nobility gained a foothold in Ruthenia, the peasantry remained predominantly committed to its own faith and distinct culture. The Catholic Church and the King were happy to leave the situation as it was.

Future generations have honoured Kazimierz by according him the title of 'Great', 'Wielki' in Polish. This was in recognition of his contribution to the consolidation of the Polish kingdom. Reforms introduced by Kazimierz Wielki placed Poland in the ranks of the leading European states. While it is debatable whether his contribution was unique, nevertheless by building on the process which his father had initiated, his reign marks a high point in Polish medieval history. In the first place Kazimierz had to build political unity. This was a slow process of breaking down of the independence which had been enjoyed by local princes and dukes. His own elevation to the status of king did not always meet with approval and Kazimierz had to contend with challenges to his authority and with regional particularism. He was as capable of brutality against those who defied him as he was of conciliation, in particular if the loyalty of an individual could be obtained by these means. Most provincial dukes and princes were forced to accept the loss of autonomy, and in return for submitting to the authority of the King gained entitlement to their lands as Crown vassals.

Parallel with the establishment of Crown authority came the need for state administration. What traditions and procedure had been established under earlier rulers had been lost. Territorial unity inevitably meant that a common administrative and judicial system had to be established. From 1346 reforms continued in phases. The Piotrków and Wiślice statutes dealt with civil and criminal law and reforms of the judiciary. The need to clarify the application of traditional laws went hand in hand with the imposition of new laws. In his need to codify laws, Kazimierz Wielki reflected the general European trend to define the status and obligations of all sections of society to central authority. He had also himself come to appreciate the importance of a comprehensive body of legislation. As head of state, Kazimierz had to think of devolution of authority to appointed administrators. This became a pressing need once his control over areas had been consolidated. Thus he appointed the so-called *starosty* as administrative representatives of royal authority in the regions.

Kazimierz had been exposed to the sophisticated Hungarian court and learned from his dealings with the Papacy and his adversaries the importance of having well-informed and educated advisors and legislators. He encouraged schooling and used those who had been trained in West European universities. The need for legislators was so pressing that he secured a Papal Charter for the establishment of a university in Kraków in 1364. While civil law, canon law, medicine and liberal arts were to be taught at the new university, Urban IV was not inclined to devolve authority over matters relating to the Church by allowing the teaching of theology. But education was not only a means of securing advancement. We know that sons of the wealthy landed gentry travelled to distant European universities as part of a process of growing up and gaining life experience. Whereas Prague University attracted a high proportion of students from Poland, some travelled as far as Italy to attend universities with established reputations. There is also evidence that by the end of the fourteenth century, in addition to the already existing cathedral schools, which provided standard teaching of key subjects such as arithmetic, music, geometry and astronomy, a chain of parish elementary schools had also been established. Obviously, it would be wrong to speak of a literate society, but literacy and education appear to have become an essential prerequisite for involvement in state matters and an accomplishment much sought after by the wealthy nobility and the Crown.

Military considerations remained paramount in Kazimierz's mind throughout his life. He was never free from the need to either defend his father's achievements or to consolidate them by further conquests. Thus the need to finance wars waged at various times throughout his reign required a regular income. Crown lands were the obvious source of revenue. Additionally, all subjects were obliged to pay dues. A high proportion of these obligations had predictably lapsed during the period when central authority had collapsed. Kazimierz thus increased his revenue by the frequently practised method of renewing and reclaiming lapsed obligations. These measures invariably raised hostility.

By the beginning of the fourteenth century the landed settlement on the so-called 'German laws' became increasingly the norm. Whereas previously peasants were obliged to make payments to the landowner or Crown in kind or to work on the estate, these new laws, based on German models, moved towards converting these payments into annual cash payment, the so-called tithe. This was seen as an encouragement for peasants to produce a surplus but also allowed for the accumulation and increase in peasant wealth. The new pattern of relations between peasants and landlords was also seen as more progressive and likely to encourage better agricultural practices and, as a result, higher yields. After the ravages of the previous century and the depletions caused by the Black Death, landlords were keen to settle peasants on their estates. Kazimierz encouraged both settlements on German laws and colonisation of new land, all the time seeking to increase the Crown's revenue.

The growth of trade, as Poland lay now on the crossroads of flourishing north–south and east–west trade routes, provided Kazimierz with an opportunity to increase revenue by levying customs payments. The exploitation of rich salt mines in Bochnia and Wieliczka remained a royal monopoly and the King increased the amount of salt which was mined and sold.

Poland's military strength depended as much on her economic resources as it did on the King's ability to adapt to new styles of warfare and to new threats. By extending the obligation of military service to all knights, the nobility and village headmen a regular supply of manpower was guaranteed. Townspeople had the duty to participate in the defence of towns, while the clergy, who in principle were forbidden to bear arms, had a duty to fund the employment of a replacement. Kazimierz's rule is associated with a building programme, which was intended to guarantee the security of the kingdom by surrounding it with stone fortifications. A continuous network of strongholds, forts and redoubts was supported by further fortifications as a fallback line of defence. Present-day travellers through Silesia and the Kraków district can still see remnants of some of the more spectacular defensive castles constructed at the time, though many were destroyed during the Swedish wars.

In view of the general turbulence in the Church's relations with various monarchies prevailing in Europe, notably the Papacy's quarrels with the King of France and continuing conflicts with the Emperor, Kazimierz's relations with the Church were relatively uncomplicated. The occasional Church condemnation of the King's personal life could be ignored as Kazimierz made sure that the Archbishop of Gniezno supported him. Successive bishops of Kraków had been hostile to him and favoured the Bohemian kings, though in the end Kazimierz was able to secure an appointment favourable to himself. The crucial issue was his, and earlier his father's, support for the Papacy in disputes with the Emperor. The payment of the Peter's Pence tax continued to predispose the Papacy sympathetically to the Polish Crown and as a result, in disputes with the Teutonic Knights, the Poles could count on favourable, if not necessarily effective or even enforceable, pronouncements.

The legal status of Jews had been earlier defined, but Kazimierz is generally portrayed as being sympathetic towards their presence on Polish lands. They were granted two charters in 1334 and 1364 which confirmed their status. Modelled on charters which had been granted in the Bohemian lands, these defined Jews as Crown subjects, and as a result protected by the Crown. The Jewish community was granted full autonomy in matters relating to their faith and community. Kazimierz welcomed Jews into Poland, mainly because they were seen as successful bankers. Laws stating what rate of interest they were allowed to charge regulated Jewish financial activities. Nevertheless during the reign of Kazimierz, the first anti-Jewish pogroms took place. In that respect what happened in Poland reflected a pattern of developments which had taken place elsewhere, in particular during the spread of the Black Death plague through Europe. As the epidemic spread Jewish communities were attacked on the suspicion that they had either directly or indirectly caused the disease. On the whole outrages committed against the Jewish community in Polish lands tended to be spontaneous and generally were not approved by the authorities, who, in view of the exchequer's dependence on the Jews' financial activities, did not want to see their flight from Poland.

The Black Death and the general state of insecurity led to splinter movements emerging from within the Christian Church. Flagellants and similar mystical groups made their appearance briefly during 1261. But more threatening to the Church's authority were radical challenges to the Papacy's increased drive for internal discipline, obedience and theological uniformity. The Church's extensive involvement in secular matters, which went hand in hand with the consolidation of Church wealth and displays of splendour, caused a reaction from within the Church ranks. In 1318 the Pope appointed two Inquisitors to deal with heresies which had manifested themselves primarily in the Silesian region. The Weldenses, Beguines and Berghard heretics had two issues in common; namely the condemnation of Church wealth and of organised observance. The Inquisition's investigations were only partially successful. In spite of the burning at the stake of a number of heretics, ideas critical of organised observance and Papal authority continued to be articulated even from within the Church.

When Kazimierz died, the boundaries of his kingdom seemed secure, but the crucial issue of succession which had the capacity of destroying all that he and his father had achieved remained unresolved. Upon this depended the immediate future of the Polish kingdom.

3

· · · · · · · ·

The Jagiellonian Period

In medieval times the death of a king, in particular one who did not leave a successor, always created preconditions for instability. In the case of Kazimierz Wielki, those difficulties had been anticipated and at least in principle, arrangements had been put in place to forestall a challenge to the Crown's authority. Kazimierz, whose fecundity was not in doubt, had the misfortune of not leaving any legitimate male heirs. In the fourteenth century this matter could not be overcome without difficulties. The concept of hereditary monarchy was too well established to allow for the replacement of one king with another, in particular one not directly related to the deceased monarch. Before his death Kazimierz had decided to appoint his nephew Louis of Hungary, the son of his sister Elizabeth, to succeed him. But a condition was attached to this agreement, namely were Louis to die without a male heir, the matter of succession should once more be decided by the Poles. Shortly before his death Kazimierz adopted another of his nephews, Kaźko. He clearly had hoped that in the event of Louis dying without legitimate male issue this nephew would succeed to the Polish throne.

Signs of dissent among the Polish nobility already preceded Louis' enthronement in Kraków Cathedral on 17 November 1370. On hearing of his uncle's illness Louis hastened to Kraków, where he was greeted by a delegation which informed him that the royal burial had already taken place. The custom of the day was for the crowning of the successor to take place first and for the burial of the deceased king to follow. Haste cannot be explained by health considerations. In the Middle Ages putrefaction of the body of the deceased was a familiar phenomenon which by itself would not have affected ceremonial obligations. This was an unmistakable sign of internal opposition to Louis. Louis tried to garner support by making commitments not to introduce new taxes and to lower taxes for arable land, but the nobility knew that they were in a strong position to trade favours for support. Louis was going to be an absentee King of Poland. Although his mother stayed in Kraków to see to his affairs, the opposition was not satisfied with this arrangement. While Kraków and Małopolska supported union with Hungary, Wielkopolska opposed it, looking to a possibility of one of the remaining Piast princelings becoming king. Just in case, Kaźko was bought off by Louis by a grant of the district of Dobrzyniec. Another pretender from the Piast line, Władysław Biały of Kujawy, initially supported by sections of the Wielkopolska nobility, faced major obstacles. The fact that he was a monk and that the Pope refused to release him from his vows was but one of those unresolved problems. Louis was able first to outmanoeuvre Władysław Biały, whittling down his support, and then to buy him off. By 1377 Władysław and Kaźko relinquished their claims to the Polish throne.

But Louis never fully concentrated on the newly acquired Polish Crown. Indeed, the recent honour was relatively unimportant compared to others which extended the influence of the Hungarian Crown throughout the Balkans as well as Eastern Europe. Hence his rather opportunistic approach to Polish affairs. During Louis' 12-year rule, some of the conquests made earlier by Kazimierz were traded in to strengthen the Hungarian Crown's position. Thus Louis renounced the Polish Crown's claim to Silesia as part of a deal which secured him the support of the Czech Luxemburgs. His daughter Maria was betrothed to Sigismund of Luxemburg. The Rus territories were incorporated into Hungary, where Louis reversed many of Kazimierz's more enlightened policies towards Jews. During Louis' rule Orthodox Christians suffered persecution. In due course Masovia and Pomerania drifted away from the Polish Crown because of conflicts with Louis.

At the end of his life Louis too faced the problem of not having a male heir. He was survived by two daughters and had obtained the agreement of the nobility that the oldest would be crowned as 'king'. It was unthinkable that a queen should rule in her own name. What Louis had obtained was an assurance that his daughters would succeed, but it was still their husbands who would be the rulers. Louis had to make sure that their marriages would strengthen both daughters' positions. Naturally the Polish nobility took a lively interest in the succession issue. It was realised that the remaining Piast princelings lacked the determination and status to lay claim to the Polish Crown.

It was therefore accepted that whatever decision was made concerning the succession to the Hungarian Crown would affect the fate of Poland. The nobility also knew that they stood to gain further privileges, as Louis would be bound to seek their support and approval for whatever decision was made. As the Hungarian Crown concentrated on the succession issue, the governance of Polish territories was left in the hands of appointed plenipotentiaries. The power of the nobility grew and so did their anticipation of better things to come when their support for the appointed successor was requested. In 1374 their efforts were crowned with success. By the Pact of Košice Louis was assured on his death that one of his daughters would be allowed to succeed to the Polish throne. But the Polish nobility drove a hard bargain. They demanded and obtained assurances that the kingdom's borders would not be reduced, and that they would not be obliged to bear arms in wars outside the borders of the Polish kingdom. All taxes paid by the nobility on their estates were abolished and taxes paid by the peasants whose holdings were on ecclesiastical or nobles' estates were reduced from 12 *groszy* per *lan* to 2. The nobility was also assured that all Crown appointments would be made from the ranks of the local nobility. The implications of the Košice privileges were momentous. The Crown's income would be reduced and the nobility's obligations to support military campaigns would be limited.

When Louis died on 11 September 1382, the first signs suggested that there would be no conflict over who was to succeed him. His oldest daughter Maria, who had married Sigismund Luxemburg, had been nominated to the Polish throne and the younger, Jadwiga, betrothed to Wilhelm, son of Leopold Habsburg of Austria, was to take the Hungarian Crown. But Louis' widow decided to change these arrangements. She was aided by members of the Hungarian nobility, who opposed the Luxemburg connection and planned to have Maria in Buda in order to isolate her husband and then remove him. In Poland there was also anxiety about the consequences of the princesses' marriages. Jadwiga's betrothal had not been consummated, as was the custom in those days, due to the fact that she had not reached puberty. This gave the Polish nobility the hope that were she to be nominated to become Queen of Poland, they would still be able to influence the choice of husband. For the nobility and the Church this situation also held out the prospect of the prolongation of the interregnum when they could further strengthen their position and weaken that of the central authority.

In 1383 as a result of an agreement concluded between the assembly of Polish nobility and a Hungarian envoy, Jadwiga was accepted as the future Queen of Poland. But the matter was not entirely settled. An unexpected pretender to the Polish Crown emerged in the person of Ziemovit, the Piast prince of Masovia. Between the time when she was named as the heir to the throne and her arrival in Kraków in 1384, Jadwiga's future was still not clear. The Wielkopolska nobility was inclined to support Ziemovit, or at least to consider Jadwiga on the condition that she married Ziemovit. A plan to kidnap her and forcefully marry her to Ziemovit failed. In the end Jadwiga's mother realised that if she procrastinated, the Polish nobility might make their own choice, and she allowed her daughter to go to Poland. On 15 October 1384 she was crowned Queen of Poland.

There was, of course, still the outstanding issue of Jadwiga's as yet unconsummated betrothal to Wilhelm Habsburg. The Polish nobility resented this arrangement and when the hapless fiancé arrived in Kraków on 15 August 1385 to bed his future wife, his way to her bedchamber was barred and he was made to leave Poland. The choice of Jadwiga's husband was deemed too important a matter and not even her deceased father's wishes, little more the young girl's preferences, stood in the way of the matter being reopened. The Polish nobility made sure they had the freedom to make a choice they considered appropriate. Jadwiga's feelings on the matter were of little consequence, even though she was known to oppose the final choice made on her behalf. And who could have blamed her, for the nobility decided that this bright and highly educated young woman should marry a man three times her age and a heathen to boot. The decision to enter into an agreement with the Lithuanians was made by the Małopolska nobility. They thought in terms of incorporating Lithuania into the Polish kingdom and furthermore of securing for themselves opportunities for enrichment which would come in the wake of royal grants. On 14 August 1385 in Krewa an agreement was signed between the Lithuanians and representatives of the Polish Crown. In return for a commitment to restore the Polish kingdom to its previous borders, the Lithuanian ruler Jogaila, who on betrothal took the name Jagiełło, was to become King of Poland. On 11 January 1386 he was elected king. Jadwiga's hand in marriage was part and parcel of the deal. As part of the marriage arrangement he agreed to convert and to lead Lithuania towards the Church of Rome. Some of the Lithuanian nobility had already been accepted into the Orthodox Church.

It is difficult to overlook the fact that the union, however advantageous to Poland and Lithuania, was made at the expense of the young woman's personal happiness. Jadwiga had been brought up at the Hungarian court, one of the most enlightened in Europe. She was literate and exceptionally well educated. From an early age she had been prepared to one day become Queen of Hungary. By all accounts she was a spirited and enlightened woman, fully aware of her position. Jagiełło was an illiterate warrior king. Whereas Jadwiga had been brought up in the environment of knightly chivalry and enlightened discourse, her husband had no time for such rituals, and was even by the standards of the time, neglectful of personal hygiene. Nevertheless, the Queen's youth and robust health gave hope that a new royal dynasty would emerge from this union, thus securing Poland's future, and that was what the Polish nobility wanted.

By marrying the Queen of Poland, the Lithuanian ruler consolidated the union between Poland and the Duchy of Lithuania. Commitments made by both sides were spelled out precisely in the Krewa Agreement, confirming the political importance of the act. Jagiełło undertook to reconquer lands recently lost by the Polish Crown, firstly the Rus territories, but also Pomerania and Silesia. Of great importance was the fact that Lithuania, which had the capacity to become Poland's main enemy and rival in the east, thus joined Poland in a common political destiny. The choice had been for the Poles to either defeat the Lithuanians or to join them. The union was certainly very advantageous to both sides. The Teutonic Knights, who at a stroke lost their excuse for the conquest of the Lithuanian territories, now became the common enemy. In the international arena, Rome's support and approval for the Christianisation of Lithuania was a matter of considerable importance. The Teutonic Knights, who were fully aware of the implication of the union, mounted a propaganda war against Jagiełło, allying themselves with Jadwiga's rebuffed fiancé. But the Poles were able to take advantage of disarray in Papal affairs, because a conflict had just broken out between two contenders to the Papacy. The Poles took the side of Pope Urban VI against Clement VII. Urban, whose case was stronger, was loath to alienate the Poles and therefore endorsed Lithuania's acceptance of Christianity. This reduced the Teutonic Knights' argument, which rested on the claim that the conversion of Lithuania had been superficial and therefore could not be accepted as real. Notwithstanding the Papal pronouncement, the Knights continued to take a more than lively interest in

Lithuania, trying to extend their conquests and attempting to stir up an uprising. They had good reasons for trying to discredit the Polish and Lithuanian arguments. The need to conquer and convert pagan tribes was the rationale for the Knights' state. Were it to be accepted that this process was completed the Knights' role would be redundant. In fact the Knights had established a state which they did not intend to abandon and their ambitions grew with conquest. In 1390 the confrontation between the Knights and Jagiełło was fully established and would continue throughout his rule. Military and diplomatic skills were utilised in this conflict, with both sides attempting to gain support in European capitals.

When Jagiełło took up residence in the royal palace in Kraków he became fully preoccupied in Polish affairs. In the mean time a relative of his, Vytautas (Witold in Polish), headed a Lithuanian movement against the union with Poland. The potential for difficulties between Poles and Lithuanians had always been there. In those days Lithuania was not the small Baltic-based state we know now, but a large sprawling entity, embracing lands from the Baltic to the Black Sea. Most of the population inhabiting the area had converted to the Orthodox Christian Church. The Rus nobility was angry at the Lithuanian nobility's determination to keep them out of all decision making. This rivalry pushed the Lithuanians towards a union with Poland, which although not entirely to their liking, strengthened their hand in their dealings with the Ruthenians. But even among the Lithuanians, some did not welcome the union with Poland. While Jagiełło was preoccupied in Poland, discontent brewed in the Lithuanian lands, fuelled by rivalry between the Polish nobility, greedy for Lithuanian lands, and by Lithuanians' anxiety about being sidelined. In these circumstances the Teutonic Knights hoped to benefit from conflicts between the two.

The hope that the union would lead to the establishment of a new royal dynasty in Poland, which would have strengthened Jagiełło's position, was put in doubt, because for seven years Jadwiga did not become pregnant. Tragedy struck on 17 June 1399 when Jadwiga died after having given birth to a daughter who only survived a few days. In 1402 Jagiełło was able to bolster his position by marrying the granddaughter of Kazimierz Wielki. But in reality his situation was already clarified by the fact that no dissent had emerged to his continuing role as King of Poland after Jadwiga's death. On account of the numerous privileges granted to the nobility over the last centuries, the Polish Crown was to all purposes an elected one. Jadwiga was a descendant of the Piast dynasty, but she could not be the ruler of the kingdom, while her husband, who was ruler, had no hereditary or dynastic claim to the Crown. Poles had an emotional attachment to Jadwiga, though in reality she played only a minimal role in policy making. Fortunately for Jagiełło, the Polish nobility backed him, appreciating the need for unity and centralisation. The only person who had earlier posed a threat to his position, Ziemovit, had made his peace with the King and renounced his claim. In 1401 Jagiełło clarified further the nature of Poland's union with Lithuania, by defining relations between the two states and between himself and Witold. The latter became Jagiełło's plenipotentiary in Lithuania, with the title of Grand Duke. In Lithuania Jagiełło continued to be the hereditary ruler, so naturally he was loath to give up his secure position there, for an insecure one in Poland. In the mean time the Lithuanian nobility obtained an assurance that were Jagiełło to die without legitimate male issue, they would be consulted on matters relating to the succession to the Polish throne. The agreements established the principle that the two states were of equal importance. This concession smoothed relations between the two, reducing rivalry and tension. More importantly it brought the two states together to deal with the continuing menace posed by the Teutonic Knights.

The opportunity to square up to the long postponed fight was sought by the three protagonists. Relations between Poland, Lithuania and the Teutonic Knights' state had always been difficult. But the union between Poland and Lithuania made the conflict so much more urgent for the Knights. Time was not on their side. With Lithuania becoming closer to Poland and entering into diplomatic relations with Western European states, the Knights' excuse for further conquest became increasingly doubtful. In 1403 Pope Boniface IX decreed that the Teutonic Knights were wrong in attacking the newly converted Lithuanians and that their actions were detrimental to the Christian cause. With this edict all Crusading activities against the Lithuanians should have ceased. Instead the Knights tried to consolidate their territories. In 1407 the new Grand Master Ulrich von Jungingen initiated an aggressive policy towards Poland. By purchasing from Sigismund Luxemburg, King of Hungary, the territory of the New Mark, wedged between Wielkopolska and Pomerania, the Knights gained an easier route to the west. The Poles, irritated by the Knights' opportunism, viewed this as an act of aggression. The Teutonic Knights decided to strike first at the Poles, the stronger of the two enemies.

In Poland, the desire to resolve the long-drawn-out and inconclusive state of rivalry with the Teutonic Knights was also gaining
support. Thus the Poles were ready for a confrontation once the Polish
nobility felt confident that the Lithuanians would join in an attack on
the Knights, and would not be tempted to negotiate a separate peace.
The pretext came when in 1408 an uprising broke out in Żmudź
(Žemaitija) territory, which Witold had earlier handed over to the
Knights in return for peace. This acquisition brought the Knights
closer to the order of the Knights of the Sword in Livonia and gave
them a springboard for further attack on Lithuania. Witold decided to
support the local people against the Knights and as a result embarked
on an open conflict. In Poland this meant that the nobility had to give
the King approval for a war in support of Lithuania. On 6 September
1409 the Knights despatched a declaration of war to the Poles. On 8
October after first skirmishes between the three protagonists had taken
place an armistice was negotiated suspending all military action until
25 June 1410. Time thus gained was utilised by all sides to gain allies
and international support.

The Teutonic Knights were better placed to secure international
support. By virtue of the order's membership and contacts they were
able to appeal to West European monarchs and nobility. A call was put
out for knights to rally to the order's banners to fight against the infidels. By presenting this as a continuation of the East Prussian Crusade,
thus an opportunity to gain Papal dispensation, the Teutonic Knights
gained political and material support. West European knights flocked
to the Knights' side, motivated by the belief that the conflict would
offer opportunities for jousting, combat with other knights and ultimately glory and booty. Political considerations played a part in the
support given to the Knights. In their contest for support, the Knights
had an obvious advantage which wealth gave them. The Hungarian
and Bohemian kings were in need of money. Sigismund, the
Luxemburg King of Hungary, sided with the Knights. He hoped to
become the Holy Roman Emperor, though the desire to claim the
Polish Crown played a more immediate role. His brother, Vaclav King
of Bohemia, also decided to throw in his lot with the Knights. But the
Teutonic Knights had failed to obtain the full support of Konrad von
Vietinghoff, the Grand Master of the Knights of the Sword in Livonia.
He had not been too pleased about the Teutonic Knights' confron-
tational policies, which endangered his precarious alliance with
Lithuania. The Knights of the Sword had their sights set on the

Principality of Pskov. In order to succeed they needed either Lithuanian support or at least their disinterest. Konrad von Vietinghoff, when asked for help by the Teutonic Knights, pleaded his commitment to a truce signed with the Lithuanians. His failure to militarily support the Teutonic Knights tipped the balance in favour of the combined Polish and Lithuanian forces.

The Poles and Lithuanians played the same game, though they were not able to make use of the extent of political support which the Knights had. In 1409 a Polish delegation made its way to the court of Henry IV of England, only to be told that he supported the Knights. In relation to the Papacy, the Poles seemed to have struck lucky. Towards the end of 1409 a conclave of cardinals met in the Italian town of Pisa to resolve the schism which continued to tear apart the Church. They repudiated the two pretenders to the Papacy, Benedict XIII and Gregory XII, and in their place elected a new Pope, Alexander V. He had earlier spent some time on missionary duties in Lithuania. Jagiełło, banking on the new Pope's familiarity with the state of relations between the Poles, Lithuanians and the Teutonic Knights, immediately recognised the new Pope. In the circumstances, Alexander V did not give his support to the Knights' call to aid their Crusade against the infidels in the east. But since few at this stage recognised him as a rightful Pope, this advantage was only of limited value. At the same time Jagiełło and Witold made peace with Muscovy and with the Masovian princes who though reluctant to anger the Knights, honoured their feudal duty to aid their lord, the King of Poland, by sending troops to assist him. In the military confrontation with the Knights, the Poles also used Swiss mercenaries and Tatar units provided by a pretender to the leadership of the Golden Horde, who had earlier sought sanctuary in Lithuania.

Historians have pointed out that the two sides approached the inevitable conflict in a distinctly different spirit. The Knights depended on the participation of West European knights to join them. The Teutonic Knights represented a formidable and experienced military force, but not numerous enough to face a major conflict with the combined Polish–Lithuanian forces. Mercenaries were brought in to aid the Knights. Polish historians have recently pointed out that in addition to generally underestimating the enemies' ability to plan for a major confrontation, the Knights viewed the war in different military terms. They prepared for a war of open confrontation, in which knights would be bound by a strict code of conduct, which governed such confrontations in the West. Each knight fought with his retinue and his servants. He decided when to take booty and generally did not pursue a defeated enemy. He also decided when to leave the battlefield.

Jagiełło did not feel bound by these rules. To him and the Lithuanian and Polish nobility this was a long-awaited confrontation with an enemy. He depended on a *levée en masse*, forming a more disciplined armed force. Extensive planning had preceded the confrontation. Jagiełło, acting as the military leader of the combined Polish and Lithuanian forces, considered fully the terrain, used intelligence sources to assess the enemy's strength and movements and ultimately utilised the element of surprise, all alien to the chivalric code of conduct accepted by West European knights. In more than one way the conflict was one between two sides committed to distinctly different military doctrines.

The military confrontation, which in Poland is referred to as the battle of Grunwald, took place on 15 July 1410. It is frequently described as the most important military battle of the medieval period. Its unusual feature was that it took place between two Christian forces. On one side stood the Teutonic Knights numbering approximately 500, experienced military men, well armed and confident of their political and military power. Though precise figures are difficult to ascertain, it is possible the Grand Master of the Teutonic Knights had at his disposal additionally a cavalry of 16,000 and an infantry of 5,000 men. The nobility from areas controlled by the Knights and an undefined number of foreign guests and volunteer knights were attached to the Knights. Mercenaries from Switzerland and other European states strengthened the side. The Grand Master Ulrich von Jungingen personally led his men into battle. Of critical importance was his decision not to take the offensive but to fight a defensive war. The Knights calculated that the combined Polish–Lithuanian forces would move to Pomerania and that the major engagement would be on the left bank of the Vistula.

The Poles and Lithuanians, who, it is generally agreed, prepared themselves better for the conflict, were led by Jagiełło and Witold. On 30 June the Polish and Lithuanian forces met and moved to Prussia hoping to surprise the Knights near their major stronghold of Malbork. This manoeuvre had been made possible because a pontoon bridge had been prepared to cross the Vistula. Jagiełło's tactic was to avoid a confrontation with the Knights for as long as possible and to use the element of surprise. In the morning of 15 July the Grand Master, having caught up with the Poles and Lithuanians, decided to take up positions to prevent them from moving further towards Malbork. Near the village of Stębark (Tannenberg) the Knights awaited the Polish and Lithuanian units. Jagiełło, who had been forewarned of the waiting enemy, accepted that the battle was inevitable. But at this point the Polish king used to the full the fact that the enemy was eager for a confrontation. He procrastinated and the Knights and their units were obliged to stand in the growing heat waiting for the enemy to approach. Normally the Knights would expect the enemy to accept the challenge and enter into combat. But while individual knights challenged the enemy to individual combat, which was a preliminary to the major conflict, Jagiełło refused to move his units to the battlefield. Finally, the Grand Master despatched emissaries to the Polish camp bearing two naked swords as a symbol of the challenge to battle. The gesture, which was all part of the ritual of medieval warfare, irritated the Poles with its imputation of cowardice and the battle could no longer be postponed.

At midday, when the units of the Teutonic Knights had stood since early morning in the summer sun, the Lithuanians emerged from the cool of the nearby woods and proceeded to battle. The hostilities lasted approximately 7 hours. In the first place the Knights scattered the Lithuanian units, which fled from the battlefield. An attack on Polish units followed but was not successful and a protracted fight ensued. Jagiełło, who was forbidden by the Polish noblemen to participate in the battle, gave orders from a nearby hillock. By the evening, when the most ferocious battles between the Polish units and the Knights appeared likely to result in a Polish victory, the Grand Master and all his commanders entered into the mêlée. They all died in the final bloodbath. By nightfall, the Polish–Lithuanian victory was assured. Many of the wounded, left on the battlefield, died during the night. In the morning the Poles recovered the body of the Grand Master and those of three other high-ranking Knights and returned them to Malbork. The exact casualty figures are unknown and in future years both sides strove to either minimise or inflate them, according to the need. But the Teutonic Knights' records refer to 202 Knights having fallen in the battle and of an additional 18,000 men, including mercenaries and guests knights from Europe, perishing. Polish chroniclers make reference to 50,000 fallen in battle and equal numbers taken into captivity. There is need for caution in treating these figures too literally, the phrase 'thousands and thousands' might well have denoted 'lots and lots'.

There is no denying the importance and enormity of the battle. Nor is it possible to deny the Poles and Lithuanians their victory. They had been better prepared for the confrontation, and military decisions made earlier and on the battlefield resulted in a well-deserved victory. The supremacy and supposed invincibility of the Knights had been destroyed. Although Jagiełło was not able to follow up the military victory with a total rout of the Knights, they never regained their prestige. After burying the dead on the battlefield the Polish and Lithuanian armies proceeded to lay siege to the Teutonic stronghold of Malbork. But by 22 September they had to call it off. They had no siege machines and Malbork was a formidable fortress. Jagiełło also realised that he needed to follow up his military victory with political consolidation. Most of the major Prussian towns now accepted that the Knights' power was broken. With the destruction of their stranglehold Prussia would come to terms with the Poles and the Lithuanians, but not yet. In any case, the army showed sign of restlessness and there was a need to allow the nobility and knights to return home. On 1 February 1411 a peace treaty was signed with the Teutonic Knights in the town of Toruń. The main, if rather modest, achievement of the treaty was the return of Żmudź to Lithuania. The Knights' hopes of establishing absolute control over the Baltic coast were destroyed.

In the coming years the emphasis shifted to obtaining a victory by diplomatic means. In 1414 an international gathering took place in Constance to try and resolve the continuing schism within the Papacy. Delegates from the whole Christian world tried to resolve the painful dilemma that three individuals claimed to be the rightful Pope, Gregory XII in Rome, Benedict XIII in Avignon and Alexander V in Pisa. The Knights and the Poles used the opportunity to present their cases for adjudication. Taking advantage of the complex dealings which inevitably accompanied all attempts to break the Papal deadlock, the Polish delegation, carefully chosen for its intellectual ability, suggested that the Knights' continuing claim to fighting a just war against the pagans was wrong. Polish jurists put forward a theory that pagan states existed before the birth of Christ and therefore had a right to exist and that conquest as grounds of conversion was not justified. These arguments reflected the growing acceptance that neither the Pope nor the Holy Roman Emperor had absolute authority to claim pagan territories as theirs. Martin V, the Pope, who was chosen to replace the pretenders, only partly accepted the Polish arguments. By failing to support unequivocally the Knights' argument of ownership on grounds of conquest and conversion, he nevertheless left open the possibility of a change of policy. This was a qualified victory for the Poles. The Teutonic Knights' road east had thus been barred. On 2 September 1422 a new peace treaty was signed between the two. Its most important achievement was that it defined the border between Prussia and the Lithuanian state. This provision remained valid until the turbulence following the end of the First World War created a new state of affairs.

The end of the power of the Teutonic Knights accelerated separatist movements in Lithuania. Jagiełło was unwilling to relinquish his position as hereditary ruler of Lithuanians, but neither Witold nor the Lithuanian nobility accepted subordination to the Polish Crown. In 1420 the first signs of Lithuanian independence manifested themselves in initiatives in foreign relations. Witold became involved in the question of the succession to the Principality of Muscovy, mainly because he took up the case of his grandson Vasily Vasilevich. In his relation with the Czech state, Witold supported the Hussites. But as long as Witold was alive, these separatist tendencies were kept under strict control and were not allowed to affect his relations with Jagiełło.

With Witold's death on 27 October 1430, the conflict burst into the open. The immediate background was the question of succession in Lithuania, but that issue was closely linked to the succession issue in Poland. Jagiełło had been fortunate to sire three sons when he was in his seventies. Two survived but Jagiełło realised that it was very likely that he would die before they came of age. To strengthen their claim to the Polish throne he tried to obtain the commitment from the Polish nobility that one of his sons would be allowed to succeed him. But the Polish nobility refused to swear an oath to the young princes, instead seeking to reaffirm the principle of an elected monarchy by demanding confirmation of all privileges granted to them earlier. Jagiełło was unwilling, but possibly also unable, to assure them that they would have a say in matters relating to Lithuanian succession. Witold's death immediately brought to the fore the controversial issue of Lithuania. Jagiełło reluctantly accepted the Lithuanians' decision to choose his younger brother Świdrygiełło as ruler. Świdrygiełło had a long history of disloyalty to his older brother and opposition to Polish dominance. Not surprisingly the Polish nobility tried to veto his appointment. In February 1431 war broke out between Poland and Lithuania. When the, still unbowed, Teutonic Knights tried to take advantage and attack Poland, both protagonists quickly signed an armistice. At the end of

September 1432 Jagiełło supported a coup, which overthrew
Świdrygiełło. The Catholic faction gained the upper hand in Lithuania.
For the time being the union continued, though the Lithuanian boyars
had succeeded in wresting from the Polish nobility equal rights in
determining the issue of succession in their country.

On 1 June 1434 King Jagiełło died, having caught a cold on a trip
to the woods to listen to the nightingales. His four marriages had run
the usual gamut, including the mid-life crisis marriage to a proverbial
'floozy', the widow Elizabeth Granowska who had an unusually vivid
past. But the important point was that from his last marriage he had
two surviving sons. Władysław III Jagiellończyk (Ladislaus of Varna,
1434–44), on becoming the King of Poland, was only ten. His election had been guaranteed by an earlier agreement between the King
and the nobility. On 10 November 1444 Władysław died in a reckless
attack on Turkish forces in the battle of Varna. During his brief reign
Poland had become involved in unwise attempts to secure the
Bohemian and Hungarian Crowns. In the mean time central and royal
authority in Poland suffered. Relations with Lithuania deteriorated
and advantageous opportunities in Prussia were not followed up. The
exchequer was depleted, but income continued to decrease as the
nobility and the Church made the most of the situation by pressing for
further reductions in their obligations. Nevertheless Władysław and
his advisers were well aware of the need to pay close attention to
events taking place on Poland's southern, south-eastern and south-
western borders.

The Papacy, no longer necessary to confirm succession but still a
powerful influence in ecclesiastical politics in Poland, remained as
divided as always. Earlier attempts in Constance to find a candidate for
the Papacy acceptable to all factions only resolved certain problems.
The nomination of Pope Eugene IV was accompanied by rivalry
between the Church Council and the new Pope over the question of
supremacy. The Council maintained that the Pope was merely the head
of the Council, while Eugene insisted that his position was above the
Council. To strengthen his position the Pope concluded an agreement
with the Eastern Church, at the time desperate for help against the
Turks. By the act of Union signed on 6 July 1436 the Orthodox Rite
Christians accepted the authority of the Papacy. In return Eugene
called for a campaign to defeat the Turks. In the mean time the
members of the Church Council who disagreed with Eugene's appointment and his attempt to reduce the authority of the Council appointed

their own Pope, Felix V, who naturally accepted the supremacy of the Council over that of the Pope.

In Poland these developments had a profound influence, reducing the authority of the Papacy and threatening the creation of an independent national church. The Church in Poland became to all purposes autonomous. The Church hierarchy became more conscious of opportunities offered by internal developments, seeking to maximise the Church's role in internal affairs. A selective approach to the Papacy allowed the bishops to benefit from the patronage of either Pope, though in principle the Polish hierarchy supported the Council, a view fully backed by the theologians at the University of Kraków.

Meantime in Bohemia, a movement which articulated more fully the growing criticism of the Church, emerged to threaten the very theological foundations of the Christian Church. Jan Hus' movement, which started with the disapproval of the Church's sale of indulgences, its political aspirations and its financial wealth, took root first in Bohemia, but gradually spread to neighbouring states. Silesia and parts of southern Poland became strongholds of the Hussite movement. Its main supporters were the lesser nobility, deeply critical of the growing wealth and power of the Church and the burden of taxation, which they had to pay. The man who tried to exploit the various strands of international, theological and internal problems in order to secure for Poland a place in the ranks of European powers was Cardinal Zbigniew Oleśnicki, Bishop of Kraków. In the first place he made sure he was appointed guardian to Jagiełło's young sons. Oleśnicki pushed for the ten-year-old Władysław to be crowned King of Poland before he reached the required age of 15. His allies were the powerful Małopolska nobility, determined to retain privileges and administrative posts. The opposition, when it coalesced, contained a high proportion of those who were Hussites, or were at least sympathetic to the Hus doctrine.

In 1437 Sigismund Luxemburg, King of Bohemia and Hungary, died. He had hoped that Albrecht Habsburg of Austria would succeed to both thrones. But the Hussite faction of the Czech nobility decided to approach Władysław to become King of Bohemia. Unwisely, the proposal was accepted, embroiling Poland in an unnecessary war with the Austrians, Hungarians and Catholic Czechs. The military campaign in Bohemia turned out to be an expensive disaster. But the international situation became even more complicated when, in 1439, conflicts between Pope Eugene and the Council came to a head at the same time as Albrecht Habsburg who had been crowned King of Hungary, died. The Hungarian throne was infinitely more important to the Poles than the Bohemian one. Oleśnicki had not been enthusiastic about the campaign to secure the Bohemian throne, because he had all along wanted Władysław to unite the Polish and Hungarian kingdoms. The Hungarian nobility found the prospect of a Polish candidate to the throne in Buda attractive. They were reluctant to allow the Habsburgs to claim the throne on the basis of inheritance, whereas an elected king, which is all that Władysław would be, offered rich rewards in the form of privileges. The matter of succession was made so much more complicated by the reluctance of the pregnant widow of the deceased Hungarian king to go along with the plans. When a son was born, the Poles and their Hungarian supporters became embroiled in civil war against the Queen, now determined to defend her infant son's right to succeed. Two years of fighting further depleted the Polish exchequer. Władysław became King of Hungary, though only until the baby boy came of age. The victory was only partial, as both sides realised that it was necessary to end the conflict and to concentrate on the Turkish threat.

In 1443 the Hungarians, urged on by the Papal legate Cesarini who represented the interest of Eugene IV, undertook to attack the Turks. The decision was an unwise one as the Hungarians had successfully rebuffed an earlier Turkish attack and it was only on the Pope's suggestion that they decided to launch the Crusade. The first campaign was unsuccessful because the Venetians who had promised to attack the Turkish forces from the sea, mainly to cut them off from the Turkish mainland, kept their ships in port. By 1444 the bulk of the Polish Church hierarchy decided to throw in its lot with the Council faction and thus against Eugene, who was responsible for starting the war against the Turks. A delegation was despatched to Władysław in Buda to ask him to return to Poland and take care of urgent matters there. Unfortunately, inspired by Cesarini's crusading spirit, the young king led another military campaign against the Turks. On 10 November, he was believed to have been killed in battle. Since his body was not recovered, rumours about his survival circulated for some years after the battle of Varna. The Turks claimed to have the young king's head skinned and then pickled in honey, which made identification difficult. In any case, since the head displayed by the Turks was brown and fair-haired, whereas Władysław had dark hair and was light-skinned, these rumours continued. Only in April 1445 was it decided to elect a successor. Uncertainty about the fate of Władysław and the youth of his brother explain the delay. It would be another two years before Kazimierz (Casimir IV, 1446–92), was crowned. This time was utilised to clarify and negotiate his precise legal position in Poland and in Lithuania. Although the young Kazimierz insisted that he was the hereditary ruler of Lithuania, an entitlement derived from his father, the Lithuanian nobility had come to view itself as separate from the descendants of Jagiełło and wanted to make its own choice. In 1446 both sides accepted a compromise solution, in which Kazimierz was crowned elected King of Poland, and hereditary King of Lithuania. Henceforth Lithuania was treated as an independent state but in a union with Poland.

Władysław's ten-year absence from Poland created insurmountable problems for his successor. State finances had been badly affected by the international adventures. Expenditure was three times greater than income. This was due to Władysław being obliged to pay the Polish nobility for their participation in the Bohemian and Hungarian wars. The Polish nobility had no duty to assist the King in foreign wars; he therefore had to pay them the going rate for mercenaries. This he did by issuing promissory notes against income from Crown lands. The Crown had as a result lost its financial independence.

During Władysław's lifetime relations between the Polish Crown lands and Lithuania were complex. The Lithuanian side repeatedly sought to redefine its relations with Poland. While stresses and tensions prevailed, the issue of a separate Lithuanian monarch was repeatedly, though unsuccessfully, raised. On a number of occasions Lithuanian separatism threatened Polish interests, most notably during the protracted war with Prussia when they showed a reluctance to attack the Teutonic Knights. A number of historians have tried to account for the fluctuations in Polish–Lithuanian relations which by the end of the fifteenth century seemed to have settled. Two factors might account for this process of stabilisation. One interesting explanation is that the Lithuanian nobility, previously a warrior caste, whose power and wealth depended on conquest, underwent a change and became more preoccupied with their landed estates, and thus less inclined to war activities. Another explanation relates to the growth of Muscovy. At the beginning of the century Tatar influence over the Russian lands weakened, allowing for the emergence of leaders who were no longer cowed by the military and political power of the Golden Horde. The most active of the new eastern princes was Ivan III

Vasilevich, ruler of Muscovy who, in the second half of the fifteenth century, consolidated his hold over Riazan, Pskov and Novgorod. Lithuanian attempts to enter into agreements with the Golden Horde and Crimean Tatars, hoping that they would oppose the growth of Muscovy, came to nothing. The power of the Golden Horde was weakened by internal rivalries. Their attack on the borders of Muscovy were wasteful, but in the long term failed to prevent Ivan from consolidating his power base. Lithuania too, because of the loss of the nobility's military prowess, refused to mobilise for war. Thus Lithuania's expansion to the east ended. The Poles were only too happy for this to happen, as they had not been inclined to assist the Lithuanians in their conflicts with the emerging eastern power. They were more preoccupied in events taking place in Prague and Buda, which offered opportunities for the expansion of Polish influence into Central Europe.

On succeeding to the throne Kazimierz's initial concern had been to re-establish Polish control over Pomerania and Prussia. During the period 1435–54 relations between the Polish Crown and the Teutonic Knights had been relatively stable. In 1435 the Treaty of Brześć ended a period of conflict between the two, which had been precipitated by the Ruthenian ruler Świdrygełło laying claim to the Lithuanian throne. Świdrygełło, Jagiełło's younger brother, briefly Lithuania's Grand Duke, attempted to foment anti-Polish uprisings and to claim the throne for himself. This led the Polish Crown to take military action against him. During these earlier conflicts Świdrygełło sought Tatar assistance. He was equally willing to ally himself with the Teutonic Knights. Only when the Poles defeated him did the Teutonic Knights accept the need for stability in relations with the Polish Crown. In 1453 relations between the Teutonic Knights and their subjects became confrontational, due to the harshness of the Knights' rule and growing criticism of their power and its abuse. But in Prussia sections of the economically and politically influential communities grouped into associations, which then cooperated to represent their interests to the Knights. In 1435 the Teutonic Knights had just emerged from a particularly turbulent period of internal strife during which various sections of the order fought each other for influence and for the right to appoint the Grand Master. The recent Grand Master Conrad von Erlichshausen was determined to revive the order's power. When in 1453 leaders of key Prussian towns combined with the landed gentry to form a Prussian Union, with the aim of reducing the power of the Knights, the scene was set for a bruising confrontation. The Prussian Union appealed to the Polish king for assistance. In 1454 victory seemed assured, as most of the towns declared in support of the Prussian Union, disarmed the Knights and destroyed their fortifications.

But Kazimierz was not a skilled military leader and his campaign was hampered by the lesser gentry using his call for levies as an opportunity to secure privileges, similar to those already enjoyed by the Church and the wealthy nobility. The campaign became bogged down, dragging on for 13 years, at the end of which the gentry had been successful in extracting assurances that the Crown would no longer have the right to call a mass levy without their prior agreement. Thus the King's ability to wage war was further reduced, unless of course, he was prepared, on each occasion, to grant further concessions, thus continuing to extend the gentry's privileges. By 1461, the King abandoned the levy as a means of raising an army and instead depended on mercenary forces. This and the appointment of an inspired commander, Piotr Dunin, allowed the Poles to secure Prussia and Pomerania. War ravaged the Prussian territories to the point where the Prussian Union was only too glad to see the end of hostilities. In 1466 both sides agreed to a peace treaty signed in the town of Toruń on 19 October. Poland gained Pomerania, the district of Chełmno and Michałów. Malbork, the seat of the Teutonic Knights, earlier relinquished by Czech mercenaries and the town of Elbląg remained in Polish hands. The district of Warmia became the property of the bishopric of Warmia, whose appointment was to be determined by the Polish king. The Teutonic Knights retained their possessions in Prussia but were cut off from the west by Polish lands. All territories held by the Knights on the left bank of the Vistula became a fief of the Polish Crown and the Grand Masters were to swear an oath of fealty to the Polish king. The Teutonic Knights, who had always drawn recruits from the German territories, were now to accept Polish knights into their ranks, but on the condition that at one given time only half of the Order would be Polish. Although in due course and unwillingly, the Teutonic Knights were forced to accept the Polish conditions, in Prussia a strong desire for independence from the Knights and from Poland had taken root. Long-term German colonisation and a distinctiveness which had always been present in the region, meant that there was no desire to come under the Polish Crown.

Kazimierz's rule marked the high point of Jagiellonian dynastic ambitions. His marriage to Elizabeth, daughter of Albrecht Habsburg, allowed him to lay claim to the Bohemian and Hungarian thrones.

Elizabeth came from a tradition where dynastic considerations had played an important role. But the fact that the couple had six sons and five daughters made it so much more important for them to spread the family's influence and to provide for each child. This was the time when ruling families were only too happy to encourage monarchist myths, which put stress on the uniqueness of royal bloodlines. In this case it would enable the King to secure thrones for sons and would at the same time extend his political influence. In that respect the medieval period was a time when the idea of the durability of dynastic connections over military or political ones was widely accepted.

Whatever Kazimierz's ambitions for his sons, his plans would not have been successful had appropriate opportunities not presented themselves. In 1458 the thrones of Bohemia and Hungary once more became vacant. The Habsburgs had wanted to claim both, but to their anger, the nobility preferred to elect local men. In Bohemia the Hussite George of Bodebrad became king. In Hungary Matthias Corvin was elected to the throne. The first faced problems immediately as the Pope opposed the decision. While initially Kazimierz refused to become involved, internal conflicts between the Czech Catholic nobility and supporters of George led him to reconsider the matter. The Pope wanted the Polish king to put forward his son's candidacy, but Kazimierz would only agree if the Pope first granted his approval of the Peace of Toruń with the Teutonic Knights. The Wielkopolska nobility, sympathetic to the Hussite cause, was not willing to give the King their support against the Czech king. But in 1471 following George's death and after extensive negotiations involving the Papacy, the Habsburgs, the Bohemian and Polish nobility, Kazimierz's oldest son Władysław became King of Bohemia. While these negotiations were taking place a faction of the Bohemian nobility, that did not support George but disagreed with the nomination of the Polish prince, approached Matthias of Hungary to become also King of Bohemia. At the same time in 1471 a number of Hungarian magnates, disaffected with Matthias' preoccupation with the Czech issue, and unhappy about his neglect of the Turkish threat to the Hungarian border, approached the Polish king with the request that he allow his second son Kazimierz to be nominated to the Hungarian throne. A first attempt to defeat Matthias failed in 1474. When in April 1490 Matthias Corvin's death brought forth again the question of succession to the Hungarian throne, the Jagiellonian King Władysław of Bohemia pitched in his bid against his younger brother Jan Olbracht's claim to the throne. The younger Kazimierz, whose candidacy to the Hungarian throne had been put forward in 1474, had in the mean time died. Only the threat of Maximilian of Austria grabbing the Hungarian throne brought the warring brothers to their senses and the Bohemian and Hungarian thrones were once more united in the person of Władysław Jagiellończyk.

When Kazimierz Jagiellończyk died on 7 June 1492 he hoped that his son Jan Olbracht would be chosen King of Poland and the next son Aleksander would take over Lithuania. At the time of their father's death neither was married which boded ill for the future. Aleksander obtained the Lithuanian nobility's approval immediately, but Jan Olbracht had to deal with opposition to his election to the Polish throne. By 27 August 1492, he fought off his younger brother's Zygmunt's claim and that of his older brother Władysław, King of Bohemia and Hungary. On 23 September he was crowned Jan Olbracht (John I Albert, 1492–1501), King of Poland.

Theoretically, the Jagiellonian dynasty now dominated Central Europe. The reality was very different and Jan Olbracht's foreign initiatives came unstuck because of his brothers' limited support for his policies. In 1484 he decided to confront the Turks, whose increased control of the Black Sea coast threatened to choke Poland's trade routes. But plans for a war against the Turks were linked with his plans to secure for his younger brother Zygmunt the throne of Moldavia. Attempts to draw Władysław into the plans failed and instead Jan Olbracht turned to his other brother Aleksander. Neither he nor the Lithuanian nobility were keen on the plan. Anxiety about relations with Moscow meant that they gave Jan Olbracht only qualified support.

Relations with the Polish gentry were of crucial importance if the King was to raise a mass levy. His father had successfully fought to decrease the importance of the nobility by allying himself with the *szlachta* (gentry), as the lesser nobility were increasingly known. Jan Olbracht increasingly came to depend on that social stratum. He was, though, made to pay a high price for their support. In a series of meetings, culminating in the Piotrków rally, the King was forced to confirm earlier concessions. Since the gentry were preoccupied with the economic viability of their estates, the King agreed to laws which limited the right of the peasants to leave and made it more difficult for other landowners to harbour runaways. This was the culmination of a long process whereby the peasants progressively lost their personal freedom and were obliged to work long periods on the lord's estate. Laws forbidding townspeople to purchase land strengthened the power of the gentry further. The gentry's privileges now defined them as a separate and distinct section of society, enjoying extensive privileges and exceptions.

Jan Olbracht finally confirmed the power of the gentry by formalising the deliberations of the nobility. These meetings had their origins in the early stages of the emergence of kingship, and had been used by the rulers to confirm taxes, the waging of wars and elections of successors. But the Jagiellonians attempted to regulate them, first by calling district meetings and then assemblies of the nobility from all of Poland. A two-tier decision-making structure had already emerged during Kazimierz's rule. The Sejm was a meeting of the *szlachta* and the Senate represented the Council, the power base of the powerful magnates. Kazimierz and his son also aimed to destroy the power of the wealthy nobility and thus used the Sejm to obtain the support of the *szlachta* for their decisions. The creation of a more formal structure of decision making placed power in the hands of the *szlachta* at the expense of the Crown and the wealthy nobility.

In his confrontation with the Turks the concessions made to the gentry proved to be of little value. When in 1497 Jan Olbracht raised a mass levy and proceeded along the river Dniester and towards the Prut, his army was routed even before facing the full force of the Turkish army. Having exposed his military weakness, Jan Olbracht henceforth had to contend with periodic Turkish and Tatar attack on his southern border.

On 17 June 1501 Jan Olbracht died without legitimate issue. It is now suspected that he might have contracted syphilis, which accounts for his not having had any children and long periods of ill health. On 4 October, his brother Aleksander (1501–6), King of Lithuania, was chosen as King of Poland, thus once more placing Lithuania and Poland under one ruler. But the Jagiellonians' rule of Poland was coming to an end. When Aleksander died without issue in 1506 the youngest of the brothers Zygmunt I Stary (Sigismund I the Old, 1506–48), became king. The final Jagiellonian king was Zygmunt August (Sigismund II August, 1548–72), who succeeded his father Zygmunt Stary in 1548. He too died without issue, leaving his youngest sister Anna as the only surviving Jagiellonian.

During the course of the sixteenth century processes initiated earlier were completed or codified, which has led historians to see the period as the end of medieval times and the beginning of modern history. The consolidation of the power of the *szlachta* was finally confirmed in 1505 at the meeting of the Sejm in Radom. There Aleksander famously accepted that no legislation affecting the gentry's interests could be instigated without their approval. The act, which is usually referred to as the *Nihil novi* code, was a legal confirmation of the existing state of affairs, which reinforced the power of the gentry and limited the authority of the Crown and the high nobility. During the rule of Zygmunt Stary his second wife the Italian Bona Sforza tried to reverse some of the measures which limited the power of the Crown. Bona came from a political tradition in which the power of the monarch was stronger and she attempted to consolidate the Crown's financial, administrative and political authority. Her efforts earned her the hatred of the court circles and the gentry. Polish historians stress her penchant for intrigues, and recourse to poison as political tools. Contemporary historians have been kinder to her and point to her political objectives. But her efforts failed and with Zygmunt Stary's death she left Poland.

Territorial stability reached its peak at the end of the Jagiellonian rule of Poland. Wars continued to be waged but only as a means of warding off threats to the kingdom's security. The Prussian threat was the most important unresolved issue during the reign of Jagiełło's sons and grandsons. Prussia continued to be seen as a German outpost. The Knights' resentment threatened to push them in the direction of any anti-Polish coalition. The Teutonic Knights in fact never fully accepted the condition of the Toruń Peace. In particular they resented Prussia becoming the feudal property of the Polish Crown. In order to avoid swearing an act of fealty, they appealed to the Pope to reverse the peace. Depending on what were the Papacy's other objectives, the Knights were either promised support, or had those promises withdrawn. Not surprisingly therefore, the Prussian issue continued to preoccupy successive Polish kings. In 1519 the Teutonic Grand Master Albrecht von Hohernzollern-Ansbach, supported by the Holy Roman Emperor Maximilian, decided to wage war against the Poles. War activities ended after 15 months and negotiations followed. In the mean time a new, and far more dangerous, threat appeared in Prussia. The Reformation gained support in the region and Albrecht, who supported it, decided to secularise Prussia. New negotiations with the Poles were conducted on the basis of a request that the Polish Crown agree to Prussia becoming Albrecht's hereditary property, for which he would swear an oath to the Polish king. At the root of this surprising development were economic factors. The Knights needed to deal with the economic crisis which had overwhelmed the order. Albrecht's public conversion to the Lutheran creed ended Catholic support for their cause. Henceforth Albrecht was dependent on Poland and naturally ceased being a threat.

While in the last years of Jagiellonian rule Poland's western border was stabilised, the eastern and south-eastern borders continued to change, in most cases due to loss of territories. The emergence of the Moscow-based state at the end of the fifteenth century led to constant conflicts. Both Jan Olbracht and Aleksander tried to reduce tensions, but the dynamic nature of the Tsar Ivan IV's policies and an increasing desire on the part of the rulers of areas east of Lithuania to look to Moscow inevitably reduced Polish and Lithuanian influence. During Zygmunt Stary's rule Moscow entered into alliances with the Turks and encouraged the Tatar tribes of the Black Sea region. In 1537 Poland and Lithuania signed a peace with the ruler of Moscow. But in 1538 a new threat emerged from the south, where Sahib Gerej became a virtually unchallenged ruler of Crimea. Turkish support for Sahib posed a challenge to Poland and Lithuania. But neither was able to devote resources to waging a war against the massed ranks of the Crimean Tatars. The Lithuanians continued to be preoccupied with conflicts with Muscovy, while Zygmunt wanted to keep his hands free to deal with Hungary. Fortunately, anxious about events in Russia, the Turks saw advantages in avoiding conflicts with the Poles and Lithuanians. Although during the reign of Zygmunt August the south-eastern borders were frequently raided by the Tatars, no full-scale invasion took place. After 1551 the Turks replaced Sahib with Dewlet Gerej who established better relations with the Polish king. The Tatar rulers were kept at bay by frequent gifts and bribes which the Poles were prepared to make as a price of continuing peace. In the fifteenth and sixteenth centuries the Islamic world was ever present on Poland's borders, and the cultural, military and intellectual interaction between the two was considerable.

4

Reformation and Renaissance in Poland

The Jagiellonian rule is generally seen as marking the end of the medieval period and the beginning of modern times in Polish history. This assertion does, however, need qualifying. Many aspects of Polish political, economic, religious and cultural life, which had evolved during the late fifteenth and sixteenth centuries, were obvious continuations of developments which had already started earlier. But at the same time there is no denying the fact that this was a time when new ideas challenged the Christian view of the world and brought forth the Classical culture and knowledge of Greek and Roman times. Poland was affected by these intellectual trends, as was most of Europe. Because of Poland's proximity to Hussite, Calvinist and Lutheran centres Polish churchmen and thinkers were fully aware of the religious and political ideas advanced by these movements. Within Poland, parallel to the religious debates taking place in other states, a challenge to the Church's political power and monopoly over all aspects of spiritual and cultural life was emerging. At the beginning of the sixteenth century Poland was ready for the Reformation. At the same time academics at the University of Kraków, inspired by classical texts, developed scientific theories and expanded the boundary of knowledge. Extensive contacts with other centres of learning facilitated the exchange of ideas and stimulated further debates. But the Renaissance, though enriched by ideas from Bohemia, Italy, France and Germany, flowered only briefly in the Kraków University and within the intellectual community.

The Jagiellonian rule had been a time of relative stability. Thus at the end of the fifteenth century the Crown and the nobility became increasingly preoccupied with internal matters. The gradual emergence of the lesser nobility, the gentry, as a political force might have complemented this gradual reorientation from conquests and consolidation of borders to an increased awareness of events taking place within the kingdom. It has been suggested that the nobility, no longer dependent on booty and conquest, would henceforth look to their estates for means of gaining funds. This in turn meant that they would be determined to either bring new labour to work on their land or alternately seek to force the peasants to compulsorily till their land. The trend was thus towards the enserfment of the hitherto free peasantry. The most important changes would nevertheless be associated with the growth of towns and the emergence of the town community, not only as an economic force but more importantly as a community which sought to influence political decision making. Their economic power came from the increased volume of foreign trade. Kraków and Lwów benefited from the west–east trade in particular because of the growth of demand in the now rapidly expanding markets in the east. Lublin and Poznań and Gdańsk also continued to expand. Other towns of significance were Nowy Sącz, Bochnia, Krosno and Sandomierz. These towns derived their wealth from the increased volume of foreign and internal trade. But the towns' political power was expressed in their ability to demand toll payments on goods coming into the towns and trade taking place in their markets. In due course towns were able to increase their income by establishing monopolies over goods produced and traded. Internal town administration required the wealthy burghers and traders to arrive at a workable consensus. Towns thus developed some form of internal consultative fora and with that sophisticated financial systems. This in turn led to the emergence in the towns of wealthy burghers who had both the knowledge and economic power to become involved in political issues, initially on a regional but ultimately also on a wider level. The powerful burghers of Kraków had already earlier been able to make their views known in matters relating to the choice of monarch. During the Reformation, wealthy town dwellers were more critical of the privileges enjoyed by the nobility and the Church and thus were more likely to consider dissenting religious views.

By the fifteenth century Poland was affected by political and intellectual developments taking place in the East and West of Europe. The fate of the Papacy, most importantly the ongoing rivalry between the Papacy and the Holy Roman Emperor, and political developments in Germany, Hungary and Bohemia were of great importance to Poland.

But at the same time conflicts with the Tatar hordes and the growth of the Turkish threat had a bearing on Poland's fate. Developments in the east, mainly the emergence of the power of Muscovy, faced Poland with a new threat that would increase over the following centuries. Thus Poland was never entirely focused on Western Europe. For West European states the year of 1492, the date when Christopher Columbus landed in the Antilles, marks the symbolic end of the medieval period and the beginning of modern history. For Poland that date had no immediate meaning. Poland had not benefited directly from the Mediterranean economic and cultural developments. Therefore the reorientation from the Mediterranean to the Americas, which was so important to Southern and Western European states, was of little relevance to Poland and did not in itself alter the prevailing balance of power in Central Europe. At best, 1492 had only a slight symbolic significance for Poland. Likewise the Renaissance and the Reformation, two powerful intellectual forces which deeply affected Western European states, had an impact on the Polish kingdom; nevertheless both flourished only briefly. Their influence on Polish cultural life has to be appreciated on the background of other forces for change.

During the Jagiellonian period Poland's borders and political system had evolved and stabilised to a point that, one could argue, marked a seminal point in state building and political maturing. Thus the marker symbolising the division between medieval and modern history could be placed after the death of the last Jagiellonian. The rule of Zygmunt I Stary (1506–48), whose Italian wife Bona brought Renaissance culture to the royal court, could be seen as the turning point. Their son Zygmunt II August (1548–72) was prepared for the responsibility of ruling a kingdom which was very different from his father's and most certainly would have been unrecognisable to his great-grandfather. In the 1520s Renaissance culture was absorbed by the royal court and the households of the wealthy nobility who had travelled to the West. By then the gentry and wealthy townspeople, who were unlikely to have had direct experience of cultural and political developments in the West, appear to have also taken up new ideas and been exposed to different cultural trends. The critical years of change in Poland were those from 1492 until 1572. This was the time between Jan Olbracht's election to the Polish throne and the death of Zygmunt II August, the last Jagiellonian king.

Kazimierz Jagiellończyk had prepared his sons for their future roles in a manner which can be seen as characteristic of the late medieval period. Even then most confident European rulers knew that their successors would have to face a complex world. Royal education was not haphazard or incidental. It involved the acquiring of a clearly defined set of skills and accomplishments. In the case of the six princes there is more information about their education and preparation for the future than has been the case with earlier royal children. It would appear that both their father and mother had appreciated the need for formal schooling. A formidable team of teachers had been assembled to provide this. The princes were expected to be literate, but also aware of the world around them. Teachers chosen to teach them had special areas of knowledge and educational skills. The renowned historian Jan Długosz was placed in overall charge of the young princes' education. An Italian, Philip Buonacorsi, known also as Kalimach, taught them Latin. Jan Welsa, professor of liberal studies and medicine, completed the team. By all accounts the princes' education was by the standards of the times, extensive and up to date. The sons of the nobility could have expected to receive, even if not so thorough, nevertheless a formal education which in some cases would have been followed by a spell abroad to attend foreign universities.

Zygmunt August, the son of Zygmunt I Stary by his second wife Bona Sforza, was prepared for his future role as king by his mother. Her ideas went well beyond that of gaining support for her son's election to the throne. In the West the conflict between the state-building and centralising power in the Crown, and the nobility's political demands for self-determination and defence of their privileges, had advanced much further than it had in Poland. Bona arrived in Kraków with clear ideas on the way the authority of the Crown should be firmly maintained and increased and on how to reduce the privileges of the nobility and the gentry. In the first place she set out to enrich herself but simultaneously she strove to improve the Crown's financial situation, which was in need of administrative and fiscal reforms. The purpose of these reforms was increased administrative efficiency, but in particular stronger control over Crown lands and revenues which would, in turn, increase the Crown's authority. Some historians suggest that her approach to politics was governed by Machiavellian ideas, to which she would have been exposed in Italy, and which she tried to pass on to her son. Her son was educated in a humanist tradition, speaking both Polish and Italian even if, regrettably, he never mastered the Russian language, which the majority of his Lithuanian subjects would have spoken. Bona had wanted her son to continue the dynastic struggle with the Habsburgs, which her family had pursued in Italy, and the marriages of her son and daughter were to be part of that master plan. As it turned out, some of her political plans had less relevance to Polish realities. On succeeding to the throne Zygmunt August had to alter his attitudes and political objectives from those acquired from his mother, being more responsive to the realities of the Polish kingdom and the Duchy of Lithuania which he ruled.

One of the main distinguishing features of the political system which had evolved in Poland during the late fifteenth and sixteenth centuries was the degree to which the nobility had been able to assert its authority over the Crown. In Poland the Crown's authority continued to be weakened rather than strengthened, as had been the case in the German areas, in particular in the Habsburg domains. The Jagiellonians had initially depended on the landed magnates for support. But, by the end of the fifteenth century, in an attempt to free themselves from the domination of that stratum of the nobility, they courted the support of the wealthy burghers and lesser nobility, the *szlachta*. The result, as has been shown in Chapter 3, was increased devolution of policy making to the Sejmiki, the provincial assemblies of the gentry and then to the Sejm, the all nation assembly. By the beginning of the sixteenth century the *szlachta* had made sure that the King was not able to raise an army for military action without their prior agreement and that they would not be expected to support him militarily if he waged wars outside the boundaries of the kingdom. These concessions enabled them to influence foreign policy decisions, but also made it possible for them to affect foreign policy choices and to demand even further release from obligations to the Crown. Each time the King wanted to take military action anywhere other than the kingdom the nobility had to be paid for bringing their men to the battlefield. At the same time the gentry were constantly anxious that the Crown and the powerful nobility could combine to outmanoeuvre them and to impose financial burdens upon them. They were jealous of the lucrative court appointments which the magnates were able to secure for themselves. While in principle they called for increased accountability and respect for accepted and agreed laws and procedures which they wanted confirmed in written codes, in reality as a social group they were motivated by self-interest which, in most cases, was very short-sighted. Thus by the end of the sixteenth century Poland had evolved the unique political system whereby the *szlachta* enjoyed unusually extensive rights to have a say in most matters of state.

The enhanced rights of the gentry did not automatically lead to increased Crown accountability and respect for law. On the contrary, at the beginning of the sixteenth century sections of the gentry calling itself the 'Executive' Camp demanded the codification of Crown dues, which they claimed were excessive. In reality, exploited by the more astute magnates, the gentry split into factions. Instead of becoming a stabilising force, they and their agitation became a source of weakness. While they claimed to be fighting for consultation and accountability, in practice they sought to gain rewards for supporting the King's policies. The King's dependence on the nobility to raise an army was the single most contentious issue in the Crown's relations with that social group. In the course of the sixteenth century the Crown realised that this had become a source of Poland's military weakness. The nobility started using each call to arms as the starting point for further negotiations for concessions. But the alternative was for the introduction of a form of taxation to replace the levy, which would then allow the Crown to either pay to build up a standing army or to hire mercenaries. Most other European monarchs had moved in that direction as part of the general trend of reducing the nobility's stranglehold over the Crown. This issue was taken up by the Executive Camp who wanted to avoid making any contributions to these military reforms and instead wanted the Crown to finance a standing army from income from Crown properties.

In 1537 the gentry added another demand to their previous list of grievances. This was the confirmation of the principle of elected kingship. Until then the gentry's participation in decision making concerning the succession to the throne tended to be symbolic, and it was the magnates who effectively determined the matter. By 1573 the idea that the election of the King should be approved by an assembly of all the nobility, had taken root. The gentry's direct participation in the election would change the way the matter was decided. From being a carefully considered issue, controlled by the magnates and the leading families of the land, it would become something between a national festival and an auction, during which foreign princes or their representatives placed bids for the Polish Crown in return for concessions.

Economic stability undoubtedly underpinned these political changes. In the sixteenth century Poland became the main supplier of grain to Europe. The port of Gdańsk at the mouth of the main navigable river which flowed through the Polish lands, became the chief outlet for the grain for export. The establishment of Polish control over

Prussia and Gdańsk stimulated this trade further. The landowners had a powerful financial incentive to increase grain production. While they were loath to become involved in trade, seeing this as incompatible with their noble status, trade in grain remained the nobility's monopoly. During this time the destruction of most of the primeval forests was completed in order to increase the area of cultivated land. The landed nobility used its political power to push for legislation which further decreased the rights of the peasants, as they now sought to tie the labour force further to their estates and to increase peasants' obligations to work on their land. In 1538 the nobility demanded that townspeople should be forbidden to buy land. While legislation was introduced it was never possible to fully implement it. The nobility fought further to restrict the right of the towns to levy customs payments and demand toll payments. For themselves they sought to be released from all payments when moving their grain. Their jealousy of the growing power of the towns extended to demands for restrictions on the power of guilds which had been able to set prices for goods produced in the towns. The conflicts between the nobility and the burghers extended to attempts to prevent the latter from enjoying their wealth by introducing sumptuary laws which would restrict the burghers and their wives in the wearing of fashionable clothes and displaying their wealth. While in many cases such legislation was introduced, its implementation was never possible.

Most important political demands were increasingly made by the *szlachta*. Their self-preoccupation with narrowly perceived interests, their calls that they should be released from the obligation to pay taxes and dues, were accompanied by loud pronouncements of patriotism. They demanded the direct incorporation of Prussia and Lithuania into Poland. In reality they would have wanted to see the rights of the Lithuanian nobility reduced and to take over and colonise Prussia and Lithuania.

In relation to the Church, the *szlachta*'s political programme coincided with the main thrust of the Reformation. In Poland the Church's growing wealth and aggressive involvement in politics had consequences not dissimilar to those which had manifested themselves in other European states. At the beginning of the sixteenth century the Church's determination to increase further its wealth and the powers of the ecclesiastical courts was generally noted with anger. So was the Church's desire to avoid all taxes and duties and to seek further exceptions whenever opportunity allowed. The gentry demanded that the power of ecclesiastical courts be limited and that the state should not be forced to implement decisions made by those courts. This in particular applied to accusations of heresy. There was a growing resentment of the burden of taxation levied by the Church, in particular because as a landowner the Church had benefited from rising grain prices, while at the same time refusing to pay any taxes to the Crown. The fact that the Church hierarchy was seen to be fully enjoying its wealth did little to maintain its standing in society. Debates taking place in Germany and Bohemia filtered into Poland with ease. Whereas Hussite ideas were already known in Poland, Calvinist and Lutheran doctrines took root more swiftly. Lutheranism, which was seen as the ideology of the townspeople, on the whole did not appeal to the gentry, who frequently toyed with Lutheranism and then progressed to declare themselves in favour of the Calvinist doctrine. At the same time an indigenous movement sprung up in Poland, mirroring those which had evolved in the neighbouring states. The Polish Brethren, who subsequently were also called the Arian movement, were a more radical Christian movement which addressed religious and social issues.

At the beginning of the sixteenth century religious tolerance was the norm in Poland. It would have been unwise for the Jagiellonians to follow any other policy, in view of the dominant role of the Christian Orthodox Church in the Lithuanian territories. At least to start with the state condemned the Reformation. During the period 1520–25 Zygmunt Stary did introduce legislation which appeared to prepare the ground for the persecution of heretics. A Royal Commission was set up to investigate cults which advocated a purer form of Christianity. The Church feared that this would result in a reversion to Judaism. In reality the King did not implement his own edicts and was known to oppose the Church's attempt to prosecute heretics. His son Zygmunt August took a more active interest in the Dissenter movements. At his initiative a delegation was sent to Rome to discuss with the Papacy, unsuccessfully as it turned out, the establishment of a national church. At the same time the royal household remained committed to Catholicism. Thus as long as the new Christian doctrines did not threaten the unity of the state, the Crown and its legislative role, there was no incentive to support inflexible and intolerant internal policies. Prominent Calvinists and Lutherans held Crown positions and the last two Jagiellonian kings were known to be openly sympathetic to their views. In Poland the Catholic Church remained dominant and in spite of numerous quarrels between the Crown and the Church, the establishment of a national church was on more than one occasion considered but not pursued. In Poland, Catholicism remained the faith of the ruling monarchy.

When Zygmunt August was crowned in 1548 Poland was a country of complex and diverse religions. The Church in Poland had already shown a tendency to drift away from the Papacy, caused principally by the complex state in which the Papacy found itself in the fifteenth century. The Church leadership was seen as corrupt and lacking in religious commitment. The Polish Church's ability to withstand the ideas of the Reformation was further weakened by its own dilemmas as to whether to remain with the Papacy or to establish a national church. A petition addressed to Pope Paul IV by the Polish delegate requested that permission should be granted for mass to be celebrated in Polish, and that the national synod be convoked in Poland. Interestingly, it also requested that priests should be allowed to marry. These proposals were naturally turned down, but only by the middle of the sixteenth century were these ideas dropped. The Papacy had not been successful or consistent in tackling challenges to its authority and it was only after the Council of Trent in 1563 that it responded with increased vigour to the theological threat posed by the Reformation. The decisions of the Council were accepted by the Polish Church and formed the basis of its Counter-Reformation. The arrival of the Jesuit order in 1564 boosted the confidence of the Catholic Church in Poland. The Jesuit order which had been established in 1540, uniquely among religious orders, owed its obedience directly to the Pope and not to the local bishop as would have been the norm with other religious orders. Thus the Jesuits could be depended upon to be the obedient servants of the Papacy, in this case specifically to implement the Council of Trent decisions on Catholic dogma and organisational reforms. On arriving in Poland they initiated a widespread propaganda campaign to counter the Reformation ideas. They were in particular active in education and publishing.

Dissenter ideas of all varieties found a ready audience in Poland, though unity was never forged between them, thus weakening the impact of the Reformation here. Historians point to the flowering of Protestant ideas in the sixteenth century, but it did not lead to mass conversions even though anticlerical sentiments were strong among the gentry. The royal household and the Jagiellonians remained staunchly with the Catholic Church. A number of prominent magnates, though, did become Dissenters. Peasants and the poorest gentry also

remained Catholic, though the *szlachta*, as a group, was most suscep-
tible to the ideas of the religious Dissenters. Nevertheless it is estimated that at the height of the Reformation in the mid sixteenth
century no more than a seventh of the gentry defined itself as
Dissenters. Małopolska and Silesia had the highest proportion of
dissenting congregations, while Masovia had the lowest. A puzzling
feature of the Polish Reformation would seem to be the fact that a
majority of the gentry's delegates to the Sejm were Dissenters. This is
explained by the fact that these were usually the best-educated people,
most likely to be militant in their opposition to Church privileges, a
point generally supported by all the gentry irrespective of their faith.
The Arian sect was one of the more interesting examples of radical
religious ideas which briefly prevailed in Poland. They called for a
return to true Christian values, by which they meant a classless society in which all people were equal. They opposed violence and as a
symbol of their commitment to peaceful methods of resolving
conflicts, wore wooden swords. The Arians nevertheless remained a
minor group within the Dissenter movement.

Although attempts were made to build a united Protestant Church
during the 1570s, these efforts failed. Led by Jan Łaski, a campaign
had been waged throughout Poland and Lithuania to obtain first the
support of Zygmunt August, and then to secure legislation, to give the
Protestant Church the same rights as were enjoyed by the Catholic
Church. In the first aim the Dissenters failed, even though the King
was known to be sympathetic towards the Calvinist movement. In
1570 the Lutheran, Hussite and Calvinist churches did agree to come
together, to the exclusion of other Dissenter movements including the
anti-Tridentine Catholics. But this was as far as unity could be forged.
An unwillingness to compromise on principles of religious dogma
stood in the way of organising one church. Thus divided, the Dissenter
movements failed even to have the laws on heresy abolished. In any
case by 1572, when the King died, the Counter-Reformation had
consolidated its strength and managed to stem the growth of Dissenter
movements. As an eminent historian of the period Henryk Łowmian-
'ski stated, 'The Reformation was a passing episode in the history of
Poland.'

The emergence of new religious debates was part of the general
cultural and intellectual trend, which affected the whole Christian
world. Notwithstanding the heresy laws, religious tolerance and the
absence of discriminatory laws allowed for Dissenters from states

where they had been persecuted to seek shelter, however briefly, in Poland. Their presence gave a boost to developments which had already started earlier. Since the Counter-Reformation led to the persecution of religious Dissenters in France, Germany, Switzerland and the Netherlands, some travelled to Poland in search of asylum. Communities of Anabaptists settled in Prussia, Mennonites in Żuławy. Jews fleeing the Inquisition and Hussites persecuted in Bohemia found refuge in the Polish lands. Some travelled to Poland to attend religious schools as was the case of those who came to the Arian centre in Raków. The arrival of foreigners was a positive factor in the history of the Polish kingdom. These people brought with them not only new ideas on religious issues, but in most cases contributed to the development of the humanist intellectual traditions. In addition to the already noted presence of Italians at the royal court in Kraków, individual scholars either briefly visited or settled in Poland. Polish printing houses produced translations of well-known Reformation texts and religious books in Polish. Until then religious books were written in Latin, limiting their readership to men of the Church or few of those who had benefited from any education.

The Jewish community also benefited from religious tolerance. The size and organisational structure of the Jewish community in the Polish and Lithuanian lands grew slowly. By 1500 it possibly comprised no more than 15,000 members. With the community, religious and social provisions became more complex and sophisticated. Possibly due to the general security and relative absence in the Polish–Lithuanian Commonwealth of the persecution which was at its height in West European kingdoms, the Jewish community expanded by natural growth and small waves of migration. By the beginning of the sixteenth century Jews in Poland tended to follow the pattern of West European Jewish communities supporting schools, ritual baths, abattoirs, hospitals, cemeteries and a variety of charitable foundations. This was in addition to their maintaining theological schools, synagogues and rabbis. Individual communities were given full responsibility to discharge the communities' dues to the Crown and state. Yiddish, a form of ancient German, increasingly became the language of Polish and Lithuanian Jews. Although remnants of the Eastern Jewish Khazar kingdom had survived in Lithuania, the Jewish community increasingly defined itself as Ashkenazy, thus West European. The last two Jagiellonian kings encouraged the arrival of Jews in Poland and in particular in Lithuania. During this period Jews became firmly associated with moneylending, tax farming, i.e. tax collection in return for a fee which represented a percentage of taxes collected, trade and artisanry. While attacks on the Jewish communities did take place these tended to be caused by economic rivalries, precipitated for example when a Jewish moneylender took farms or land from debt defaulters. The Counter-Reformation introduced new elements into Christian–Jewish relations. For the first time rumours started to circulate about Jews abducting Christian children whose blood, according to rumours, was needed for the making of Passover bread, desecrating the Catholic host and trying to convert Christians. Zygmunt August disapproved strongly of any attempts to persecute the Jews and was known to take the side of Jews accused of ritual crimes. And although discriminatory legislation was introduced in Lithuania in 1566 obliging all Jews to wear distinct yellow hats, the Crown had little desire to support these attitudes, in particular because the Jewish community was seen as making a very important contribution to the economy. Although subject to discrimination, the fate of Jews in Poland and Lithuania was still better than in England or the West European states.

In the sixteenth century culture and its development were no longer confined to narrow social groups which had both the financial means and leisure to act as patrons of culture. The gentry's increased participation in politics brought an awareness of the significance of broader social, economic and political developments. Theological and political debates which in earlier centuries might have been confined to ecclesiastical, university and court circles, were now of interest to the gentry and wealthy burghers. But culture in all its manifestations was no longer confined to the capital and spread beyond the boundaries of the main towns. A notable feature of the sixteenth century was the emergence of educated and well-informed individuals from provincial estates and smaller towns.

A whole variety of factors contributed to the cultural flowering in the Polish kingdom. Both easy contact with other states and the desire to be better informed played a role in that process. Trade and individual travel added to the easy exchange of ideas. In the sixteenth century the establishment of Polish control over the port city of Gdańsk meant that it became an extensively used conduit for increased trade and travel between the Polish hinterland and the Baltic coast. The earlier established University of Kraków acted as a magnet, attracting students and scholars. On her deathbed Jadwiga had donated all her personal jewellery to the University. The University's reputation was fully established by this time. In addition to providing opportunities for students from Poland, foreign students also were drawn to Kraków. The fact that Latin was the language of tuition in all European universities made it possible for scholars to teach and benefit from teaching at foreign universities. Mathematics, astronomy, theology, and Classical languages were all taught at the Kraków University. But, by 1525 the University became associated with conservatism and failed to respond to demands for new ideas and interpretations. The King had not heeded calls for the University to be restructured and its professors were accused of being stuck in old ideas and not appreciating the importance of new debates based on humanism and the study of Classical civilisations. Its prominence among European universities thus diminished.

Not all university students came from privileged backgrounds. The Kraków burghers frequently complained of students' rowdy behaviour and the fact that many supported themselves through begging, thus being a burden to the community and bringing the town into disrepute. Women were forbidden to enrol under the penalty of death. There is one recorded case of a girl being discovered as having disguised herself as a boy and enrolled at the university. When found out she was tried. Fortunately the death sentence was commuted to life banishment to a nunnery where in due course she established herself as an outstanding abbess.

During the Renaissance period education was treated seriously. Education meant not merely learning Latin and the basics of theological debates. It extended to the study of science and history. The Renaissance stressed the importance of a systematic approach to learning, based on observation and research. Thus the study of mathematics was considered particularly important. Geography, history and the natural sciences all benefited from this new approach to learning. Renaissance scholars looked to Greek and Roman texts for broader knowledge. The study of Aristotle was as important as was that of old Hebrew texts. For that purpose Classical Greek, Latin and Hebrew were taught at the University of Kraków. Polish intellectuals and scholars corresponded with foreign scholars. The writings of Erasmus of Rotterdam were extensively published and discussed within the university and educated communities in Poland.

Among Polish scholars of the time, the writings of Andrzej Frycz Modrzewski are central to the Polish Renaissance. He advocated education as a means of learning and cultural self-improvement. But in his work *On the Reform of the Commonwealth* he went further by explaining the connections between education and good governance. This was not necessarily the view taken by the magnates and the gentry, who considered administrative functions as a means of self-enrichment or alternatively as a means of defending vested interests. Nevertheless during the sixteenth century the extension of educational opportunities and improvement in the intellectual quality of those employed in the increasingly expanding state administration, meant that the state and its complex relationship with the Crown and the subjects became the focus of intellectual enquiry. Education ceased being just a preparation for the priesthood and became a prerequisite for the holding of Crown and state functions as well as an attainment in its own right. Humanist colleges called academies were established in a number of towns, notably Gdańsk and Toruń. Both the Dissenter religious movements and, as part of the Counter-Reformation, the Catholic Church came to appreciate the need for better and more widely available education. As has been already noted, the Jesuits were particularly active in setting up schools in most major towns. In 1579, a new university was opened by the Jesuits in Vilnius.

The nobility and the wealthy burghers were frequently able to finance their sons' further education by a period of travel and study abroad. In the past churchmen and theologians had travelled to Rome. For those not connected with the Church travel and study beyond the boundaries of the area of their birth were a new trend and clearly reflected an interest in the humanist ideas emanating from Italy. The universities of Padua and Bologna were particularly popular with the Poles. For the Calvinists and Lutherans travel abroad was usually connected with attempts to extend their understanding of those religious movements and to forge contact with their main proponents. They headed for Wittenburg, Leipzig, Marburg or Heidelberg. By the same token the Counter-Reformation motivated young Catholics to travel to Vienna, Graz or Freiburg, all renowned centres of a fightback against the Reformation. England on the whole did not attract much interest during this period. An exception was Jan Łaski, who travelled first to England and then to Scotland. In Poland he had been the leading proponent of the unification of the Dissenter churches into a Polish Protestant Church. In that aim he had not been successful. He had more success in Britain where he was instrumental in setting up the Church of England and the Church of Scotland before returning to Poland.

Production of paper and the rapid development of printing presses encouraged the new intellectual trends. The first paper mills appeared in Poland at the end of the fifteenth century, the one in Prądnik near Kraków being possibly the first. The revolutionary expansion of printing explains the spread of culture, both across social groups and beyond the main centres of learning. Initially Latin was the main language of cultured discourse. But with the development of printing houses and increased demand for books, publications in Polish appeared in increasing numbers. The Reformation and the Counter-Reformation boosted printing, as pamphlets and books were aimed at a broader audience. The Calvinists and Arians were particularly interested in printing the Bible in the vernacular. But the Jesuits quickly learned to use the printed word as a means of fighting back and they too opened their own printing houses. Centres of learning and towns where Dissenters opened their schools all had their printing houses. Printers were interested in producing important religious and non-religious translations of famous foreign thinkers. But with equal astuteness they noted the growth of demand for Polish language texts. This accounts for a move towards publishing in Polish rather than Latin. This outburst in publishing declined with the Counter-Reformation, when the Papacy initiated the idea of keeping a list of books and authors of which the Catholic Church disapproved. The Index, as it was called, limited production of Dissenter books but also made public the Church's disapproval, on moral and political grounds, of some of the books.

As has been mentioned, the Reformation was a time when intellectual developments went beyond the narrow confines of religious discourse. Biernat of Lublin's book *A Brief Description of Aesop's Life and Some Other Affairs of His*, published in 1522, is an outstanding example of a work which broke with past conventions and addressed everyday dilemmas. In it the author shows how the philosopher turned to reason in his search for understanding. Biernat went further in suggesting that, by depending on divine explanations, man abdicated responsibility for enquiry. This approach to learning is the essence of the Renaissance. This approach explains why mathematics, natural sciences and history, subjects which offered rational explanations for natural phenomena, were all avidly studied during this period. The new approach was summed up in the assumption that man was to be rational and to act responsibly. New criteria of proof in logic, philosophy and science were thus expected.

In scientific work, Copernicus' theory is an outstanding example of rational thinking which unintentionally challenged the Church's doctrine of the origins of the Universe. In his book *De Revolutionibus Orbitum Coelestium*, published in 1543, Copernicus rejected the assertion that the Sun orbited around the static Earth. But it was not just his conclusions but also his method of proof, which marks him as a Renaissance man. His theory was based on observation and mathematical calculation. Not having set out to do so, he challenged the Church's monopoly of interpretation on the subject. There was no denying the revolutionary implications of his theory. Galileo would in years to come continue research initiated by Copernicus. As a Renaissance man, Copernicus had enjoyed an extensive education. Born in the town of Toruń in 1473, he first studied in Kraków but then travelled to the universities of Bologna, Padua and Ferrara. His astronomical observations had been conducted while he was in Fromborg in Warmia. His interests extended to engineering and he is credited with building a water supply system for the town. He also studied economics and finance. During the period 1519–30, Copernicus acted as a delegate of the Warmia diocese to the Prussian Sejmik, which had been discussing monetary reforms. In this connection Copernicus published two works dealing with the role of currencies in the economy. His theory, which was entirely original and only loosely based on Aristotelian principles, asserted that there are four causes for civilisations collapsing: conflict, mortality, drought and depreciation of currency. His conclusions were based on economic considerations, namely that where two currencies circulated, the one with the lower content of precious metal would replace the stronger one in circulation. This phenomenon, which was subsequently similarly noted by Thomas Gresham in Britain, arose because stronger currencies were hoarded while the public would try to pass on depreciated coinage in exchange for goods (or the better currency). Copernicus' advice to the Royal Commission led to the establishment of stable currency in Poland and Prussia.

Other branches of science followed a similar, if not so spectacular path. In 1517 Maciej of Miechów published a book on Eastern Europe entitled *Tractatus de duabus Sarmatis Asian et Europiana*. The author, who was the rector of the University of Kraków, presented in this widely translated volume a study of the geography and ethnography of Eastern Europe. His maps were scientific and based on observation and logical deduction. He rejected the previously held myth that all rivers originated in mountains, pointing out that this was patently not the case. What he did in reality was develop the science of geography and cartography in which he refused to recognise the existence of mythical countries and instead stated boldly that further research and exploration were needed. Maps and books on the geography and flora of the region were produced in Poland as part of the trend towards scientific observation. Interestingly, although scholarly books appeared in Latin, more accessible editions in Polish were also produced.

The driving force behind the debates on politics was the turbulent nature of relations between the gentry and the Crown. The Renaissance both encouraged and justified attempts to codify a body of laws which would be both just and fair to all. Andrzej Frycz Modrzewski in his book *De Republica Emendanda* advocated that societies be studied scientifically. He opposed the existing feudal order and rejected the idea of absolute obedience, which it and the Church suggested. He wanted arbitrariness and prejudice to be abolished and instead advocated the establishment of an ideal state where the rights of individuals would be balanced against their social obligations. According to him, the purpose of laws was to prevent anyone from using offices for self-enrichment. While Modrzewski's theories were associated with the Executive groups within the gentry, he in reality supported the establishment of clear codes which would protect all people, not just the gentry, against the arbitrary whims of the monarchs. He was equally opposed to restrictions of the rights of the burghers and peasants. While his concept of an ideal Commonwealth could nowadays be described as Utopian, he came to his conclusions by attempting to understand how society worked and how it could be improved. While he accepted that there might be circumstances where the King might need to take over absolute powers, he believed that the monarch's actions should also be open to scrutiny. According to his theory, a body of philosophers was, in all circumstances, to guard the common good. Modrzewski advocated educational reforms which would establish a rational and secular educational system. Although a devout Catholic, Modrzewski rejected the authority of the Papacy and wanted to see the creation of a national church.

The Jesuits were uniquely aware of the importance of the printed word in the Catholic Church's fight against the Reformation. The writings of Piotr Skarga were a good example of the intellectual quality of the Counter-Reformation. In his *Sejm Sermons* he made it clear that he considered it the state's duty to protect the subjects from Dissenter ideas. He rejected all suggestions that religious tolerance was a sign of progress. At the same time Skarga was deeply critical of the priests' loose morals and failure to set a good example. While hostile to all non-Catholic faiths, he disapproved of rabble-rousing and calls for the imposition of the death sentence against heretics, who he believed should be converted by example and persuasion.

As has been suggested earlier, during the Renaissance period publishers showed themselves receptive to what would now be called consumer demand. They took the lead in providing books in Polish and ones which frequently were on subjects which were of popular interest. For the first time literature and poetry were extensively published during this period. The best-known writers of that period were undoubtedly Mikołaj Rej and Jan Kochanowski. Both addressed real dilemmas faced by human beings and wrote of the beauty and sadness of life. Kochanowski's *Treny*, a series of poems on the death of his beloved daughter, are as moving to a present-day reader as they must have been to readers in the sixteenth century.

The Renaissance took music out of the purely formal religious and court setting, where it had been practised earlier. Songs and music for organ and lute, instruments that became very popular, were published during that time. Among a number of composers, Jan of Lublin who composed the *Tabulature* for organ is seen as an outstanding contributor to Polish musical development. Music making and singing as a pleasurable activity were encouraged by these publications. There is also evidence that folk themes and tunes were borrowed and adapted for a more sophisticated audience.

While the wealthy burghers and nobility participated in the intellectual developments of the time, it is interesting to question whether they actively encouraged culture for the broader community, or merely thought of self-improvement. The royal court naturally set the tone, but it would appear that the Jagiellonians were not particularly interested in acting as patrons of the arts. Bona, uniquely, was determined to bring to Poland examples of Italian culture, and the rebuilding of the Wawel royal castle in Kraków is entirely due to her efforts. But neither Zygmunt I Stary nor Zygmunt August showed any interest in nurturing local talent. As numerous foreign visitors noted, the latter had a passion for very expensive jewellery and fine clothing, but that was as far as it went. For this failure to make the royal household a centre of artistic and cultural life, the humanists condemned both monarchs. It is notable that Rej and Kochanowski after a period at the royal court, returned to their respective estates. Both made references to lack of culture in the King's immediate entourage and castigated the wealthy for their hypocrisy and philistinism. But the magnates and the wealthy burghers looked to the royal court for examples of splendour and modelled their lifestyle on what they observed in the castle in Kraków. Conspicuous display of wealth thus masqueraded as worldliness and culture. The lifestyle of the archbishops and bishops differed little from that of the nobility, which accounts for the Dissenters' condemnation of the Church and of its wealth and power.

The rebuilding of the royal castle certainly set the tone for the nobles, as building a sumptuous palace in the most up-to-date style was a guaranteed way of making an impression. Italian models and architectural styles were the most popular. The Italian Giovanni Trevano conducted the reconstruction of Wawel castle. The Zygmunt Chapel in Kraków Cathedral is recommended as a particularly fine example of Renaissance architecture. This and the Wawel galleries designed by Franceso Fiorentino and Bartholommeo Berrecci were frequently imitated. The Pieskowa Skała castle built for Stanisław Szafraniec and Baranów castle commissioned by the Leszczyński family, were closely modelled on Wawel. Zamość, Łańcut and Nieśwież castles are also good examples of the Italian style so admired by the magnates. Apart from these incidental examples, it is generally considered that, in architecture, the Renaissance period was not as inspiring as other branches of culture.

The Renaissance directly or indirectly influenced the lifestyle of the nobility. The nobility as a whole and the wealthy burghers were affected by European-wide developments. Poland experienced and participated in the political and intellectual life of Western Europe. Education, consumption patterns, cultural and religious contacts all drew the wealthy and propertied classes into Europe-wide trends. But the daily life of most of the burghers, the peasants and poorest nobility were little affected by these changes. The townspeople in some cases became more aware of political issues and consciously pursued them, though at this stage not successfully. The gentry to a larger than hitherto extent participated in political and cultural activities, even if in most cases these were confined to the local assemblies. These nevertheless addressed issues of national relevance and made representations to the Sejm.

Women's position in society continued little changed, though the daughters of the nobility frequently did benefit from some home tuition. They might be expected to have some basic education, but if literature is to be accepted as giving a true picture of male preferences, a docile and obedient girl continued to be the male ideal within the nobility and wealthy burghers' families. Bona's direct and forthright involvement in politics and her administration of Crown properties drew criticism, because her actions did not conform to the stereotype of a queen's role, which was still confined to that of producing a number of healthy sons. Within the urban communities men were expected to be in charge of financial matters. As always, it is difficult to gauge whether in reality such rigid divisions prevailed. Women had the right to hold property in their own names, and the dowry and the morning-gift, a one-off payment made by husbands to their wives on marriage, was treated as entirely theirs to dispose of. Only in 1577 did the Church manage to establish its monopoly over marriages, when Church ceremonies and blessings became the norm. Interestingly during the Counter-Reformation women's rights were strengthened, as it was recognised that in matters of faith, women were more conservative and respectful of the Church hierarchy. Therefore the Church for the first time tried to reach a female audience.

The poor gentry, whose lifestyle might be very similar to that of the peasantry, the peasantry and the poorer strata of the town-dwelling population had little access to the cultural life enjoyed by their betters. They might have been indirectly affected by these events, but it is dubious that they would have been active participants in any of the new activities, cultural or educational. Their dwellings and patterns of life, when they did alter, did so most likely because of changing patterns of economic activity, wider availability of goods or because of the prevalence of a cash economy, which meant that goods, purpose made, could be purchased, rather than made for the person who ordered them. Thus while the gentry strove to limit what were seen as the arbitrary demands of the Crown and state, the poor fared worst, since the gentry tried to consolidate their economic and political power by limiting the personal and economic freedoms of the peasants. The word 'free' when applied to the description of a Pole, invariably was applied to the nobility and not to the community as a whole. Enserfment of the peasants became increasingly the norm in the Polish kingdom and in the Grand Duchy of Lithuania. Wealthy towns were better placed to resist attempts to limit their rights. Although the gentry frequently succeeded in having discriminatory legislation introduced, their inability to have it fully, if at all, implemented allowed the towns a degree of autonomy.

The Reformation in Poland was a brief religious flowering at the end of the Renaissance. Although an interesting period in the history of sixteenth-century Poland, its impact was nearly entirely confined to cultural developments. Religious disputes remained peaceful and free of strife. However, both the Reformation and the Counter-Reformation led to the widening of political, religious and intellectual debates. Importantly, Poland remained committed to Catholicism and in Europe, which gradually divided along new religious lines, this had important implications for the course of future Polish history.

With the end of the Jagiellonians came the end of dynastic rule in Poland. Although neither the Piast nor Jagiellonian dynasties were hereditary, there was always a marked preference for the candidate to the throne to belong to the ruling dynasty. Only when that proved impossible did the magnates consider alternative choices. At the same time the Crown failed to establish its authority, instead becoming increasingly dependent on the broader mass of the nobility. The emergence of the *szlachta* as a major factor in all debates concerning appointment of successors and the waging of wars had a profound impact on Poland's place in regional politics and the internal political structures.

As each pretender to the throne sought approval from the nobility, so matters of state, traditionally decided by the King in close consultation with the powerful magnates, were devolved to the assembly of the gentry. These in turn came to be manipulated by the magnates, contributing to paralysis of state decision making. The result was not a larger degree of Crown accountability, but stalemate.

In foreign affairs the interests of the Jagiellonians, after a brief period when Hungary and the kingdom of Bohemia were of direct concern, narrowed down to defence of purely the interests of the Polish kingdom and the Duchy of Lithuania. The days when the Jagiellonians thought in terms of a Great Slav kingdom were over and the henceforth the boundaries of the kingdom would stabilise.

5

The Polish–Lithuanian Commonwealth

During the sixteenth century two processes, occurring simultaneously, marked the symbolic transition of Poland from a medieval to a modern state. The first was the establishment of the Polish–Lithuanian Commonwealth. The second was the transformation of a kingdom still based on a single ruling dynasty, into a commonwealth of the nobles in which the King was elected. Both processes had culminated during the latter part of the sixteenth century, though their roots can be traced back at least to the election of Jagiełło as King of Poland.

During the whole of the Jagiellonian period the Polish Crown was engaged in cross-border disputes that gave geographical definition to its state. In Bohemia and Hungary the struggle against the Habsburgs took place. At the same time the emergence of the state run by Teutonic Knights required successive Polish kings to focus on political developments in that region. The emergence of the Grand Duchy of Lithuania and the possibility that it could ally itself with the Teutonic Knights, created preconditions whereby the Polish kingdom had to constantly keep developments in the north and north-east under close observation. The growth of the power of Muscovy, and the challenge it posed to Lithuania, was also a source of concern for Poland. Throughout this period, and influenced by these developments, the final form of the Polish–Lithuanian Commonwealth was gradually taking shape.

The incorporation of Masovia into the Polish state had been proceeding piecemeal throughout the fifteenth century. Successive Polish kings had been reluctant to subordinate it, partly because they did not have the military power to do so, but also because they were reluctant to take action which might lead the Masovian Piast dynasty to ally itself with the Teutonic Knights, rather than to become part of the Polish kingdom. In 1526 the last of the Piast dukes died without issue and this enabled Zygmunt Stary to complete the incorporation of Masovia into Poland. The area had grown in importance after Prussia adhered to Poland. Although the local nobility was opposed to Poland's policy of absorbing Masovia, in reality the region had enjoyed close contacts with Polish Crown territories and a process of colonisation by Poles had been taking place throughout the past century. During the latter part of the sixteenth century the royal court increasingly gravitated towards Warsaw, making it an informal capital of Poland.

With the Toruń Treaty of 1466 Prussia, previously held by the Teutonic Knights, was divided into two. The part retained by the Knights was referred to as Ducal Prussia and became the feudal possession of the Polish Crown. In 1525 Albrecht Hohenzollern-Ansbach negotiated an agreement with Zygmunt Stary whereby the Order of the Teutonic Knights were secularised. The Polish king accepted Albrecht's hereditary rights to Prussia. In an act, which is usually remembered more for being the subject of an overblown painting by Jan Matejko, Albrecht swore an oath of fealty to the Polish king. This was an unusual provision at a time when the feudal system was on the wane, but assured Albrecht's loyalty to Poland at a time when it would still have been impossible, if not imprudent, to try and incorporate Ducal Prussia into Poland. In reality neither the Teutonic Knights after the signing of the Toruń Agreement nor Albrecht were willing to accept subordination of Prussia to Poland and invariably did all in their power to reverse it. In 1563 Zygmunt August, preoccupied with unfinished conflicts against Russia and Sweden in Livonia, gave Albrecht permission to appoint another branch of his family, the Brandenburg Hohenzollerns who ruled Pomerania, the right to succeed in Ducal Prussia. On his death, Albrecht was succeeded by his son Albrecht Friedrich who showed signs of mental instability. This allowed the Brandenburg Hohenzollerns to lay claim to the Duchy in 1603. By these means Ducal Prussia was alienated from the Polish kingdom. In 1660 Ducal Prussia was annexed by Brandenburg.

The remainder of Prussia, which was usually referred to as Royal Prussia, was incorporated into Poland in 1569. A strong sense of separateness remained in the district and at times this led to open opposition to the Crown's policies. The port town of Gdańsk had the confidence and political acumen, not to mention the economic strength through its Hanseatic connections, to become a major player in royal policies in the Baltic. But the port jealously guarded its independence. During Zygmunt August's rule Gdańsk refused to supply the King with ships to help military action in Livonia. The city feared that profits which it hoped to derive from the ongoing conflict would be reduced because the Polish Crown would claim some of the spoils. The city also strenuously opposed the King's attempt to create a Crown fleet. Even a royal charter failed to break the city's monopoly over all maritime matters.

Within Royal Prussia conflicts between the nobility and the particularly strong urban communities became especially pronounced during the second half of the sixteenth century. The Prussian nobility wanted the Sejmik, the local assembly of nobles, to adopt laws modelled on Polish ones, which would give them increased rights at the expense of urban interests. But, within Prussia, the burghers formed a powerful group and could not be easily sidelined. They countered by campaigning for laws which would allow the nobility to be tried in accordance with common law. Where the nobility had the privilege of only being tried in their own courts, these were always more tolerant of the nobility's misdeeds. The Prussian burghers were more politicised than their counterparts in the Polish towns, calling for constitutional reforms. At the same time, the Prussian nobility and urban dwellers were capable of uniting against the Polish Crown on confessional lines. The majority of the Prussian inhabitants were either Calvinist or Lutheran and therefore agreed on the point that the Catholic Polish Crown should not be allowed to encroach upon their religious and social institutions.

During Zygmunt August's reign, Polish interest in the Baltic coast increased. Several factors account for this. Albrecht Hohenzollern was interested in extending his influence into Livonia where the Teutonic Knights' one-time allies, the Knights of the Sword, increasingly succumbed to Protestantism. But Zygmunt's main concern was the spread of Russian influence into the region. Tsar Ivan IV, ruler of Muscovy, wanted to expand Russian trade with Europe through the Narva River and thus needed to destroy the trading monopoly of the two main Baltic ports of Riga and Gdańsk. Zygmunt August was very much interested in developments in the area. His plans for a major military confrontation came to nothing because the Crown was short of money and the nobility only reluctantly supported the conflict which embroiled Poland and Lithuania in war with the Russians during the years 1557 and 1561. Had the Polish king been successful in his plans the Crown's control of the Baltic coast would have been extended and the Baltic trade would have provided much needed revenue. Zygmunt August's plans did not work out and he failed to obtain a decisive victory. By becoming involved in Livonia, the Poles and Lithuanians became involved in wars with Russia and rivalry with Sweden. In 1561 the King of Sweden captured the port of Reval, marking the starting point of Swedish rule in Estonia. For the time being the matter was unresolved, mainly because the Russian thrust had weakened due to Tatar attacks on Moscow. These developments nevertheless exposed the precariousness of Poland's access to the Baltic.

The completion of the process of unification between Poland and Lithuania was the most important achievement of the sixteenth century. In December 1568 representatives of both sides met to bring to a conclusion what had been constantly discussed and debated since Jagiełło became King of Poland. In the long term both sides appreciated the need for unity and the most recent conflict with Russia over Livonia underscored this point. The outstanding issue was the precise way in which the two were to be co-joined. It has to be appreciated that this was not a process of conquest or subjugation but the coming together of two kingdoms. Unity would require guarantees that neither side would be treated as a minor partner and that historic and legal differences would be respected. After extensive negotiations, which lasted until July 1569, the final form of the union was agreed. Henceforth Poland and Lithuania formed a Commonwealth of Two Nations, Polish and Lithuanian. Having the same monarch united the two. There was to be only one Sejm, but various parts of the Commonwealth were allowed to choose representatives to the Sejm in different ways. The principle of unanimity of decision making was accepted in the Sejm, though at this stage this was still intended to ensure consensus in legislative matters. In due course this became an important and much hallowed principle which the gentry took to mean as giving any individual the right to destroy any legislation which he or his group did not wish to see implemented.

Although Poland and Lithuania agreed to form a Commonwealth, inherent in the agreement was the assumption that the distinctiveness of each would be retained. Thus no attempt was made to impose one model or to envisage uniformity, let alone centralisation. Poland and

Lithuania were to have different coins though of the same value. But both were to retain their own judicial systems and armies. Poland and Lithuania were to have separate finances and the Crown would make appointments to administer separately each section of the Commonwealth.

Within Lithuania opposition to the union had been mainly concentrated around the powerful Radziwiłł family, though even they had to accept defeat when they realised that they were incapable of mounting a defence against Russian incursions against Lithuanian interests. But the Crown had to make some concessions mainly to the Lithuanian magnates, who demanded that the royal estates held by the magnates should not be returned to the Crown, a right demanded by the Polish gentry to weaken the power of the magnates and of the Crown. The *szlachta* felt that by rewarding the loyal magnates with concessionary leases of Crown estates, the state exchequer had been depleted. Whereas in the Polish Crown territories this process had been partly reversed, the Lithuanian magnates blocked similar reforms being implemented. Thus a higher proportion of great estates persisted in Lithuania, while in Poland, under pressure from the gentry, the Crown reclaimed its lands. Zygmunt August successfully pressed Lithuania for the return to Poland of Podlasie, the palatinate of Volhynia, Bratslav and Kiev.

With hindsight it is difficult to judge who benefited more from the creation of the Commonwealth. Undoubtedly, both had been coming closer since Jagiełło became King of Poland, but it is possible that the growth of the Russian threat forced the final decision. At the same time the King's own desire to neutralise his opponents within Poland and to undermine the Lithuanian magnates' desire for independence, by appealing to the Lithuanian gentry, could also have played a role in the final decision. As it turned out, the unexpected result of the union was that the central authorities grew weaker. The gentry had a first taste of its new powers when the King died in 1572.

Previously, although in principle the nobility had a say in the choice of successor, this had not been an entirely free choice. Dynastic considerations remained the most important criteria when the magnates decided who was to succeed to the Polish throne. But in 1572, with the death of Zygmunt August, the Jagiellonian line had died out. The Piasts who presented themselves for consideration to the throne had a very weak claim or were too insignificant to be realistically considered. Although Zygmunt's middle-aged sister Anna was available, no one seriously considered electing her as Queen of the Commonwealth. The nobility were faced with a genuinely free choice but also with no precedent to fall back on to assist them in the process. In the circumstances, the election of successive kings was surprisingly orderly.

In the first place there was general consensus that the Archbishop of Gniezno should take the lead. It was agreed that he should act as Regent and then call for local assemblies of nobles to make their representations. The nobility grouped in regional blocs to discuss how to proceed with electing a new king. Regional confederations of the gentry undertook to maintain law and order while the Senators undertook to make sure that the safety of the Commonwealth was not imperilled. A number of issues caused discord. Anxiety about Catholic dominance and foreign policy choices were very important considerations. But, impressively, the period of interregnum was not used to settle old scores. During the first interregnum a number of procedures were put in place which would henceforth govern the election of each next king. The basic principles – these would come to be known as the *Henrician Articles* – were a list of minimum and non-negotiable demands put to each prospective monarch. An elected king was expected to swear to uphold the elective principle and to make a commitment to maintaining all privileges which the nobility enjoyed presently. He would have to support the principle of religious tolerance. All his decisions were to be verified by a group of Senators. He had no right to levy new taxes or to declare war, as these were matters which only the Sejm could agree. The elected king had the duty to convene the Sejm at least twice a year. In addition to the *Henrician Articles*, the prospective monarch was expected to sign a list of personal undertakings, the so-called *Pacta Conventa*, which were negotiated with each candidate separately and varied depending on circumstances preceding the elections. These gave the nobility scope for extracting further concessions and commitments.

During the first election, the rights of all those who had a claim to the status of a nobleman to participate in the decision making directly and in person was confirmed and henceforth upheld. The process of electing the next king took place at a full gathering of the nobility in Warsaw in 1573. Those wishing to be considered were not allowed to attend in person, though their agents did and they entered into protracted bidding, freely making promises to the assembled nobility and trying to outdo other candidates. In addition to a number of lesser

Piasts an interesting number of foreign monarchs bid to become King of Poland. Tsar Ivan IV made a feeble attempt on his and his son's behalf. The more serious contenders were Ernst Habsburg, Archduke of Austria, King Johan Vasa of Sweden and Henri Valois, brother of the King of France. The magnates and the Catholic Church supported the Habsburg bid. The gentry, mindful of the Habsburgs' policy of strengthening royal rule, decided on Henri (1573–74). This proved to be a disastrous choice. His brief sojourn in Poland between January and June 1573 descended into a farce. On arrival Henri quickly alienated the Poles. Only 24 years old, he seemed reluctant to proceed with marriage to the 50-year-old Anna which had been part of the deal. Instead he shocked his hosts with his preference for the company of young painted men of his entourage. He made no decisions of state, other than to draw heavily on treasury funds which he merrily gambled away in long card games with his friends. On hearing of his brother's death he slipped out of Poland and returned to Paris, never to come back. His kingship lapsed when he refused to heed Polish calls for his immediate return. A three-year interregnum followed during which decision making was paralysed by Henri's refusal to relinquish formally the throne of Poland, but also by the nobility's lack of decisiveness and their disagreement.

In 1575 as the Senators and the nobility debated what to do next, a group in the Sejm took matters into their own hands and convened a new round of meetings with a view to electing the next king. The Habsburgs once more put forward their candidate, which was the Emperor Maximilian II. The Senators chose him, but the gentry, who believed that the Senators had wrongly usurped the right to make this decision, chose Stefan Batory, Prince of Transylvania and pretender to the Hungarian throne. The two contenders to the Polish and Lithuanian throne fought a brisk war, but Maximilian's death in November determined the outcome in Batory's favour.

Stefan Batory (1575–86) was everything Henri Valois had not been. There is no doubt that the gentry made a choice which went beyond dynastic and foreign policy considerations. Batory was a military man. He was austere and forthright. He displayed political acumen and military leadership. The Polish gentry felt that his aspirations overlapped with Polish interests. Transylvania had been conquered by the Turks and became a principality of the Ottoman Empire. But the Turks had little interest in converting the region, whose inhabitants were a mixture of Orthodox Christians, Catholics, and religious Dissenters, mainly Calvinist and Lutheran. Batory's long-term hope was to wage war against Turkey, but also to destroy the Habsburg claim to the Hungarian throne. These two aims generally overlapped with Polish and Lithuanian plans, even if there always existed differences about priorities. When Batory received the Crown of Poland he undertook to wage war against Muscovy, which increasingly threatened the Commonwealth's interests around the Baltic coast.

Batory's rule re-established strong central authority, though all his internal and foreign policy decisions were always motivated by his prime aim which was the Hungarian Crown. Thus, though his rule was generally supported, the gentry and magnates always looked distrustfully at his actions, uncertain whether he was placing Hungarian objectives above those of the Commonwealth. In his internal policies Batory avoided direct conflict with the gentry, as this would have made it difficult for him to raise taxes for wars. But at the same time he made sure that the authority and the prerogatives of the Sejm were not increased, as this would have constrained his freedom. Thus, rather than seek the approval of the Sejm for contentious matters such as increases in taxation, he appealed directly to the district assemblies, which could be more easily persuaded to support the King. He was happy to see the creation of tribunals of the nobility, which reduced further the power of the Crown over the nobility, but he also soothed the gentry's anxieties. This in turn guaranteed their support for some of his objectives. By appointing outsiders to key administrative and military posts he reduced his dependence on the local nobility, which in effect meant that he was able to limit their ability to extract concessions from him. But this facilitated the growth of powerful families which owed their wealth and elevation entirely to the King. The Zamoyski family rose to prominence in this way during Batory's reign.

Batory was first and foremost a soldier. That was why the Poles elected him, and in that respect he did not disappoint them. But in the process of preparing the ground for the pursuit of war against the Russians he made a number of decisions which in the long term proved to be detrimental to Polish interests. By keeping him short of money, the nobility left the King little option but to sell those interests when a convenient purchaser appeared. The port city of Gdańsk and Prussia had refused to recognise Batory's election. Batory's response was to attack the city militarily and economically. When both failed, in return for a payment of 2 million Polish złotys, he annulled the 1570 charter which had given the Crown a monopoly over all maritime policies and subordinated the port to Poland. Further concessions followed. They resulted in the weakening of the legal ties binding Gdańsk to Poland and reducing the Crown's rights to build a military fleet in the Baltic without the port's prior agreement. In 1577 Batory accepted Georg Friedrich of Brandenburg's claim to act as custodian and heir of his cousin Albrecht Friedrich of Prussia, who succumbed to mental illness. The Brandenburg claim was recognised in return for a much needed fee. But the effect of this last decision was to hand over Ducal Prussia to Germany. The Polish route to the Baltic went along a narrow strip of land, with Pomerania on the west and Duchy of Prussia on the east.

In 1578 Batory embarked on preparations for war against Ivan IV. With that in mind he reformed and overhauled the military system. In addition to the creation of a standing infantry, he supported the use of a professional cavalry. His preparations for the campaign against the Russians were impressively thorough. In August 1579 his troops secured victories by capturing Polotsk and finally in 1581 Pskov. In January 1582 both sides settled for a negotiated peace. Batory gained Livonia and Polotsk. The Polish and Lithuanian Commonwealth's successes caused Sweden to take action and to secure Eastern Livonia (Estonia). But for the time being the Russian thrust had been fore-stalled.

Just as Batory started preparations for a campaign against the Turks, he succumbed to a sudden illness. On 12 December 1586 he died. Poland once more faced the need to elect a new king. The period of Batory's rule had manifested the positive and negative aspects of deci-sive monarchist rule. The nobility were increasingly dividing into two camps, one in favour of strong central authority, and the other, distrust-ful of the possible losses of their privileges and freedoms, in favour of using the elections and the bidding which would accompany them to limit the next monarch's powers.

In 1587 after a bitterly contested election Zygmunt III Vasa (Sigismund III Vasa, 1587–1632), heir to the Swedish throne, became King of the Polish and Lithuanian Commonwealth. This was the beginning of a period where Swedish issues came to dominate Polish politics. The reason for this was that in 1594 on his father's death Zygmunt III was crowned King of Sweden. Lutheran Sweden never-theless opposed a Catholic king. In 1600 the Swedish parliament dethroned the King and replaced him with his uncle who was then crowned Carl IX. Zygmunt III never gave up his claim to the Swedish throne and many of his policies within the Polish and Lithuanian Commonwealth stemmed from his preoccupation with that priority.

In 1632 Zygmunt III died and in the elections which followed his son Władysław was chosen to become King of Poland and Lithuania. He was crowned Władysław IV Vasa (Ladislaus IV Vasa, 1632–48). Like his father he refused to relinquish his claim to the Swedish throne and when in 1632 the Swedish King Gustav Adolph died, Władysław hoped to realise this claim. Unfortunately for his plans, the Swedes preferred to choose Gustav's daughter Kristina as queen. When his wife died Władysław IV asked for Kristina's hand in marriage. He was turned down. As far as he was concerned, his plans for succession to the Swedish throne were postponed but not abandoned. In 1648 Władysław IV died unexpectedly. His young son predeceased him by a few months. Thus Władysław's younger brother Jan II Kazimierz Vasa (John II Casimir, 1648–68) was then elected to succeed to the throne of the Polish and Lithuanian Commonwealth. He too refused to relinquish the family claim to the Swedish throne. In 1654 Queen Kristina abdicated and embarked on a life of aimless travelling through the royal courts of Europe. But Jan Kazimierz failed to push his advantage and the Swedes elected Carl X Gustav as king. Seizing the opportunity offered by Poland's difficulties in a war with the combined Turkish and Tatar forces, Carl X invaded from the north. Only in May 1660 was the war ended by the Treaty of Oliva. By that time Polish territories had been devastated by the long war and by the Swedish armies. Poland thus paid a heavy price for the Vasas' preoccupation with the Swedish succession. Not surprisingly the gentry tried throughout to forestall conflicts with Sweden, fully realising Poland's vulnerability to attack from Russia and Turkey.

The Vasas did not work well with the Sejm, nor did they accept the constraints of the political system. Their foreign policy required a strong military presence, and extended wars underlined all the more the need for a method of raising revenue for an army and for its equipment. Since the nobility distrusted the King's objectives, they did their best to limit the monarch's freedom to declare and pursue wars. Zygmunt III was suspected of wanting to abandon the Polish–Lithuanian Commonwealth and return to Sweden. His conspicuous Catholic piety and preference for Catholics when making appointments offended the Polish nobility used to a less discriminating religious policy. His attempt to build up an army and finance it by a more regular system of taxation raised the gentry's suspicions about his willingness to be accountable to the Sejm. It is generally admitted that Zygmunt III was temperamentally incapable of working with the gentry and had brought some of his problems upon himself by being unnecessarily difficult in his dealings with the Sejm and local assemblies.

Władysław IV was a military man but, even in times of troubles, he failed to gain the support of the gentry. While he is credited with over-hauling the structure of the army, introducing new strategic ideas, modernising and preparing it for war, he nevertheless was criticised for his adventurous attitude towards foreign policy and for lack of accountability. His successor Jan Kazimierz, in his dealings with the Sejm, benefited from successive wars which made it easier to gain the Sejm's approval to raise taxes for the purpose of building up the Commonwealth's military capacity. His own conviction that the Crown should be strengthened was by then shared by sections of the nobility. The first use of the principle of *liberum veto* to wreck a bill caused the King and political thinkers to consider reforming the polit-ical system. Jan Kazimierz was nevertheless inconsistent in his attitude towards the *liberum veto* principle, using it to spoil bills which he had opposed. His argument that the succession should be agreed before the death of the previous king, a principle with which many were inclined to agree, was defeated because it was known that he and his wife wanted to impose Henri Jules, Duc d'Enghien, on the Commonwealth. In 1668 Jan Kazimierz, facing a strong anti-royalist block within the Sejm, hatched a plan whereby in return for a French bribe which enabled him to retire to France, he abdicated. He had hoped to clear the field for the election of Philip Wilhelm, Duke of Neuberg.

The gentry's response to calls for reforms of the political system was not uniformly hostile. The provincial Sejmiki were at times will-ing to agree with proposals put to them by the Crown. But the Vasas faced one major disadvantage in that their motives were generally distrusted. Their preoccupation with Swedish affairs and pro-Habsburg foreign policy, which found expression in dynastic marriages, caused the *szlachta* to suspect ulterior motives behind the King's reforming zeal. In spite of promising that they would renounce their claims to the Swedish throne, once they were elected, Władysław IV and Jan Kazimierz refused to honour that promise. In the circum-stances the gentry saw themselves as custodians of Polish interests, and the elected kingship gave them plenty of opportunities to stress this role. Antagonism between the gentry and the Crown was heightened because the Vasas were Catholics and the community of the gentry represented a religious diversity and was generally predisposed towards tolerance. The monarchs' dependence on foreigners, frequently military engineers and strategists, tended to be viewed with distrust, even if these were men whose role it was to reform the Commonwealth's fighting capacity. Nevertheless in spite of the turbulent nature of political life, it is surprising to note that the gentry was not always disruptive. What they asked for was that the Sejm make all state offices accountable. They demanded respect for laws and transparency. These were the reasons for the convening of gatherings, which usually crystallised around a particular call or slogan, or the most immediate problem. In most cases the gentry was exercising the right forcefully and frequently violently to disagree with the King and form associations to pursue their policies. Nevertheless during the second half of the seventeenth century the principle of *liberum veto*, which in practice meant that any one individual member of the assembly had the right to veto decisions made by the Sejm, was so widely used as to make the passing of any laws impossible. When a degree of national unity prevailed, this right to dissent from the majority was rarely used, but at times of conflict between the Crown and the gentry it became a means of attacking the King and limiting his power. After 1650 the increased use of the veto to scupper all decisions of the Sejm, became symptomatic of the state of internal anarchy.

During the Vasas' rule, the Commonwealth was in a state of near permanent conflict. When, in 1611, Gustav Adolph succeeded his father Carl IX as King of Sweden, relations between Poland and Sweden took a turn for the worse. Gustav was determined to take advantage of Poland's involvement in war with Russia and against the Turks to consolidate Sweden's position around the Baltic. The beginning of the Thirty Years War divided Europe into Protestant and Catholic camps. Gustav was a crusading Protestant and determined to consolidate the German states of his co-religionists. The Polish–Lithuanian Commonwealth, though not directly involved in the Thirty Years War, was a factor in Gustav's strategic calculations. Zygmunt III was Catholic. He was also the brother-in-law of the Catholic Habsburg Emperor Ferdinand. The opportunity was too good for Gustav to overlook. Zygmunt's continuing claim to the Swedish throne and rivalry between Sweden and the Commonwealth over the Baltic coast were but added incentives for a Swedish attack.

In 1626 the Swedes attacked Royal Prussia, capturing several cities and ports in Livonia and Prussia. They also acquired the right to levy a duty of 3.5 per cent in the port of Gdańsk. Since neither side was entirely free to concentrate on their dispute a truce was negotiated in 1635.

In 1655 the Swedes resumed hostilities. The situation had dramatically changed since 1635. The Thirty Years War had ended and the Swedish army, mobilised, trained and confident, but definitely not willing to disband, was on the lookout for another confrontation. The Swedish exchequer had been emptied during the rule of Queen Kristina and conquest promised to patch up that hole. Furthermore Carl X Gustav, who succeeded to the Swedish throne after Kristina's abdication, knew that Jan Kazimierz the King of Poland did not have the full support of the Polish and Lithuanian nobility. Carl Gustav was therefore counting on the nobility's indifference towards Jan Kazimierz's continuing claim to the Swedish throne. Furthermore by then Poland was involved in a protracted conflict with Russia and the Cossacks.

The Swedish attack on Poland was so much more successful because the Swedish king had, as a result of the Treaty of Westphalia which concluded the Thirty Years War, obtained western sections of Pomerania. This gave Carl X Gustav the advantage of being able to attack from the west and north. The attack was militarily and politically a great success. The 40,000 strong Swedish army swept through Wielkopolska and Lithuania. The Polish and Lithuanian nobility, distrusting their king, refused to allow him to raise an army. A number of prominent nobles, notably the Radziwiłłs, declared in favour of the Swedes. The Swedes occupied Warsaw and Kraków, with the Polish and Lithuanian nobility accepting that the Swedish king could be a replacement for the previous one. Jan Kazimierz had not been a popular monarch which made this act of transfer of loyalty appear less treasonable. The fact that the Commonwealth was at the time facing a combined Russian and Cossack attack which continued until the Peace of Andrusovo in 1667, made the Swedish invasion impossible to defeat.

But the Swedes made the mistake of behaving like conquerors. In due course opposition to their rule crystallised around Jan Kazimierz, who had managed to evade the Swedes. Eventually the nobility rallied around him. The fact that Carl X Gustav failed to pay his soldiers naturally decreased their fighting spirit and increased pillaging, which further alienated the Poles. The Swedish determination to hold on to Poland was decreased by guerrilla warfare waged by the Poles. In 1659 and 1660 the Swedes were pushed out of Poland. The events of the Swedish conquest of Poland are described as 'The Deluge' (Potop). One of the high points of the Swedish invasion, it is believed, was an attack on the monastery in Częstochowa which held the most holy of Polish Catholic icons, the picture of the Black Madonna in 1655. Historians are far from uniform in agreement as to that event. Some see it as a key turning point in the war, rallying the Poles behind a symbol of national unity. Other have suggested that the event was of scant contemporary significance but had acquired legendary meaning after the nineteenth-century writer Henryk Sienkiewicz portrayed it as a high point of patriotic endeavour in his spirit-rousing historic novel entitled *Potop*. The Swedes were nevertheless defeated and by the Treaty of Oliva, signed in May 1660, relinquished all conquered territories while Jan Kazimierz renounced his claim to the Swedish throne.

Events unfolding on the eastern borders caused the Vasas a lot of problems and repeatedly faced them with perilous military situations. Initially Zygmunt III was unwilling to enter into any agreements with Moscow, wishing to keep his options open for his pursuit of the throne of Sweden. There were many reasons pushing the two towards an accommodation, most obviously the threat posed by Tatar raids. Only after the Swedish throne was usurped by his uncle was Zygmunt III willing to establish direct relations with the rulers of Moscow. But in the east, the four horsemen of the apocalypse seemed to have been unleashed upon Russia. The country succumbed to famine, wars, uprisings and the plague. The so-called 'Times of Troubles' started with the death of Ivan IV. He was succeeded by his son Fiodor. Fiodor's younger brother Dmitri, whose legitimacy was in doubt, had earlier disappeared in unexplained circumstances. In 1598 Fiodor died and the boyars declared Borys Godunov, Ivan's brother-in-law, as tsar. When in 1605 he died unexpectedly the countryside descended into chaos. Peasant uprisings challenged the state on several occasions. Young men appeared claiming to be the long-lost Dmitri. In Russian folk tradition such miracles referred back to the belief that the Tsar is the defender of the peasants against the narrow interests of the nobility. Not surprisingly the appearance of these pretenders coincided with famines and peasant uprisings. For the Polish and Lithuanian nobility the upheavals following Ivan's death offered an opportunity not only to push Muscovy away from the Baltic but also an unexpected chance to secure the Russian throne. Religious fervour played a part in this thrust east. Only a few years earlier the Patriarch of Jerusalem made his way to Moscow and declared Moscow to be the Third Rome (after the real Rome and Byzantium). As the Moscow Patriarchate was created, the Jesuits in the Polish–Lithuanian Commonwealth extended their ambitions to conversion of the Orthodox Christians.

In 1604 a military force led by a Polish magnate Mniszek, moved to capture Moscow. Mniszek's expedition had the support of Zygmunt III, who offered the pretext of assisting one of the pretenders to the Crown of Muscovy. A newly revealed young Dmitri was opportunely married off to Mniszek's daughter. Polish units did reach Moscow, but in May 1606 they faced a setback; in a mob attack Dmitri was killed and most Poles were either killed or imprisoned. Mniszek and his entourage finally got away. Chancing upon another pretender they took up his cause. In 1609 Russia was once more invaded by a joint Polish and Lithuanian force. By that time Sweden took an interest in the events unfolding in Russia, and the Russians appealed to them for help. Only in January 1619 was a peace treaty signed by the Polish–Lithuanian Commonwealth and Russia. Briefly the Russian boyars had renewed a proposal, which the Lithuanian boyars had favoured in 1600, that would have entailed the Polish king, or his son, becoming Tsar of Russia and uniting the three states under one crown. Discussions had proceeded quite far on that subject and in 1610 Zygmunt III's son Władysław accepted the title of tsar. But the majority of the Russian boyars were not prepared to accept such a solution. Instead, after a prolonged period of civil war, which further devastated the country, Mikhail Romanov was chosen as Tsar of Russia, thus precluding the creation of an interesting, but in reality impossible, regional union.

In Poland, the campaign against Russia was viewed with distrust. The Turkish and Tatar threats were considered more important. Even Zygmunt and his son had doubts about the adventure, mindful that any victories would bring them into direct confrontation with the Swedes. In reality, the Vasas would have wanted to pursue a more active foreign policy in the west. Instead, they found themselves drawn into problems east of the Commonwealth. Nor were the rewards commensurate with the effort. All that was secured from the Russians was the Principality of Smolensk and smaller areas in the vicinity.

In 1632 after Zygmunt's death, while the elections of the next king were taking place, Lithuania and Russia clashed. This was described by both sides as preventive military action, while all along both continued to declare their commitment to the 1619 treaty. Once the new king was in place a full-scale campaign against Russia was restarted, but this time with the help of Cossack units. Once more only limited progress was made and both sides agreed to sue for peace. Failure to secure a military victory led Władysław IV to relinquish his claim to the Moscow throne and recognise Mikhail Romanov as the Tsar of all Russia. Attempts to draw the Russians into a joint war against Sweden were not successful, nevertheless Władysław IV was free to concentrate on war with Sweden.

The next crisis with Russia occurred when Władysław IV died in 1648. Moscow took action out of a growing awareness that the Polish–Lithuanian Commonwealth was becoming weaker. In 1648 the conflict between the Commonwealth, the Cossacks and the Tatars worsened. In Moscow the possibility of Cossack and Tatar unity was viewed with anxiety. This brought the Commonwealth and the Russians together. But, even though both sides tried to settle all grievances, these proved too difficult to resolve. The Russians felt that the Poles had shown them little respect and felt in particular aggrieved by the publication in Poland of books lauding the previous king's military victories over the Russians. Talks broke down in 1652. As a result Moscow let the leaders of the Cossack rebellion know that it was prepared to accept their desire to become the Tsar's subjects. The Ukraine was thus incorporated into the Russian Empire, though the Cossacks were promised autonomy. Jan Kazimierz tried to decrease the impact of these events by negotiating with Turkey, where anxiety about a Cossack alliance with the Russians was a strong motive for trying to decrease tension between Turkey and Poland. In the spring of 1654 a joint Cossack and Russian attack on Lithuania was initiated. The Commonwealth was badly prepared for the war and in due course Smolensk was captured. In August 1655 Vilnius was taken, after which it is estimated that 30 per cent of its population was massacred. Tsar Alexy Romanovich declared himself ruler of Lithuania. But like Jan Kazimierz, the Tsar was anxious about the growth of Swedish power and thus reopened negotiations with the Polish–Lithuanian Commonwealth. But any alliance between the Polish–Lithuanian Commonwealth and Russia was viewed in most European capitals with deep anxiety. The full force of diplomatic disapproval was used to prevent a Polish–Lithuanian alliance with Russia. The French supported Sweden. The Habsburgs did not want to contend with a powerful rival in the East. Even the Papacy, fearful of the spread of the Orthodox Christian faith into Western Europe, opposed the rapprochement.

In 1660 war was resumed. Briefly the Commonwealth appeared to have the upper hand, but in reality neither side could deliver a decisive victory. Both sides knew the Turks and the Tatars posed the bigger real threat and that unity would be beneficial to them both. Negotiations were opened but dragged on for a long time, culminating in the Peace of Andrusovo signed in January 1667. Ukraine, where the Cossacks had tried to play off the Russians against the Lithuanians was finally divided, with Poland holding the areas west of the Dnieper. The Russians retained areas beyond the river and the town of Kiev. The Commonwealth's claim to parts of Courland in the north was confirmed. It was then assumed that the Tsar wanted his son to stand for election as King of Poland and Lithuania, an idea which would have been supported by the Orthodox nobility of Lithuania. Both sides pledged support in the event of a Turkish or Tatar attack. They were also committed to suppression of any further Cossack uprisings. In May 1686 both sides signed an Eternal Peace. Rivalry between the two ended but at the same time all attempts at unity also ended. Henceforth the fate of the Polish Crown drew the Commonwealth into the Habsburg sphere and with that away from cooperation with Russia.

During the rule of the Vasas the eastern parts of the Commonwealth were affected by religious turbulence. This led to the emergence of the Uniate Church, which turned out to be small but significant evidence of the continuing desire by Christians to re-establish the unity lost with the split between Rome and Byzantium. In 1589 after the fall of Constantinople, Moscow attempted to assume the leadership of the Orthodox Church. To many this was an unacceptable step towards russification. Nor were the Lithuanian Orthodox Christian leaders willing to support the Moscow Patriarchate with funds. Within the Ukraine the wish to remain separate from Moscow was particularly strong. At the same time in Rome the idea of reuniting the two churches had never been abandoned entirely. Thus in 1596 came about the Union of Brześć. In return for recognising the authority of the Pope, most of the Commonwealth Orthodox bishops obtained guarantees that the Eastern rite would be recognised. To the architects of the Uniate Church this was to be but a starting point of a process which was to culminate in the two churches coming together. Unfortunately, even within Ukraine religious leaders felt uncomfortable about the theological and political implications of the union. One of the most important Ukrainian magnates Konstanty Ostrogski continued to support generously the Orthodox Church, opposing the Uniate movement. Nor were all Orthodox bishops willing to accept the authority of the Pope. Within the Church of Rome, views were split on the Uniates. While Rome remained loyal to those who joined it and has through centuries honoured its commitment to recognising the Eastern rite, the Church remained small, confined nearly entirely to the Ukrainian population. The majority of the Orthodox, most notably the rapidly growing Cossack communities, remained loyal to the Orthodox Patriarch in Moscow.

Poland and Lithuania had learned to live with the threat posed to their eastern and south-eastern borders by the Tatars since the thirteenth century. By the fifteenth century the nomadic marauders had settled and, although raiding continued to be an important element of their lifestyle, a Tatar state had been established on the shores of the Black Sea. By 1478 the Ottoman Turks subjugated the Tatars, transforming them into vassals of the Ottoman Empire. The relationship between the two nevertheless continued to be turbulent. For the Poles, Lithuanians and the rulers in Moscow the important political aim was to keep the Turks and Tatars divided. This was not always easy to achieve. The Turks and Tatars were united by religion and shared hostility towards the Polish and Lithuanian Commonwealth and Russia. At the beginning of the sixteenth century hostilities broke out between the Tatars, who were supported by the Turks, and the Commonwealth which used the newly emerging Cossack communities to defeat the Tatar push into Poland. The larger picture was of the Polish–Lithuanian Commonwealth rivalry with Turkey, but in reality this was usually fought through their proxies. The Ottoman Turks directed the Tatars, while the Poles tried to control the Cossacks, pushing them into conflict with the Tatars.

The Cossack communities emerged in the fourteenth century in the wild steppes of Ukraine and the area of the Dnieper River. These were territories to which runaway serfs fled and where adventurers headed. Although by the fifteenth century the Commonwealth officially sponsored colonisation of the region, the remit of the state did not reach to Cossack territories. Numerous attempts by the Crown to exert its authority failed, because the settlements, which developed on the borders of Ukraine and beyond the Dnieper, had evolved as military communities. The need to defend their homesteads against Tatar raids had forged a highly militaristic culture, disdainful of all authority. The Cossacks were formidable fighters. By the second half of the fifteenth century and throughout the sixteenth, the Commonwealth hired them during times of war and conflict. The Cossacks were therefore unwilling to accept relegation to the status of peasants. This placed the Crown in a quandary. On the one hand it felt uncomfortable about the free Cossack communities. But, on the other, it was only too willing to hire them, in particular because of continuing disputes between the Crown and the gentry over taxes, which prevented the Vasas from building up and financing a standing army.

The Crown settled on dividing the Cossack communities into registered Cossacks, who were to enjoy all the privileges enjoyed by free men in return for which they would be obliged to bear arms, and the remaining Cossacks who would be disarmed and degraded to peasant status. In implementing this obviously very risky policy, the Crown blundered. The decision as to how many Cossacks should be registered was made inconsistently. Initially it was calculated that 6000–7000 registered Cossacks would provide an adequate pool of fighting men. But wars with the Swedes and Russians, and the defence of the Commonwealth against Tatar raids created an enormous demand for experienced soldiers. At the time of the campaign which took the Poles up to Moscow, approximately 20,000 Cossacks were enlisted in the Polish army. But when military campaigns were finished the Crown tried to once more reduce the number of registered Cossacks. This, and the frequent failures to pay their wages, caused disaffection in the Cossack communities.

At the beginning of the sixteenth century the Zaporozhian Cossacks (Cossacks from the further reaches of the Dnieper River) started menacing Turkish communities on the Black Sea. Varna and Trebisond were sacked. In 1615 they reached Istanbul. At the same time by the beginning of the seventeenth century what had earlier been a natural democratic community underwent a gradual transformation into an economically and politically more complex society. Demands for the recognition of their status as soldiers went hand in hand with calls for political rights similar to those enjoyed by the Polish and Lithuanian gentry who also had the right and duty to bear arms. Several localised Cossack uprisings acted as a harbinger of what was to come. In 1648, what started as a private conflict between Bogdan Chmielnicki, leader of the Zaporozhian Cossacks, and his Polish neighbour became an uprising, which engulfed the whole of Ukraine. The Polish army was ignobly defeated at Korsuń, Piławce and at Żółte Wody in May 1648. Chmielnicki's Cossacks attacked Catholics, Poles and Jews. Jews were frequently employed as estate managers by the Polish nobility and thus attracted the Cossacks' particular hatred. Reprisals taken by the Polish landowners against the Orthodox and Cossack communities were as savage as those inflicted by the Cossacks. When Chmielnicki combined forces with the Tatars he posed a deadly threat to the Commonwealth.

The death of Władysław IV offered respite as the Cossacks waited for the election of the new king to see whether he would accept their demands. But the successor Jan Kazimierz resumed military action against the Cossacks and the Tatars in 1649. In June 1651 the Commonwealth army secured a victory near Beresteczko, only for the Cossacks to regroup and resume fighting. In 1653 Chmielnicki appealed to the Russians for protection and Tsar Alexander Mikhailovich agreed that their territories should come under Russian rule. Since the Commonwealth and Russia were at war this was an agreement which neither side expected to outlast the next peace treaty. Poland's problems increased as the Swedish invasion of 1655 required a regrouping of forces. Fighting continued until the Swedes were forced to withdraw out of Poland and the King was able once more to concentrate on the combined Russian and Cossack threat. The signing of the Andrusovo peace treaty with Russia in 1667 marked the end of the conflict with the Cossacks. What had been Cossack territories were divided along the line of the river Dnieper and Zaporozhe was administered jointly by the Russians and the Poles.

The end of the Cossack uprising came about not merely because of the end of the wars with Sweden and because Russia allowed the Commonwealth to concentrate on resolving the Cossack problem. Of equal importance were changes taking place within the complex Cossack community. Chmielnicki had tried to create an independent Cossack state. But his plans to be crowned hereditary monarch met with strong opposition within the community. Even though many Cossack leaders had accepted state and military positions, drawing wages and enjoying privileges, vestiges of old democratic ideas lingered making it impossible for Chmielnicki to obtain support for his efforts. Regional differences also divided the Cossacks. Since they failed to agree and build up unity this reduced their ability to negotiate from a position of strength with neighbouring states. The result was that the community could always lead uprisings but not gain independence as a stable peacetime polity.

During the sixteenth and seventeenth centuries Ukraine was rapidly colonised by Poles. But the predominant pattern of land settlement was of enormous estates. This accounted for the domination of the magnates in the politics of the region. These men frequently brought with them whole villages. They also encouraged the arrival of Jews who took up intermediate positions, such as overseers, estate managers, innkeepers and rent collectors. This association with the process of establishment of Polish control over the Ruthenian and Ukrainian communities aroused the Cossack hatred of Jews. During the Chmielnicki uprisings the Jewish population suffered disproportionately from oppression by both sides.

The end of the Vasa period is synonymous with the collapse of the power of the Crown and the emergence of a distinct culture of the gentry, which came under the name of Sarmatian culture. The *szlachta*, through the process of elected kingship and, by its determination to constrain the Crown within strict legal boundaries, had reduced central authority and had assumed responsibility for all matters of state. The next test would be for the gentry to discharge those responsibilities.

6

. . . .

Republic of the Nobility, 1669–1795

The end of the seventeenth century witnessed the emergence of a distinct Sarmatian culture among the gentry of Poland, Lithuania and Ruthenia. The name derives from the legend that this nobility descended from a 'Sarmatian' tribe, which spread from the shores of the Black Sea conquering the people of north-eastern Europe. The gentry of the Sarmatian culture believed that, in spite of their cultural, religious and ethnic diversity, they had common ancestry and that the rest of the population, notably the peasants, were a conquered people. During the second half of the seventeenth century Sarmatian culture, which was confined to the gentry, the *szlachta*, had become more defined. Contemporary historians and political leaders added pseudo-scientific and historic explanations to what was essentially only a set of common values espoused by the gentry. In the Commonwealth the gentry, amounting to approximately 7–10 per cent of the population, constituted a larger section of society than was the norm in other European kingdoms. This was due to the fact that primogeniture, whereby the estate and title would pass only to the oldest child, was not practical in Poland. Thus all sons of a nobleman were considered to belong to the nobility. Unlike their West European counterparts, the *szlachta* enjoyed extensive political and economic privileges, and most importantly had the right of a say in most matters of state, including succession to the throne.

The characteristic features of Sarmatian culture, as espoused by the *szlachta* in particular during the seventeenth and eighteenth centuries, was contempt for foreigners and other social classes, distrust of different cultures, and general xenophobia. These attitudes emerged because of the militaristic culture which prevailed in the Commonwealth which appeared to be constantly at war with its neighbours, a state which was not always easy to justify in strategic terms. Conflicts with Sweden, ongoing wars with the Tatars and Turks and latterly Cossack uprisings, focused attention on the eastern borders where Sarmatian culture was most strongly entrenched. The establishment and codification of principles governing the elective monarchies drew the gentry closely into direct rivalry with central authority. They became preoccupied with the defence of existing privileges, most notably the right to participate directly in deciding who was to be the King of the Commonwealth. The succession of elected foreign monarchs who, once enthroned, used the Commonwealth's resources to pursue their own, as distinct from the Commonwealth's, interests, further strengthened the gentry's determination to consolidate its hold over state matters. Thus, in Sarmatian culture, the protection of the gentry's freedoms, its right to express disagreement with the Crown and to take action against it, appeared as a concern to protect the state from dynastic adventures. The *liberum veto* was elevated to a general principle allowing everyone of noble rank to express his disagreement with decisions made by the Sejm and thus personally to invalidate them. The preservation of these freedoms was considered so important that their exercise was seen as overriding the need to make important decisions, which would allow the state to discharge its functions. This explains the gentry's constant unwillingness to approve any taxation measures, which would have enabled successive monarchs to maintain an army.

While they were inordinately proud of the fact that in the Commonwealth the *szlachta* had the right to elect the monarch, Sarmatians faced a dilemma, as they distrusted those very foreigners whom they elected as kings. Each round of elections allowed the nobility to bid for further privileges, which progressively eroded the Crown's authority. Once elected on the basis of having promised to respect and increase privileges, relations between the electors and the elected tended to falter. The elected kings arrived in Poland accompanied by their retinues, obviously wearing foreign clothes and behaving differently from the way the Polish and Lithuanian nobility did. This aroused contempt for foreign ways and exacerbated relations between the elected king and those of his subjects who only a month earlier, had exercised their right to determine his promotion. Henri Valois was from the outset seen as being effete and excessively preoccupied with the young men in his entourage. The Vasas, who repeatedly attempted to reform the military system, and brought with them engineers and military advisers, also incurred the distrust of the Sarmatian gentry. The gentry resented the influence of foreigners over the Commonwealth's security even though they were neither willing nor able to do anything to remedy its visible military shortcomings.

During the seventeenth century Sarmatian culture became increasingly backward looking, concentrating on the supposedly great days of the past, most notably the times of the Piast rule. An element of messianism was an integral part of this reasoning. This thinking was in particular further enhanced by the ongoing conflict with the Muslim enemies in the East. The revival of the Catholic religion after the Counter-Reformation, rivalry with the Orthodox nobility in Lithuania and conflict with the Orthodox Russians magnified the Sarmatians' conviction that it was Poland's historic destiny to uphold Christianity in the Commonwealth and to push its frontiers east. These ideas became particularly embedded in the Sarmatian culture from the second half of the seventeenth century and reached their height during the rule of Jan III Sobieski.

Whereas during the Reformation Poland upheld the right to freedom of religion, towards the end of the sixteenth century the Counter-Reformation spearheaded by the University of Kraków and the Jesuits successfully fought back. Dissenter religions had never taken root in villages which made it easier to rally the majority of the community around the Catholic faith. The towns did, however, espouse Dissenter ideas. During the Counter-Reformation it was easier to attack the burghers as laws generally offered them less protection against attacks from the state and Church. Not until 1557 when Stefan Batory established a Crown Tribunal could the Calvinist, Lutheran and Hussite nobility be tried. By imposing severe sentences on those who were deemed to have transgressed against the true faith, the Protestant nobility was in due course cowed. Publishing houses were likewise attacked and their owners were either fined or imprisoned. The disunity of the Protestant sects in Poland made it easier for the Counter-Reformation to destroy them. The Arians in any case were on doctrinal grounds excluded from the Protestant synod established by the three other Dissenter sects. By the end of the sixteenth century all Dissenter communities first in Kraków and then in other parts of the kingdom were destroyed. The Swedish invasion made it so much easier to justify the persecution of non-Catholics, in particular those of the Protestant faith. In 1658 the Arians were expelled from the

Commonwealth. In 1668 the Sejm made it a crime punishable by expulsion from the kingdom for Catholics to leave the faith. This act effectively put a stop to the further development of Protestantism in the Commonwealth. Catholicism became the religion of the Sarmatian culture. The idea that Catholicism was the true faith of Poland dates back to the Sarmatian days.

During this period the nobility's religion became showy, with the Church providing an elaborate ritual and the *szlachta* behaving with exaggerated religiosity similar to the pietism among Western European Catholics. Weeping, sighing, exclaiming and calling out the Virgin Mary's name were part of the expected performance which was justified by the claim that it was a religious and spiritual revival. One sign of the gentry's changing culture was the growth of religious intolerance.

The rejection of all things foreign narrowed down intellectual discourse. Standards of education fell. Sarmatians loved using Latin to show off their erudition, but in reality their knowledge and understanding of Latin were superficial. At the beginning of the seventeenth century Jesuit-run schools spread, challenging and replacing those which had been established earlier by Protestant communities. The educational programme of the Jesuits propagated the ideas of the Counter-Reformation, which amounted to subservience to religion, personal devotion and bigoted attitudes towards those outside their religious milieu. In due course the University of Kraków, being the centre of the Counter-Reformation, lost its position of intellectual pre-eminence. Nevertheless towards the end of the century political commentators came to appreciate the need for education as a means of steering the political debates towards reforms. While within the courts of the great magnate families love of learning was maintained and a tradition of building up libraries continued to be cultivated, the gentry generally slipped into a state of self-satisfied complacency. To the Sarmatians piety and patriotism were seen as a defence against the corrupting influence of foreign ideas. Schools either run by Jesuits or modelled on them appeared to satisfy the gentry's educational needs. The magnates, as previously, continued to benefit from wider educational opportunities and thus did not so readily embrace the ignorance of the gentry.

During the seventeenth century the gentry's style of dress became distinct; distinct from the wealthy magnates who favoured foreign fashions and from the more functional clothes worn by the wealthy town people and the peasants. The *szlachta's* main outer clothing was a cloak, usually bound at the waist with an elaborate sash. In the eastern regions the gentry wore shorter cloaks with silk, brocade or other colourful sashes. Surprisingly, in spite of their xenophobia, through extensive military and social contacts with eastern neighbours, the Sarmatians assimilated many aspects of those cultures. The sash was reminiscent of the type worn by Turks over their clothing. Furthermore, the gentry favoured shaven heads, sometimes with no more than a small wisp of hair on the scalp, a style favoured by Muslim Turkish and Tatar warriors. The wisp of hair, it was believed, would be used by the Prophet Muhammad to pull each man into heaven. In the Sarmatian culture, a scarred head usually was a sign of manliness and military prowess. During ostentatious and elaborate banquets, a true Sarmatian was expected to drain his drink and smash the goblet over his own head, thus presumably adding to the scarring.

The Sarmatians' attitude towards women was a mixture of exaggerated respect and repression. Kissing of women's hands, a habit still maintained by some men in present-day Poland, and ritualised courtesies were the norm. In reality the fate of women was far from easy. They were expected to remain at home, where the gentry's households usually had distinct women's quarters. Pious womenfolk of the Sarmatian gentry were not expected to leave home unaccompanied. In the eastern regions, seclusion, not dissimilar to that of the Muslim purdah, had become the norm. They played no open role in politics, though within the magnate families some women had strong political ideas which they were able to be made known, though mainly because of the privileged status of their families.

Outside the orbit of the gentry, the prevailing cultural tradition of this period is defined as Baroque. In architecture the trend which prevailed was for building residences which were showcases of the owner's wealth and splendour. The rebuilding of the royal palace in the newly established capital in Warsaw set the tone. Magnates and the wealthy gentry copied the castle and the royal residence in Ujazdów. The Łańcut castle of the Lubomirski magnates, Krzyżtopór of the Ossoliński family and Kruszyna castle, are all splendid examples of this trend in architecture.

In 1669 Michał Korybut Wiśniowiecki (1668–73) was elected King of Poland and Lithuania. The decision marked a victory for the gentry, keen to prevent a foreigner taking the Crown. The Senators had advocated the election of Jan Kazimierz's protégé Louis, Duc de Condée.

The alternative was the Habsburg candidate Duke Karl of Lorraine whose election would have involved Poland in a war with Turkey. As a descendant of the Piast rulers of old, and great-grandson of Jan Zamoyski, Wiśniowiecki represented the desire to set the clock back to the mythical days when Poles were ruled by their own dynasty. Though relatively well educated, he lacked drive and was more of a puppet in the hands of those who chose him. His election solved nothing as the pro-French camp plotted to remove the King.

The King's marriage to Eleonora Maria von Habsburg drew the Commonwealth into the Austrian camp and with that into conflict with Turkey. In 1669 a Turkish alliance with rebel Cossacks, who once more tried to create a state on the Dnieper, spelled trouble for the Commonwealth. In 1672 the Turks invaded and faced a deeply divided Commonwealth with a king who seemed not to know what to do. The gentry was loath to participate in fighting but was at the same time determined not to allow the King to raise taxes with which to pay for raising troops. Turkish victory was assured. Podole and large swathes of Ukraine were captured. The Polish commander Jan Sobieski succeeded in stopping the Turkish advances and persuaded the Sejm to provide funds for an army. In November 1673 Sobieski secured a victory against the Turks in Chocim. Nevertheless, the Commonwealth lacked the military strength to push the Turks back, even if their advance had been halted.

The King in the mean time roused himself enough to try and lead the troops into battle. His untimely death on 10 November 1673 once more opened the issue of elections. The military situation and a need for strong leadership made Sobieski an obvious candidate to the throne. During the rule of Jan Kazimierz he had been associated with the royal camp, and opposed Michał Wiśniowiecki's election. This could have limited Sobieski's appeal to the gentry. His inspired military leadership during the Turkish invasion transformed him into a national hero. Sobieski was an educated man. His military experience was extensive. But he was not merely a soldier. He had also been politically active in most of the great upheavals of the recent years. The French, who hoped to steer the Commonwealth against the Habsburgs, supported his election. French money had helped Sobieski in his campaign. Even after his election he continued to depend on French finance to prepare for war in the Baltic. During Michał Wiśniowiecki's rule, Sobieski opposed the strengthening of royal authority. After he was elected to become king he, unsurprisingly, changed his views, even hoping to make the Crown hereditary, so that his son could succeed him. He also changed his views of taxation and revenue collection, from initially favouring devolution of decision making on those matters to provincial diets, to advocating the Crown's right to increase revenue. In most of his efforts Sobieski had to contend with the aristocracy and Senators who continued to pursue their own financial interests. The aristocratic Pac family, which dominated Lithuania, made sure that he was never confident of Lithuanian support for his policies in the Baltic region. Within the Polish kingdom Sobieski's lack of a power base among the gentry limited all his reforming attempts. Powerful aristocratic clans with systems of patronage into which the gentry were drawn increasingly dominated the political life of the Commonwealth. This made nonsense of the gentry's claim to political freedom for they gradually slipped into coteries and cliques dominated by aristocratic interests. The Sarmatian ethos and self-interest blinded them to the possibility that what they saw to be a true republic of the nobility, was in fact becoming no more than a mass of ignorant members of the lower nobility, led by aristocratic clans, whose benefit derived most from the weakening of all central authority and a state of administrative paralysis, to which they were indifferent.

Sobieski's main foreign policy preoccupation was war with Turkey. He spoke Turkish and was well informed of the power struggles in the Middle East. This led him briefly to consider an alliance with Persia. At the same time he tried to reconquer Ducal Prussia, which he had hoped would provide revenue for the prosecution of wars against Turkey. An attempt to coordinate action with the Swedes to invade Prussia was never realised. Hampered by lack of funds, Sobieski abandoned plans for a military campaign. When faced with the extension of Swedish influence into the region, Sobieski had to negotiate for support from another powerful Lithuanian aristocratic family, the Sapiehas, who made the most of the Crown's weakness to consolidate their own influence. The need to concentrate on the Turkish threat prevented Sobieski from taking any further action in the Baltic.

The Polish–Lithuanian Commonwealth had over decades learned to live with the Turkish threat on its borders. During Sobieski's lifetime Lvóv had been besieged and it was believed that Kraków was within reach of an attack. Since the Western powers showed no desire to take action against the Turks, the Commonwealth was exposed and obliged to resist such an attack by itself. Frequent Tatar incursions only served to heighten a state of undeclared war. Jan Sobieski, although he had been able to stem its main thrust, realised that he was not able to defeat the Turks. He therefore applied himself to securing a peace treaty with the Turkish rulers. In 1677 and 1678 negotiations were conducted in a particularly inauspicious atmosphere, as the newly appointed Ottoman Vizier did not like the Commonwealth. Nevertheless by 1678 a peace treaty was agreed. The uneasy equilibrium was broken in 1683 when all signs suggested that Turkey was planning a new campaign. Sobieski had by then become disappointed with France's lack of support for his policies in Prussia. It was also suspected that the French king would not be too unhappy to see the Turks defeat Leopold of Austria as this would remove France's main rival. Poland's security considerations therefore pushed Sobieski towards the Austrian camp. A joint agreement obliged each side to provide assistance in the event of a Turkish attack. Sobieski also dreamed of reclaiming Turkey's recent conquests and, possibly, even pushing the frontier of Poland to the Black Sea. There are even suggestions that he entertained hopes of placing his son on the Hungarian throne.

When the Turkish attack took place in August 1683, its main thrust was directed at Vienna. Sobieski took command of his and allied German forces to relieve the Turkish siege of Vienna. On 12 September the Turkish forces were defeated, but Sobieski's gains were limited. The Tatars, who took advantage of Turkey's moment of defeat to capture Ukraine, thwarted hopes that territories lost in Podole and around the Dnieper would be reclaimed. Most importantly, the Turks retained the fortress of Kamieniec Podolski. The replacement of the Turkish threat by the Tatars in Podole was no gain to the Commonwealth. The signing of a treaty with Russia in 1686, which consolidated the anti-Turkish coalition, entailed further losses. Poland and Lithuania accepted Russia's claim to territories on the left bank of the Dnieper and to the cities of Kiev and Smolensk.

In years to come Polish historians frequently debated whether, by rushing to relieve the siege of Vienna, Poland had not committed a major political blunder. A sense of pique even nowadays is heightened by claims that in the city of Vienna all monuments commemorating the defeat of the Turkish siege bear no reference to Sobieski's role. The imponderable issue is that of whether by assisting Vienna Poland had not saved the very power around which German nationalism ultimately coalesced. Within the coming century Austria together with Prussia and Russia would jointly dismember the Commonwealth.

Since the Turkish invasion had not posed a direct threat to the security of the Commonwealth would it not have been more prudent to ignore the thrust on Vienna? It is unlikely that Sobieski tormented himself with those thoughts. He was a committed Christian and the attack on the Turks was, in addition to being of military importance, a Crusade against the infidels. The Pope and the Catholic clergy had campaigned extensively for the Commonwealth's participation in the war against Turkey. Staying out of the conflict was not an option Sobieski could have considered seriously. During his later years he deeply regretted that in spite of having mounted four further military campaigns, the Turks remained undefeated. On 17 June 1696 Jan Sobieski died after a long period of incapacity. He failed in his final objective of placing his son on the throne.

The election of the successor King of the Polish–Lithuanian Commonwealth further highlighted the shortcomings of the process. Of all the contenders two stood out. François Duc de Conti, the French candidate, was supported by most of the magnates, while Friedrich August Elector of Saxony, representing one of the most powerful German dynasties the Wettins, was favoured by the gentry. Sobieski's supporters threw in their lot with Friedrich August as did the port city of Gdańsk. When no compromise was reached the two camps proclaimed their respective candidates to be the next King of the Commonwealth and it was left to them to sort out the issue. Friedrich August who reigned as August II (1697–1733), converted to Catholicism just before his candidacy was put forward. He arrived in Poland swiftly and was crowned on 15 September 1697. Austria, the Papacy and the Russians actively supported him. François Duc de Conti unfortunately decided to come by sea and was prevented from landing in Gdańsk. While he waited for his followers to gather, support melted away and most proceeded to August's camp to negotiate conditions for supporting him.

August II's internal aim was to strengthen royal authority, so he could have the freedom to pursue his own foreign policy objectives. Within the Commonwealth he aimed to reduce the authority of the Sejm and the provincial diets. The Saxon throne was hereditary and it was obvious that the Crown of the Polish and Lithuanian Commonwealth would always be of secondary importance to him. In the first place he wished to enhance the authority of Saxony. A challenge to Sweden was an integral element of this plan. The conquest of Livonia was important as he hoped to secure the region for his family.

Saxony and the Commonwealth were to be united and the conquest of Silesia was essential to that plan. The Poles and Lithuanians had hoped that the well-trained and experienced Saxon army would go into action against the Turks and the Hohenzollerns. But August II had his own plans and immediately on securing the Commonwealth Crown, embarked on negotiations with the Peter I Tsar of Russia to secure his support for war against Sweden.

August II's first military engagement was against the Turks. The beginning was inauspicious as Saxon, Polish and Lithuanian commanders failed to agree on joint action. Austria, preoccupied with the issue of the Spanish throne, put pressure on August II to negotiate peace with the Turks, which he did. His grandiose plans for the conquest of Ottoman possessions and for the opening of routes to the Black Sea were quickly abandoned. But Kamieniec Podolski, the gateway to Podolia, was obtained in return for northern Moldovia, earlier conquered by Sobieski. This freed August II to concentrate on Sweden.

In Denmark and Russia August II found ready allies. Both countries shared Saxony's wish to destroy Sweden. In 1698 the three formed an alliance. But the 16-year-old Swedish king, Karl XII, proved more than a match. In alliance with Britain and France he fought back. By August 1700 Denmark capitulated. This was followed by the defeat of Tsar Peter's army at Narva in November. In 1701 fighting moved onto the territory of the Polish–Lithuanian Commonwealth. The Saxons were soundly defeated and withdrew, with the Swedes following them. In May 1702 the Swedes occupied Warsaw. August II, in the mean time, withdrew to Saxony.

The Lithuanian and Polish nobility were opposed to August's northern adventures. They rightly suspected that the war had more to do with his own dynastic polices than with any genuine threat posed by Sweden. War weariness after Sobieski's wars with Turkey played a part in this reluctance to endorse the King's adventures. When August appeared to have been defeated by Karl XII, sections of the nobility sought to pacify the Swedes and to assert the Commonwealth's neutrality. The Swedes' heavy-handed treatment of the Poles, and their pillaging of areas which they crossed in pursuit of the enemy, polarised the nobility. Some believed that an alliance with the Swedes would be advantageous because the defeat of the Russians, which was one of Karl XII's main objectives, would allow the Commonwealth to reclaim Smolensk and Kiev. Supporters of a pro-Swedish policy claimed that August II had effectively abdicated and elected a new king in 1704. Unfortunately Stanisław Leszczyński (1704–10) was generally regarded as a Swedish puppet and he failed to establish his authority. The majority of the nobility reluctantly continued to support August II, in the belief that Sweden would never respect the Commonwealth's independence. Supporters of this policy formed a Confederation in Sandomierz in 1704. A new agreement was signed with Peter I and armies were raised once more to fight the Swedes. In the autumn Karl XII, anticipating a joint Saxon, Polish, Danish and Russian attack, moved first and forced the Russians back east while he pursued August all the way to Saxony. August II saved himself by abdicating the Polish throne. This left Russia undefeated, and the Commonwealth in turmoil. Few were inclined to treat Leszczyński seriously, and the Russian Crown renewed its interest in the affairs of the Commonwealth. On 8 July 1709 the Swedes, who tried to complete their earlier successes with the defeat of Russia, found their run of victories reversed. In the battle of Poltava the Swedish army was destroyed at the hands of the energetic Tsar Peter the Great. Karl XII had to flee to Turkey.

The Commonwealth's participation in the Northern War took its toll. Not until 1715 did hostilities end. Russia's victory had allowed August II to return and reclaim the throne. In reality he was now no more than a Russian puppet. The establishment of his authority proved to be a more difficult issue. Even his supporters balked at financing an army and refused to submit themselves to much needed reforms of the state structures. In the mean time Leszczyński, who still had some support among the Polish nobility, raided Poland from Swedish-held territory. Nor was Russia's victory necessarily advantageous. The Tsar demanded that Poland relinquish the left bank of the Dnieper and also claimed the right to protect Orthodox Christians in the Commonwealth. In December 1710 Turkey attacked Russia. On 19 July 1711 Peter's troops were defeated in the battle of Pruth. Hostilities continued until 1713, but the war between Turkey and Russia unleashed Cossack uprisings, which did not end until 1715. Throughout these years foreign troops traversed Polish and Lithuanian lands while fighting each other. Famine and plague, the implacable allies of all wars, haunted Poland. Economic devastation and depopulation were widespread. Some estimate that up to 40 per cent of the population died either because of war activities or on account of economic devastation and the plague. Looting had been widespread, both by foreign troops and the Commonwealth armies whose leaders became virtual warlords. While the magnates and the wealthy nobility were able to defend their properties by raising private armies, the gentry, peasants and townspeople had no such protection. The response of the gentry and the townspeople was to turn against both the wealthy nobility and the military leaders. They formed a Confederation in the town of Tarnogród. Equally critical of the Saxons' misrule, they tried to defend Crown properties and expel foreigners. By 1716 peace was made between August II who returned to Poland, and the Confederates, who nevertheless were able to demand restrictions on the size of the army. Decisions relating to internal matters were increasingly made by various magnates negotiating with the Russians and by ignoring August II. On 1 February 1717 the Sejm approved a limited military budget. Called the 'Silent Sejm' for its failure to discuss the legislation, it merely confirmed the state of political paralysis which overwhelmed the Polish kingdom. The army which had been a menace to the population during the long wars, was to be reduced in size and the King would no longer be able to make appointments to the top military posts, the so-called 'hetmani', without the Sejm's approval.

Poland's participation in the Northern War had been an utter disaster. While the Commonwealth suffered the consequences of political and economic collapse, neighbouring states fared better. Prussia in particular benefited from the collapse of Saxony and from Tsar Peter's preoccupation with Sweden and Turkey. In 1715 Prussia went to war with Sweden and by 1720 was able to secure the port town of Stetin and Pomerania. Prussia and Russia were ultimately brought together by an interest in what was taking place in the Polish and Lithuanian Commonwealth. A weak and internally unstable Poland was advantageous to both states. By 1732 Austria was drawn into the alliance.

The latter years of August II's rule were marked by the growth of the power of several wealthy magnates and their families. The Czartoryski and Potocki families in particular came to prominence. Initially they sought power and enrichment through close association with the royal household. In due course prominent members of both families distinguished themselves in debates on the reform of the state and national renewal. By the time of August's death in February 1733 no consensus had emerged on the subject and the issue of the election of a new king once more focused the international spotlight on Poland and Lithuania.

Among a number of candidates to the Polish and Lithuanian thrones two stood out, Leszczyński, whom the French were bankrolling, and Friedrich August of Saxony, son of August II. Austria and Russia supported the latter. With distrust of foreigners running high in Poland, Leszczyński was presented as an heir to the Piast tradition. Appealing to the Sarmatian *szlachta* and astutely exploiting nationalist emotions, the French protégé was successful in his bid. On 12 September 1733 a rally of 13,000 noblemen declared him King of the Commonwealth. But the Russians did not accept this decision, and acting with Austrian and Prussian agreement forced another election rally to choose Friedrich August as king. Predictably the two declared their intention to enforce their election, but Friedrich August was more fortunate. The support of the Russian troops ensured that he was crowned in January 1734. Leszczyński, without credible French military backing, had finally to accept defeat and left for France, where as the French king's son-in-law he was allowed estates in Lunéville and Nancy.

Friedrich August was crowned August III in 1733. He died on 5 October 1763. In between, his visits to Poland were few and his concern for Polish and Lithuanian affairs limited. Although he seemed to have wanted to rule in the name of the majority of his subjects, in reality he left most matters in the hands of trusted appointees. Since decision making within the Sejm was paralysed by the liberal use of the *liberum veto*, a distant and uninterested king allowed authority to slip into the hands of the magnates who increasingly de facto ruled the Commonwealth. In the Polish Crown lands the Czartoryski clan held sway, while in Lithuania the Radziwiłłs held power. The Czartoryski group came to be known as 'the Family'. Their main opponents, the Potocki magnates, associated themselves with calls for reforms, both of the legislature and executive. But in reality even the Potockis stood to lose too much were these reforms to be implemented. With royal authority severely curtailed, and the provincial and national assemblies of nobles paralysed by the gentry's preoccupation with its own privileges, the magnates secured the support of the poor gentry for their policies. The latter were rewarded with offices or outright payments. These powerful groupings made all decisions relating to provincial and state matters.

The three largest families steered foreign policy. Their role was made so much easier by the fact that throughout his reign August III continued to be dependent on the three neighbouring powers which had made his election possible. His dependence on Russia was most

obvious, though he was never free from Austrian and Prussian interference. As the Elector of Saxony, August III tried to pursue an active
foreign policy of restoring Saxony's political position. As elected
King of the Polish and Lithuanian Commonwealth he did not have the
power to force his subjects to support his Saxon policy. Thus throughout August III's reign, in spite of his involvement in the War of the
Austrian Succession and the Seven Years War, the Polish and
Lithuanian magnates pursued policies different from that of their
monarch. Their aim was to prevent him from using Polish and
Lithuanian troops for his own policies, even when he tried to recap-
ture Silesia where a sizeable Polish community lived and which had
historic links with Poland. In the War of the Austrian Succession,
which started in 1740 and lasted eight years, August III first
supported Austria, but then switched sides twice. The Saxon army
was destroyed and Friedrich II of Prussia gained Silesia. These developments should have been of direct concern to the Poles, but contradictory policies supported respectively by the Czartoryski and
Potocki families made it impossible for an army to be raised. The
outcome of the war was that Prussia increased her power. Similarly,
during the Seven Years War from 1756 to 1763, fought by an alliance
of Russia, Austria and France against Prussia and Britain, the
Commonwealth remained neutral. Russia and Prussia made use of
Polish territories, incorporated local manpower into their armies and
in Prussia's case, depreciated the value of the currency by minting
coins from dies which had been captured by the Prussians. Russia's
attack on Prussia appeared to be advantageous to Poland, but the price
to be paid was allowing Russian troops the right of entry to
Commonwealth territories, which once granted was difficult to
reverse. After the death of Elizabeth of Russia, her successor allied
himself with Prussia. The Commonwealth was fast assuming the role
of an object of other powers' policies, neither willing nor able to
participate in or benefit from the storms raging around it.

The last King of Poland was Stanisław August Poniatowski
(1764–95), scion to the Poniatowski family. On his mother's side he
was related to the Czartoryski magnates. Though coming from the two
most powerful families in Poland, this would not have been enough to
secure the throne. His election was entirely due to the fact that during
his stay in St Petersburg as assistant to the British ambassador he
became the lover of the Grand Duchess Catherine. When Catherine
succeeded her husband as Empress of Russia, she remembered young

Poniatowski. In her design for Russia's future wars against the Ottoman Empire there was a need for a stable base. To Poland, which was to continue to be nominally independent, was assigned the role of being Russia's western security cordon. In order that Poland be able to play this role successfully, the country needed stability. Poniatowski, with his reformist zeal and a sound grasp of politics, could be counted on to understand what was expected from him. He knew that he owed his election entirely to the Russians. The task was made easier by the fact that no other credible contender had presented himself. France and Austria had washed their hands of the Polish problem, rightly reasoning that Russia was determined to pursue her objectives notwithstanding their views.

Stanisław August's rule started with a major programme of reforms introduced at the Convocation Sejm in 1764. Behind the King stood the full might of the Czartoryski family, their supporters and camp followers. The King pursued rapid and far-reaching reforms of the judicial system, established a military academy for the sons of the gentry, created treasury commissions which were to combat corruption and suspended the *liberum veto*. In the mean time 'the Family', the Czartoryski ruling coterie, proceeded to purge state and army institutions of all opponents. But neither the King nor his family reckoned on Catherine the Great's desire to maintain Poland weak. Her plan had not been for her puppet to succeed in recreating a strong and independent Commonwealth. Stanisław August tried to square his own desire for the strengthening of executive powers with his dependence on his Russian patron. The matter came to a head in 1766 when Catherine put forward a demand that all discriminatory laws against Protestants should be abolished in the Commonwealth. Her diktat was resented by the majority of the gentry, who were not willing to grant the Dissenters rights equal to those enjoyed by the Catholics. It should be stressed that discrimination against non-Catholics did not take severe forms, and was more a constraint on their advancement and holding of high state posts. Catherine had hoped that support for the Protestant cause would lead to the emergence of a strong Protestant group within the nobility, which would be pro-Russian. These demands were universally resented, both on account of the Catholicism of the majority of the nobility and because of the transparency of Catherine's designs. Catherine's simultaneous demand that the *liberum veto* should be restored was clearly an attempt to maintain a state of political turmoil in the Commonwealth. The Russian ambassador in Warsaw, Nikolai

Repnin, supported by the Prussians put these demands to the King and the Sejm. The King's opponents, who opposed his encroachment on the gentry's privileges, supported the Russians. After a warning that the Russians, if need be, would tear Warsaw 'stone by stone' the reforms were abandoned. It could be argued that the gentry assisted the Russians in weakening the King's last-minute attempts to strengthen the Commonwealth. In reality they were as much opposed to the King's plans as they were to Russian tutelage.

The matter did not end there, as there was general anger at Russian interference. The magnates and the gentry split into factions, some supporting the King, others allying themselves with the Russians. Some also distrusted both sides, but were willing to consider tactical alliances. Russian troops were stationed around Warsaw to reinforce the point. The 1768 Sejm finally accepted the inevitable. Laws discriminating against the Dissenters were abolished. At the same time all the nobility's privileges were reaffirmed, including the *liberum veto* which could be used against all Sejm decisions other than those relating to economic and state matters. The retention of the *liberum veto* allowed neighbouring states to veto legislation by paying some Polish nobleman to declare his right to veto the Sejm's decisions.

The response of the Polish gentry to these difficulties and interferences was to fall back on the old tried practice of forming a Confederation, this time in the town of Bar in February 1768. The Bar Confederation represented the gentry's last attempt to set the clock back to what they believed had been the great days of the republic of the nobility. Jerzy Lukowki, an eminent historian of the period, described what follows: 'A culturally and politically isolated noble Utopia, basking in the smug certainties of its liberty and perfection, collided with the world of diplomatic realism and international aggrandisement.' The Confederates wanted to overthrow the King and replace him with a Saxon ruler. In equal degrees they opposed Stanisław August's reforms and restrictions on their freedoms and Russian interference, in particular attempts to place the Protestant and Orthodox nobility on an equal footing with the Catholics.

Russia then initiated military action, which far from destroying the opposition galvanised the gentry. In the civil war which followed, the Russians were severely constrained by the fact that in October 1768 Turkey attacked the Empire. A long and gruelling war between Russia and Turkey dragged on until 1774 when, by the Treaty of Kutchuk Kainardli, Turkey accepted defeat. Turkey's attack on Russia had not been incidental. The Porte had in fact become anxious about the consequences of Russia establishing a stranglehold over Poland. Encouraged by France, the Porte had anticipated Russia's next move, which he rightly deduced would be an attack on Turkey, and took the initiative before Poland was safely in Russia's orbit. In the mean time the Habsburgs in Austria and Frederick II of Prussia also kept an eye on what was happening in Poland. Prussia, though not opposed to Russian interference in Polish internal affairs, felt that the civil war could lead to a wider European conflict, which could acquire a religious momentum. Vienna's attempts to benefit from the state of turmoil by imposing border rectification signalled a further need for cooperation. Thus on 5 August 1772 the three powers signed an agreement partitioning Polish territory.

As a result of the Act of Partition Frederick II of Prussia gained Royal Prussia, but not Gdańsk or Toruń. Catherine the Great took Byelorussia and Livonia. Maria Theresa, whose government had already laid claim to old Hungarian territories, now grabbed Galicia. In all, the Commonwealth lost 30 per cent of its territories. As the partitioning powers moved swiftly to integrate their acquisitions into their kingdoms, the population and government were neither consulted nor informed of what had happened. Incredulity reigned in the Commonwealth. But more humiliation awaited both Stanisław August and his opponents in equal measures. The Commonwealth was expected to approve the Act of Partition. Since neither Austria nor Prussia had a clearly defined interest in Polish affairs, Russia's role increased. Reform of the whole political and financial system now became Russia's responsibility. The Poles, including the King, were reduced to being actors in a larger play stage-managed by the Russians. The removal of Stanisław August was deemed unnecessary, even though he had failed to accept the role earlier assigned to him. However, his prerogatives were curtailed and most decision making was handed over to a newly created Parliamentary Council stacked by men handpicked by the Russian court. The Sejm and King approved the partition. All attempts to gain support in European courts proved futile.

In the years that followed Stanisław August concentrated on reforming the state financial system, instigated educational reforms and abolished ancient laws which forbade noblemen from participating in trade and manufacture. In the circumstances, it is not surprising to note that there was a high degree of politicisation of most sections of the community. Within the limits of freedom which the Russians were prepared to tolerate, debates were encouraged on political reforms. These debates were being driven by echoes of the Enlightenment spreading through Western Europe and finding their relevance to events in the Commonwealth. Hugo Kołłątaj and Stanisław Staszic in particular became prominent advocates of wide-spread reforms. Both were republicans at heart, favouring limits on royal power, and advocating a larger degree of accountability to the voters. They identified the impoverished gentry as a source of politi-cal instability and believed that they should not have the right to vote. According to their proposals only those who were genuinely free and economically independent should have the right to vote. The continu-ation of serfdom was seen by both as a sign of economic backward-ness. Both authors advocated a definition of citizenship. Unfortunately even the trauma of the First Partition did not lead to consensus within society. The Czartoryski family formed the nub of political opposition to the Russians and regarded the King as Catherine's pawn. Since they were not willing to associate with those advocating radical reforms, their opposition took the form of expressing anger at their exclusion from political patronage.

The outbreak of the Russo-Turkish War in July 1788 allowed the Poles some breathing space, as Catherine's attention was fully focused on the conduct of hostilities. In 1788, at Stanisław August's request, Catherine agreed to allow him to convene the Sejm. After it opened in October, it continued its sittings until 1792. Prussia, breaking ranks with Austria and Russia, made its success possible. The Prussians decided to warn Catherine that they would view the Russo-Polish alliance as hostile to their interests. For many Poles this amounted to support for an independent Poland. In reality this is not what the Prussians meant, even if it resulted in the withdrawal of Russian troops from Poland. While Prussia pursued her policy of trying to reduce Russian influence, reformist deputies to the Sejm seized the moment and put forward legislation which would have changed the political character of the Commonwealth. The wealthy townspeople joined the reformers in calling for a property-based franchise. The culmination of these efforts was the passing of the new Constitution on 3 May 1791 when, by astute prior planning, supporters of the reforms were able to have the boldly progressive new Constitution approved. Opponents were prevented from destroying the bill by not being informed that the Sejm would convene early after Easter.

The new Constitution introduced a parliamentary monarchy though the King was no longer to be elected. The new monarchy was to be hereditary. A complex system of checks and balances was devised to make the relationship between the King and the legislature workable and accountable. *Liberum veto* was abolished, though serfdom was maintained. The previously approved law stripping the landless gentry of its noble rank, and with that the right to participate in elections, was confirmed. Burghers were not granted political rights. They merely gained citizen's rights, which offered them personal protection but no direct involvement in state politics. There is no doubt that the authors of the Constitution and its supporters were inspired by the ideas emanating from the French Revolution. Debates on the rights of Jews proved more controversial, because even the reforming deputies were loath to grant them citizenship rights and to abolish residency restrictions. Even the great political reformer and co-author of the Constitution Kołłątaj recommended that they would have to adapt to Polish ways and accept abolishing of their communal rights. Some went as far as suggesting that Jews would have to choose between acculturalisation and departure from Polish lands. The matter was left unresolved.

During the previous year Russia's response to the Commonwealth's desire for independence had been muted. War with Turkey took precedence. A year later she was free to concentrate on the Polish problem. Once peace was signed with Turkey Catherine moved with determination to bring the Poles to heel. She found allies among the Polish nobility, in particular those who felt that Stanisław August had betrayed the most hallowed of republican principles by introducing a hereditary monarchy. Resentful of the King, and determined to prevent him from undermining the political position of the nobility, they turned to Russia for help. Unwisely, perhaps naively, but also very likely in search of reward, they agreed to head a Confederation which came to be known as the Targowica Confederation. Leaders of the Confederation, Felix Potocki, Seweryn Rzewuski, Ksawery Branicki and Szymon Kossakowski, were all men of considerable standing within the Commonwealth. They declared that they would not swear the oath to uphold the new Constitution. A high proportion of the gentry joined them. By agreement with the Confederates, on 18 May 1792 Russian troops attacked the Commonwealth. The outcome was a foregone conclusion, as the Commonwealth was militarily unprepared. The King and his ministers declared their determination to defend the Constitution, but by 23 July they joined the Targowica Confederates. A number of prominent military leaders left for exile, rather than serve the Russians. Among them were Józef Poniatowski and Tadeusz Kościuszko.

The international situation was favourable to Russian designs. Fear of the example set by the French Revolution had created a consensus among Europe's ruling monarchs. The need to fight France and to stem the spread of republican ideas created a unity which overrode dynastic rivalry. Thus Austria, preoccupied with fighting France, had no objections to Prussia taking part in the further destruction of Poland. It was agreed that Prussia should be compensated for losses of territories to France, by being allowed more territories in Poland. Russia had no problems in persuading both Prussia and Austria of the need to further consolidate the Russian hold over Poland. And although the Targowica Confederates had hoped that they would be given power once the King was destroyed, this proved not to be the case.

On 23 January 1793 Russia and Prussia signed an agreement for the Second Partition of Poland. Prussia gained Gdańsk, Toruń, sections of Masovia and Wielkopolska. Russia occupied the remainder of Byelorussia, Ukraine and Podolia. Henceforth Russian troops would be stationed in Poland and in spite of the continuation of the Sejm, the Russian ambassador in effect vetted all political decisions.

The Poles, in particular those who had supported the reforms, were unwilling to accept the situation. A number of prominent politicians who had made their way either to Dresden or Paris started planning an insurrection. Networks of conspirators flourished in what remained of the Commonwealth. The man chosen by the émigrés to head the uprising was Tadeusz Kościuszko, who had earlier distinguished himself in the fight for American independence. In March 1794 he arrived in Kraków and proclaimed a revolutionary government. What could have been but a minor challenge to the Russians was transformed into a national uprising when the small army he had raised managed to score a victory against the Russians near Racławice. In the weeks to follow Kościuszko and his collaborators faced what was to become a pattern for future insurrections. Initial successes brought with them strategic dilemmas of whether to concentrate on securing a military victory against the Russians, or whether to proclaim a national uprising with a promise of new order to come. The participation of peasants in the insurrection required their leaders to address the thorny issue of serfdom, still prevalent in Poland and Lithuania. Any attempt to abolish it carried the risk of alienating the nobility. Kościuszko was nevertheless deeply affected by the principles to which he had been exposed during the American War of Independence. On 7 May 1795 he issued his Połaniec Proclamation. This declared that peasants were to be granted their personal liberty. While he had no authority to abolish serfdom, he hoped that the landowners would reduce their compulsory labour. Kościuszko was only too well aware that having militarily supported the insurrectionists, the peasants would not accept continuing servitude.

As the insurrection took hold Prussia joined Russia. Unrealistic hopes that France would assist the Poles went unfulfilled. Nor were other countries concerned to help the Poles. Turkey declared neutrality, which freed the Russians to concentrate on quelling the insurrection. In Warsaw, in anticipation of a siege, the guilds raised military units. Berek Joselewicz led one detachment, consisting entirely of Jews. As the Russian units stormed Warsaw, the insurrectionists took their revenge against the leaders of the Targowica Confederation who were hanged. To the reformers the French Revolution acted as a model, but in due course its example would also be a warning to the wealthy nobility and burghers not to allow the radical poor to take over. During this and uprisings that followed, the question of whether to mobilise the townspeople and the peasants would become a profound dilemma. Without their support all efforts to defeat the partitioning powers would end in defeat. But by so encouraging national uprisings, the leaders would be mobilising more radical elements in society. Fear of losing control of the pace of change would be inevitable. On 2 November General Suvorov's Russian troops captured Praga, the left bank of Warsaw. In the massacres which followed, thousands of civilians perished, mainly because the General would not instruct his troops to spare women and children. As the fighting came to an end the King abdicated. Most of the leaders were either dead or imprisoned. Many fearing the inevitable retribution departed for exile.

The three neighbouring powers proceeded to the final partition. In spite of inevitable disagreements, Austria took the city of Kraków and Małopolska; Prussia obtained Warsaw, Masovia and Lithuanian territories up to the river Niemen. Russia incorporated into its borders the remainder of Lithuania. By a cruel twist of fate the Third Partition was legitimised when Stanisław August Poniatowski abdicated on the Tsarina's command. Thus the independence of the Polish and Lithuanian Commonwealth ended. More than a century would pass before an independent Poland would emerge from the turmoil of the First World War.

7

Years of Foreign Tutelage

The full force of foreign domination only hit the inhabitants of the Commonwealth after the Third Partition. The first two partitions were followed by hopes that, by military or diplomatic means, territory could be regained; the Third Partition wiped the Commonwealth off the political map of Europe. Attempts to introduce reforms, which culminated in the 3 May Constitution and the subsequent Kościuszko uprising, had mobilised the community, drawing the townspeople into direct involvement in politics and taking the debate on the future of Poland beyond that of the rights and privileges enjoyed by the nobility. Thus, when the Commonwealth was destroyed by the Third Partition a mood of despair set in, polarising society into those who, on the one extreme, believed that all was lost and that it was time to be realistic, and on the other those who wanted to fight on.

Although each of the three powers imposed its own administrative and legal systems they were in agreement on the need to destroy all vestiges of past independence. There was no natural unity between Russia, Prussia and Austria, but with French revolutionary ideas spreading through their domains, the Polish question was one over which they could not afford to disagree. Nevertheless each of the powers dealt with newly incorporated areas as they considered most appropriate. As a result, the situation in their respective Polish territories proceeded along separate routes, being entirely dependent on the decisions made in Berlin, Vienna and St Petersburg. In all three cases there was neither the desire nor the ability to destroy the nobility's power. On the contrary, attempts were made to reach some accommodation with that powerful group, while proceeding with the implementation of administrative reforms. In most cases it was the lesser gentry, the *szlachta*, usually the landless that suffered by being stripped of their noble status and reduced to peasants. This in turn had an impact on the political power of the magnates who had previously secured the loyalty and support of the impoverished gentry through direct payments and bribes. The burden of new taxation and demands for manpower for the army fell nevertheless disproportionately on the peasants and the townspeople. The magnates suffered the least, usually holding on to their property and adapting to the new political realities.

Prussia, though possessing an extremely well-organised and efficiently working bureaucracy, did not immediately impose new administrative structures upon her part of Poland. Prussia's acquisitions, which were viewed as the cradle of Polish statehood, included the capital Warsaw. Through a policy of confiscation of Crown lands, and by dispossessing those who had participated in the Kościuszko uprising, the Prussian state acquired land which was then sold to German landowners. A policy of colonisation and settlement increased German presence in ethnically Polish territories. The Prussian legal code was introduced into the new territories and German bureaucrats were appointed, thus displacing what were previously elected Polish administrators. Noble assemblies were abolished. Towns, which had enjoyed a certain amount of self-government, lost all independence and right to self-rule. All property belonging to the Catholic Church was confiscated. The Hohenzollerns were Lutherans and the monarch acted as head of the Church. Thus there was little sympathy for the Catholic Church.

A policy of Germanisation was introduced throughout territories incorporated into Prussia. The main motive for this policy was apparently an attempt to raise the cultural and economic level in the Polish areas. The idea that Prussia had a civilising mission in relation to the backward eastern territories had been a theory derived from the Teutonic Knights and was much favoured by the Hohenzollerns. The need for increased grain production added impetus to policies of integrating Polish territories into Prussia. More advanced agricultural methods were introduced to facilitate agricultural production. The Polish nobility's right to estates was not challenged, though their rights over the serfs were reduced. As a result of these policies the nobility constituted the most deeply disaffected social group, mainly because of the loss of political rights and privileges enjoyed previously.

In their newly acquired Polish territories, the Prussian administration had for the first time come in contact with sizeable Jewish communities, furthermore ones which had over centuries enjoyed a degree of autonomy. By two decrees relating specifically to the Jewish community, the first in 1797 and the second in 1831, Jews were divided into those who were to be Germanised and thus would acquire full civic rights and those who could not, and would therefore be expelled. As a result of the process of Jewish assimilation was more rapid in Prussian parts of Poland than elsewhere.

Austria, like Prussia, was an absolutist monarchy. Whereas Prussia took the road to reforms, Austria, fearful of revolutions, opposed them. Francis I, son of Empress Maria Teresa, had been forced to give up the title of Holy Roman Emperor after his defeat by the French in 1805. The Habsburgs' response to the growth of French power and to the emergence of revolutionary currents in Europe was to consolidate the monarchy and to strengthen the powers of the state. Austria stripped the gentry of its taxation privileges and took away guarantees of inviolability of person and property. Some of the worst feudal restrictions were abolished. The amount of work which the peasants had to do on the landlord's estate was regulated by law. Peasants were protected by legislation, in particular against abuses by the landlords. But as the Poles found out to their cost, Austrian rivalry with France put a strain on state finances. The burden of taxes was high and continued to increase. The lesser gentry again suffered most. They were expected to show proof of their noble rank, which they frequently did not have. Without such proof they were reduced to the status of peasants.

The Austrian attitude towards the Jewish community inhabiting most of the small towns was to encourage emigration or assimilation. Under Austrian administration Jews were forced to assume German names as a starting point of their integration into Austrian society. Jewish communities continued to function, retaining control over all religious matters. Like all Austrian citizens, Jews were obliged to perform military service.

A notable feature of the Austrian administration was the imposition of far-reaching censorship. The police controlled all postal communication and publications had to be vetted by special censorship offices, which existed in all towns. The import of foreign publications was made very difficult, while all bookshops had to obtain licences. The Habsburgs were Catholics, but they did not tolerate the Vatican's interference in their affairs. Within the Empire the rights of the Catholic hierarchy were strictly controlled, while parish priests were paid from a special fund controlled by the state. No attempt was made to limit the Church's influence over society as the state came to appreciate the importance of Catholic teaching in counteracting liberal and secular ideas. This in turn led to an accommodation with the Vatican. As a result the Vatican cautioned the Polish Catholic hierarchy against encouraging dissent and nationalist sentiments.

Russia's share of the Polish Lithuanian Commonwealth was the largest, as she had secured over 62 per cent of the partitioned territory. Areas between the rivers Bug, Dniester and Zbrucz and the lower reaches of the Dnieper formed natural borders of regions incorporated into the Tsarist Empire. Though Poles did not comprise the majority of the population, Polish culture and language had been dominant, though not exclusive in these areas. Byelorussians made up 40 per cent of the population of these regions, 26 per cent were ethnically Polish, with Ukrainians, Lithuanians, Russians, Tatars and Jews making up the remainder. The Uniate and Catholic faiths dominated the region.

Initially Russia introduced only limited reforms. There was a shortage of Russian administrators and the Empire did not have a body of codified laws. This allowed the previous courts and laws to function. From the outset religion was an issue, as the Russians attacked the Uniate Church which was seen as having betrayed the Orthodox faith. In 1839 the Uniate Church was officially abolished in the Russian Empire. The Catholic Church though under constant attack was able to survive due to the fact that the Russian rulers could not entirely ignore the power of the Vatican. The Russian Orthodox Church was the official faith and legislation favoured it in all respects. By incorporating the Commonwealth territories into the Empire, the Russians had to deal with Jews who inhabited the region. Their response was to define an area of Jewish settlement, which was roughly the area of the Commonwealth.

Although Crown lands had been confiscated by the Russians, the initial attitude towards the nobility was to pacify it, rather than to antagonise it. This was the case until the November uprising in 1830 after which repressive measures were introduced to destroy their political power and aspirations. The *szlachta*, who identified most strongly with Polish nationalism and the Catholic faith, bore the brunt of Russian policies. In addition to compulsory resettlement to the Turkish borderlands, they were recruited into the army. The wealthy nobility reached an accommodation with the new rulers with a degree of ease. Tsarist administrators saw no point in antagonising them. The peasants fared worst, as the law in the Russian Empire always favoured the landowners. In the Commonwealth serfs could not be separated from the land. In Russia they were the personal property of the landowner, who with few restrictions, could do with them as he chose.

But the French Revolution and the social and political upheavals which followed it created preconditions in the homeland and among political exiles for reopening debates on the restoration of the Polish kingdom. The Revolution represented a challenge to the old order and to the old regimes. The Revolutionary Wars of France with Austria and Prussia gave rise to hopes that France's perceived historic interest in Polish affairs could now be translated into support for the restoration of Poland. But the response of the French revolutionary government was initially cautious. There was no desire to champion the Polish cause openly, as this would be guaranteed to bring Austria, Prussia and Russia closer, a military combination which could be disastrous to France.

By 1795 two groups of émigré Poles vied for the role of representatives of Polish interests in Paris. The Agency consisted of moderate reformers who thought of extending the principles of the 3 May Constitution. The Deputation, a rival grouping, was associated with Jacobin and radical ideas. The latter linked social and political reform to the war of liberation. Both tried to maintain contact with the homeland, though inevitably these contacts loosened over time. Kościuszko's arrival in Paris in 1798 raised hopes for an insurrection in Poland to coincide with French-led military action against the three partitioning powers. The initiative was seized by a group of young émigrés who approached General Bonaparte with a request to form a Polish legion. The capture of thousands of Polish conscripts among the Austrian prisoners of war strengthened their arguments. Bonaparte's oblique statement that the partitions were an iniquity gave rise to further hopes for political support. A legion was formed in the French puppet republic of Lombardy, thus avoiding a direct challenge to the Austrians and Prussians. Fired by patriotic fervour, and inspired by revolutionary ideals, the newly formed unit looked forward to military action against Poland's foes. Led by General Dąbrowski, a legendary figure of the Kościuszko uprising, the legion, which consisted of 6000 men, acquired mythic status even before it took part in military action. A mazurka composed to celebrate it, with the rousing first lines of 'Poland has not been vanquished, as long as we live', became the Polish national anthem.

Reality was so much more painful. Napoleon Bonaparte, instead of attacking Austria, settled for a negotiation. The final peace treaty, signed in Luneville in 1801, appeared to destroy all hopes which had been associated with the formation of the Polish legions. In a final insult to the Poles, Napoleon had the two legions incorporated into the French army. In 1802 a Polish unit accompanied a French force sent to quell the slave uprising in the French colony of Haiti. In a painful twist of irony, the Poles fought slaves whose desire for liberty was in no way different from their own desire for freedom in Poland. The black leaders of the uprising recognised the Poles' tragic circumstances. When captured they, unlike the French, were not massacred but given the choice of siding with the insurrection. Unknown numbers, possibly amounting to several hundred, did so and the Poles were granted the right to land, in spite of the constitution explicitly barring white people from owning land in Haiti. Descendants of the Polish soldiers continue to live in Haiti where they are known as the *nègres blancs*. In 1983 the Polish Pope John Paul II visited Haiti and acknowledged its place in Polish history.

Napoleon's military victories nevertheless still offered the best prospect for the restoration of Poland. Thus in spite of earlier disappointments when in 1805 Napoleon defeated Prussia at the battle of Ulm, Polish leaders once more lined up to support France. The Grande Armée's further victories at Jena and Austerlitz confirmed that Poland's enemies could be defeated. When French troops entered territories which had previously belonged to Poland a groundswell of support greeted them. While the magnates still held back, carefully assessing the likelihood of a permanent French victory against the combined forces of Prussia, Austria and Russia, the population viewed the French as liberators. Napoleon made references, though still noncommittal, to the reconstruction of Poland. This and his arrival in Warsaw thawed the hearts of even the staunchest republicans, who nevertheless wondered whether the French Emperor would allow the Poles the right to self-determination. Once more legions were raised to participate in the forthcoming military confrontation with Russia. Maria Walewska, a society beauty, was obligingly provided as a mistress to strengthen Napoleon's commitment to the Polish cause. Napoleon nevertheless displayed remarkable determination not to be distracted from his own objectives. When, after a brief military campaign, a peace treaty was signed between Napoleon and Tsar Alexander at Tilsit on 7–8 July 1807, Polish hopes were disappointed. As a condition of the treaty a Duchy of Warsaw was created, comprising Polish territories granted to Prussia. In 1809, in the course of war with France, Austria attacked the Duchy. When defeated by Polish units, the Austrians accepted the loss of nearly half of their previous Polish acquisitions, which were incorporated into the Duchy. Thus Kraków became part of the Duchy of Warsaw.

The Duchy's political system was determined by a Constitution modelled on the 3 May Constitution and on French radical legislation. In reality its shape had been determined by Napoleon. Serfdom was abolished, even though, recognising Polish realities, land remained in the hands of the nobility. Although Frederich August of Saxony (1807–15) was nominated as the hereditary ruler of the Duchy, the establishment of a bicameral Sejm guaranteed that the Poles would decide all legislative matters. The imposition of the Napoleonic Code meant that in the Duchy, as in most parts of Europe administered by the French during this time, a unified system of laws replaced local and traditional laws. The progressive ideas of the French Revolution, established, among others, the principle of equality of sexes and civil marriages.

In 1812 the Franco-Russian War restarted. Even though the French army reached Moscow, Napoleon was not able to hold his position and in a winter retreat the Grande Armée struggled back to France. The Russians took over the Duchy. Until the Congress of Vienna in 1814 it remained under Russian occupation. Alexander's policies were initially lenient. He allowed Polish soldiers to return to their homes. Local administrations functioned unhindered and no attempts were made to reverse the reforms introduced during the Napoleonic period. Nevertheless Alexander did not intend to relinquish the Duchy. Neither Austria nor Prussia was in a position to displace him. This allowed him to implement long-term objectives, which had been discussed and prepared earlier among his close body of advisers.

Alexander had plans for a Russian-dominated kingdom of Poland. This in itself was not a particularly new proposal. In view of the disintegration of the Polish–Lithuanian Commonwealth the issue had in the past been discussed extensively by the Polish nobility. The real question was whether any European power would wish to see the recreation of the kingdom of Poland, in which case in what form would it be allowed to emerge. During the French Revolution and in the years which followed, progressive and radical groups looked to France. The majority of the nobility, including the magnates, considered that St Petersburg would inevitably have the largest say in the future of Polish lands. Among those Prince Adam Czartoryski was the most influential. Having first been sent to Russia as a guarantor of the family's loyalty, he became a close friend of the future tsar. When Alexander succeeded to the throne, Czartoryski was appointed Minister for Foreign Affairs. He and Alexander believed that Russia had to be modernised. As the most developed part of the Tsarist Empire the Polish territories were favoured. Czartoryski hoped that the Tsar would unite all Polish territories and create a distinct Polish kingdom, which would then be ruled by the Romanovs as a separate entity.

In September 1814 the powers which had defeated Napoleon met at Vienna to redraw the map of Europe. They faced a formidable task as French conquests had unleashed new forces which like a genie, once released, refused to return to the lamp. Any attempt to restore pre-revolutionary borders would have been impossible. Austria, Prussia and England dominated the Congress of Vienna. The new rulers of France quickly made themselves indispensable to the Congress powers and thus Russia faced the combined political power of the four. All were united in making sure that Russian influence did not extend to Western Europe. Since the Polish territories acted as a bridge between the Russian Empire and Europe, they were in agreement on the Polish question. Russian attempts to hang on to the enlarged Duchy of Warsaw were met with clear and united opposition. The final result was that although it was not possible to force Russia out of the Duchy, the four allies made sure that the now renamed Kingdom of Poland was reduced by Prussia regaining the district of Poznań and Toruń. Kraków and its immediate environs were granted a semi-autonomous status and named the Republic of Kraków. Critically, the Vienna politicians recognised the existence of the Polish state, even if they were not agreed on its independent existence.

During the first five years of its existence the Kingdom of Poland or Congress Poland, as it came to be known, had the appearance of a sovereign state even though its status and future were entirely dependent on the Russians. Its distinct character, institutions and laws were all retained, as was its army. Polish was the official language. The Constitution, which had been drawn up by Prince Czartoryski, granted the Tsar executive powers, but legislative powers were vested in the Sejm which was elected from the ranks of the nobility. Nevertheless the appointment of the Tsar's degenerate older brother Constantine as viceroy, bode ill for the future. Tsar's Alexander's commitment to progressive reforms in Russia did not last.

In the Polish territories the nobility remained optimistic that further concessions could still be secured. There was no desire for open conflict with the Russians and in general it was believed that open opposition could have dangerous consequences. However, among the young and within the progressive circles the mood was different. Secret organisations did appear within the student communities. Modelling themselves on similar societies which sprang up in most university towns in Europe, and inspired by revolutionary ideas, the students were bolder in discussing Russian oppression and means of destroying it. In 1821 student and youth organisations were declared illegal. Arrests of students in Vilnius and Kraków were followed by their being exiled to the Russian interior. Far from destroying the patriotic spirit, this had the effect of creating martyrs, whose example only fired the imaginations of successive generations of young people. After 1815 the freemasonry made inroads in Congress Poland, encouraged by the belief that Tsar Alexander was sympathetic to the movement. At one time the Grand Orient had 38 lodges in Congress Poland. Membership of the Masonic movement was particularly strong among officers. Polish freemasonry emulated French freemasons who were associated with secular and progressive ideas. Therefore membership was seen as a statement in support of political reforms and scientific progress.

In 1825 Alexander died. During the ceremony of the swearing of loyalty to his successor Nicholas I, young officers in the army staged what came to be known as the Decembrist Uprising. When this failed to ignite an empire-wide uprising, arrests followed. During the extensive investigations which followed, it was discovered that the conspirators had been in contact with Polish revolutionaries. Nicolai Novosiltsev, Alexander's personal plenipotentiary in Warsaw, who had already earned himself a reputation for the zeal and cruelty in investigating student and high-school secret societies, was put in charge of ascertaining whether seeking Polish independence amounted to high treason. Hopes that Russian rule would become progressively less oppressive diminished.

It has been suggested that economic rivalries might well also have played a role in the growing tension between the new tsar and Congress Poland. Whereas in 1815 Congress Poland was on the verge of bankruptcy, by the early 1820, state finances had been fully reformed, agriculture was once more flourishing and, most importantly, the area was experiencing the first stages of industrialisation. Directing this was Prince Drucki-Lubecki, a Pole who in 1821 was appointed Minister of the Treasury. His careful planning and his strong pro-Russian policies persuaded the Tsarist government to grant Poland special concessions. In addition to establishing a Polish bank he initiated road-building programmes and was responsible for a number of similar initiatives all intended to encourage and facilitate economic growth. But for Congress Poland the most important achievement was the reorientation of production and trade towards the Russian Empire. The developing Polish textile and metallurgical manufacture thus benefited from the low level of production in Russia, where demand was growing rapidly. By a variety of tariff measures Drucki-Lubecki reduced imports from Prussia and Austria and increased exports to Russia. But in 1830 Nicolas, embroiled in conflict with Turkey and anticipating wars with Austria, grew resentful of Poland. This in turn led Poles to reconsider their position with the Empire. Growing apprehensions within the nobility hitherto committed to cooperation with the Tsarist regime, were echoed within the community of young officers and students who felt bolder in making plans for a national uprising.

When the uprising broke out on the night of 29 November 1830 it was nevertheless a badly thought out and confused event. A number of conspirators, many of whom were junior officers, had decided to assassinate the Grand Duke Constantine. They believed that a great national uprising would follow, but had failed to think through who would lead it and what would be its programme. Constantine slipped out of Warsaw, and the conspirators had to search for a leader. None of the eminent generals was willing to assume this role. Nevertheless the Warsaw population heeded the call of the revolutionaries. The Arsenal was captured and arms distributed. Some military units joined in the uprising. Others, unclear about what was happening, proceeded to join the Russian troops. In the days which followed the full force of the folly became obvious.

While the Russian troops were withdrawn, the Sejm, dominated by the conservative and liberal nobility, tried to avoid the appearance of a revolution by declaring that all that was asked for was independence. Drucki-Lubecki and Czartoryski kept doors open so negotiations with the Russians could continue. A veteran of the Napoleonic Wars, General Józef Chłopiński, was appointed dictator. Constantine, surprisingly, refused to take military action against the insurgents. He felt that, in the first place, it was for the Poles to decide what were their objectives. But the Sejm's timorous response to the uprising brought forth a Patriotic Society which put forward a radical programme starting with the court martial of all who had been deemed 'collaborators'. On 25 January the Sejm dethroned the Tsar, declaring Poland independent. This made Russian military intervention inevitable. But as the uprising had started so it continued. The politicians dithered, unwilling to link the quest for national self-determination to peasant grievances, in particular the persistence of serfdom. This meant that the countryside remained generally aloof from the uprising. Even within the towns, traders and craftsmen, though inspired by the patriotic mood, worried about their future in particular if Poland's trade was once more to be oriented to the West. The revolutionaries appear to have made a major miscalculation when they assumed that the international situation would favour their quest. In their plans for a military confrontation with the Russians they put too much emphasis on foreign aid and intervention. Neither Austria nor Prussia, and most certainly not Britain, were willing to endanger their relations with Russia for the sake of a relatively minor Polish issue. Anxiety about the spread of revolutionary ideas which threatened the Vienna system made them cautious in supporting the Poles, even if they would otherwise have been only too willing to contribute to Moscow's difficulties. In France public support for the Poles was widespread. But since no action was taken against Russia, this was of little relevance in Warsaw.

On 5 February 1831 Russian troops initiated action against the Poles. Their advance onto Warsaw was halted by the battle of Grochów, where the Polish army showed itself to be superior to the Russian units. In May after the battle of Ostrołęka the Polish run of victories was reversed. A number of young and inspired military leaders had emerged from within the Polish ranks, notably General Ignacy Prądziński and Colonel Józef Bem. But the financial situation became difficult, affecting the military situation. Popular support waned after military defeats. The best Polish units, which fought so well in the initial battles, were depleted and conscription raised peasant opposition. On 6 September Russian units led by Field Marshal Ivan Paskievich approached Warsaw from the west. The Poles were not prepared, as they had anticipated an attack from the east. When the military collapse became inevitable, the government resigned and the army withdrew, without conceding defeat or signing an armistice. Thousands of men streamed into exile rather than accept humiliating conditions of capitulation.

Tsar Nicholas I took the view that the uprising had effectively released him from the duty to abide by previous commitments.

Congress Poland was henceforth treated as conquered territory. All vestiges of independence were removed. Most importantly the Sejm was suspended and the Polish army was abolished. The Constitution was replaced by Organic Statutes, which defined how the kingdom was to be henceforth administered. In a gesture intended to humiliate the Poles, Paskievich was appointed Viceroy and with the title of Prince of Warsaw. Although the Polish areas were henceforth tied more closely to the Russian Empire, its distinctiveness was still not entirely destroyed. The Russians did not have sufficient numbers of administrators to assume responsibility for Poland. While those who had directly participated in the uprising were severely punished, officers and soldiers were still incorporated into the Russian army. Polish administrators were likewise granted official positions. But while Polish society was forced to come to terms with the trauma, many adjusted to the situation to their benefit. Poles joined the ranks of the Tsarist bureaucracy, which offered stable employment, status and reward. Poles made careers in the Russian army, the Polish Bank and the Treasury retained institutional independence and control over the economy of the kingdom. The Napoleonic Code was retained and Polish continued to be the official language. Following the Tsar's dictum that too much education led to revolutions, the University of Warsaw was shut, and most intellectual associations were banned. Museums, libraries and collections were taken over and in most cases their collections were removed to Russia. Primary and secondary education suffered until the Crimean War when Tsarist policy towards Poland was reviewed. Publishing collapsed and few newspapers appeared, even in Warsaw. Censorship prevented any contentious issues from being debated openly.

Those who had reason to leave Poland, anticipating prison sentences, and those unwilling to accept Russian occupation, departed for exile. In what came to be known as the Great Emigration, approximately 10,000 men left Poland. Some needed to escape, others believed that exile was preferable to servitude. And then there were those who believed that through personal suffering Poland could be redeemed. The highest proportion of exiles went to Paris, where intellectual and political developments created an environment which the Poles found congenial. Britain and Belgium also welcomed the exiled Poles. The Austrian and Prussian governments were too anxious about revolutionary activities within their borders to allow Poles from Russia to linger.

The romantic notion that suffering and separation from the home-land were a necessary purgatory before Poland could re-emerge, took root among the exiles. The artistic and intellectual life of the émigré communities fostered and enhanced this sense of pain. The poetry of Adam Mickiewicz and Juliusz Słowacki focused on themes of suffer-ing, separation and ultimate redemption. In their works the image of the lost homeland was romantic and idealised. Frederick Chopin, who left Poland for health reasons, was part of that creative trend and his works drew heavily on nostalgia for the lost homeland.

A high proportion of those who went into exile had belonged to the nobility or were of officer rank. The intellectual life of the émigré community was monopolised by their preoccupations. Trauma, guilt and geographical and emotional distance from the events of the November Uprising all played a role in the reassessments of its fail-ures. This in turn affected the nature of plans for the future. In Paris, Prince Czartoryski gathered around himself politicians, diplomats and those who considered that Poland would not re-emerge as an independent state unless the international situation was favourable. They laid stress on diplomacy and international support. Since Europe was dominated by the Russo-Austrian rivalry Vienna's support was critical to their plans. Some within that grouping looked to Turkey as a means of weakening Russia.

The other group was the Democratic Society. Led by Joachim Lelevel it was more clearly inspired by the revolutionary movements of the 1820s and 1830s. These were men who were aware of contem-porary political thinkers such as Giuseppe Mazzini and Felipe Buonarroti. Modelling themselves on Italian examples, they declared their organisation to be the Young Poland movement. Their conviction in the effectiveness of revolutionary action resulted in a programme which assumed that Poland would be reconstructed when popular uprisings took place in all the partitioning states. While preparing plans for an uprising in Poland, Polish exiles participated in the vibrant political life which affected most Western European capitals. Taking the view that the liberation of all people from oppression will ulti-mately benefit the Polish cause, they participated in the Italian Carbonari movements and the Paris Commune.

Initially the émigrés hoped that the defeat of 1831 would be quickly reversed. Plans for a new uprising were hatched and agents travelled to Poland to plan and coordinate future action. All failed. The author-ities in Poland learned to exploit growing peasant hostility to their landlords. The Austrians in particular used this method to quell an attempted uprising in Galicia in the winter of 1845/46, when they encouraged and even rewarded the peasants for attacking the gentry. Within Congress Poland conspiratorial activities were generally doomed due to constant police surveillance. All those suspected of involvement in any political activities were severely punished. Thus a gap developed between frequently unrealistic plans tainted by romantic notions hatched in the relative safety of exile, and actual conditions prevailing in Poland. This in turn reduced the authority of the émigré organisations. With time they became more remote and as a result less realistic in their plans for national liberation.

The revolutionary activities which swept through Europe during the period referred to as the Spring of Nations in 1848–49 marked a watershed both for the émigrés and the conspirators in Poland. The émigré activists, in particular those within the Democratic Society, were involved in events in Paris, Vienna and Prussia. But in the homeland events took a distinctly different course. In 1848 hopes were raised when, briefly, it seemed likely that Prussia and Austria would combine to pursue a war against Russia. The émigré leaders took the initiative from Berlin and Vienna, urging the gentry in the Polish lands to prepare to support an attack on Russia. Anticipating a national uprising, they sincerely hoped that the nobility would abolish serfdom and thus gain the support of the peasants. But in the Polish lands, the landowners were more cautious. Unwilling to follow the émigrés' calls they held back. The outbreak of revolution in Berlin raised the temperature, but also created new quandaries. The German revolutionaries sought German unification and were unwilling to grant the Poles assurances that an independent Poland would be created. Unity between German and Polish revolutionaries was therefore brief. When a nationalist uprising seemed imminent in the Poznań region, German liberals initially considered it sympathetically, but in the end refused to endorse the separation of the province from Prussia.

Between March and April 1848 the situation evolved quickly. Whereas initially German liberals who met in Frankfurt to plan for German unity supported Polish demands, by April, when the King Frederick William IV authorised military action in the Poznań region, no objections were raised. In May German control had been firmly reestablished in the Polish regions. Karl Marx was unusual in supporting the reconstruction of an independent Poland in 1848 and after. Revolution overwhelmed Vienna on 13 March. Leading Poles,

supported by émigrés who flooded to Galicia, put together a progressive programme of reforms in which the abolition of serfdom figured
prominently. The Austrian response was not to oppose it but to take it
over. On 15 May the Emperor announced that in the Polish lands serfdom was abolished and that the peasants were to receive land which
they had been tilling. The Austrian authorities also exploited ethnic
conflict between the Poles and the Ruthenian peasants. When in
July 1848 elections took place, the Ruthenian community split.
Nationalists, mainly Uniates, resenting Polish dominance, declared
themselves in favour of Vienna, whereas young intellectuals saw the
future of the region closely tied to the fate of Poland. Vienna ultimately succeeded in quelling all uprisings and, by November, the
Austrian army was once more in charge of Galicia. A number of Polish
revolutionaries then moved to join the Hungarian revolutionaries.
During the last stages of the Hungarian revolution a Russian army led
by Paskievich had come to Austria's aid. General Józef Bem became
famous for his military leadership when he confronted Paskievich for
the second time. When the Hungarian revolution collapsed Bem and
some of the Polish revolutionaries fled to Turkey where they were
welcomed as potential mercenaries and where, in due course, a small
Polish colony was established.

The events of 1848/49 mark a watershed in European history, sepa-
rating the period of great revolutionary upsurges from the time of the
consolidation of the German and Italian states. Earlier it had been
believed that the destruction of the last vestiges of the *ancien régime*
would automatically lead to national liberation. The Poles were to
learn that popular revolutions were no guarantee of respect for the
aspirations of national groups. On the contrary, Austrian and German
liberals were quite capable of being every bit as chauvinistic as their
reactionary predecessors had been. As the hopes of the Polish émigrés
for a national uprising collapsed, the conservative and pragmatic leadership in the Polish lands came forward with plans for accommodation
with the authorities in the hope that reforms and economic development would lead to social improvement.

There was a certain inevitability about the way in which every
international conflict was seen by the Poles as offering another opportunity for the reversal of the partitions. When the Crimean War broke
out in 1854, Poles in the kingdom once more succumbed to the hope
that Russia would be defeated and the victors would force the Polish
Question onto the international agenda. Briefly the Austrian and

Prussian authorities were willing to encourage the Poles to raise voluntary units. In Turkey, exiles from the 1848/49 revolutions formed a legion. But the war ended too quickly and the Polish Question was specifically excluded from the list of issues to be discussed at the Paris talks which ended the war.

Within the Tsarist Empire, the Crimean defeat had far-reaching consequences. Tsar Alexander II ascended the throne with a commitment to reform the Russian political and economic system. Peace, in order to implement social changes, could be secured by either of two means, in particular in the territories acquired during the three partitions. Repression combined with absolute control of all aspects of the province's life was one method. The other was conciliation. Alexander II rightly deduced that the Polish nobility was willing to consider the advantages of the second. During the period of his rule from 1855 until 1863, when the January Uprising broke out, both methods were used to pacify the Poles. In the first place, conciliation was tried. Poles were allowed to enter the Tsarist state bureaucracy. Economic development was encouraged by means direct and indirect. The abolition of tariff barriers, and the Crimean War, stimulated the development of a capitalist economy in Congress Poland. Polish entrepreneurs, bankers and industrialists benefited from the opening up of the Russian markets. Rail links with St Petersburg and Vienna were built. Agriculture advanced, with the production of grain increasing most dramatically. Economic prosperity and political concessions militated against plans for further uprisings. These concessions created preconditions for the rise of new nationalist aspirations which, if frustrated, created a combative atmosphere. Tsarist reforms had allowed for the creation of a Medical Surgical Academy. An Agricultural Society, ostensibly dedicated to the introduction of improved agricultural methods, emerged during this time. Inevitably, through its numerous branches it became the focus for debates about Poland's future.

In 1861, following nationalist demonstrations, the police attacked demonstrators in Warsaw. Bloodshed and arrests, and finally the imposition of martial law, failed to reverse the growth of national hopes and in fact only stimulated outpourings of patriotic favour. Secret societies intensified plans for an uprising. When it broke out on 22 January 1863 plans for assuming civilian authority had been well prepared. Unfortunately, the military plans had not been so well thought out. In the run-up to the uprising two distinct leaderships had emerged, each representing different views on the way that liberty could be secured.

Marquis Alexander Wielkopolski led a conciliatory group. He and his followers believed that initial requests to the Tsar should be confined to petitioning him for the restoration of political autonomy. On the peasant issue, which came to dominate all debates on the future of Poland, they favoured a slow process of transformation from serfdom. A marginally less conciliatory group, led by another great landowner, Count Andrzej Zamoyski, emerged at the same time. They demanded concessions before they would collaborate with the Tsar's reforms. Both leaders still attached importance to mobilising international support for the Polish cause. But the events of 1861 rapidly radicalised groups of young people, bringing them into contact with the anarchist 'Ziemla i Vola' group in Russia. They concentrated on planning an armed insurrection. Russian actions, in particular the arrest of a number of nationalist leaders during Sunday services, drew the Catholic Church into the confrontation. In the two years which followed the Tsarist regime did try to make some concessions, in particular in the provision of education. The Poles were also given the right to choose municipal and local authorities. Nevertheless, police and army brutality and the heightened sense of patriotic fervour reduced the likelihood of any compromise being reached.

The January Uprising was the largest of the organised attempts to regain freedom before the outbreak of the First World War. A self-appointed Temporary National Council took the decision to start the insurrection when on the night of 14/15 January 1863 the Tsarist army tried pre-emptively to call up thousands of young men. As the fighting started a manifesto was issued calling the nation to fight 'unto death'. This time the peasant issue was fully addressed and, anticipating its vital importance in the forthcoming struggle, the National Council proclaimed the abolishment of serfdom and promised land to the landless. The insurrection had been started by the radical young who were described as the 'Reds'. Those in favour of compromises, the 'Whites', held back until April when they threw in their lot with the insurrectionists.

Militarily the situation turned out to be a disaster. In spite of the declaration on the abolishment of serfdom, nearly 70 per cent of the village population remained aloof. Warsaw led in the fight. The provinces were less willing to respond. The patchy response to the declaration was made worse by divisions within the leadership. The one brilliant organiser, Stefan Bobrowski, died in a duel with another Pole. In the international arena the Polish cause once more led to expressions of sympathy, but not much in terms of aid. Liberals, progressive-minded circles and Catholics took a pro-Polish line. The Vatican, hoping for the weakening of the Russian Empire, supported it. In France, fraternal support was expressed, though supplies could not be sent to Poland, as Prussia, led by Bismarck, took a pro-Russian line. On 8 February 1863 Prussia and Russia signed a convention agreeing to cooperation in tackling the Polish issue. Austria, though willing to benefit from Russia's weaknesses, which would have allowed further expansion into the Balkans, on the Polish Question decided not to play the diplomatic card. A stiff note of protest was sent jointly by Britain, France and Austria to the Russians. Its implications were minimal.

In the summer of 1863, as a result of conflicts within the National Council, the Reds took over the leadership of the insurrection. But the momentum had been lost. The Russian policy of rewarding generously those who remained loyal, including making provisions for widows of civil servants that did not support the Polish cause, had its effect. On 2 March 1864 the Tsarist government issued an *ukaze* confirming the abolishment of serfdom. Peasants were freed from all outstanding obligations, and were granted land which they had tilled as serfs. This decision had a great impact on the peasants who had been ambivalent about the insurrection. Lack of military success and finally shortage of funds and ammunition led to its collapse. By the spring of 1865 the Russian army was hunting down those Poles who refused to lay down their arms. Once more thousands of men departed for exile, briefly stopping in France, where the official welcome was reversed after their participation in the Paris Commune.

After the insurrection, the Tsarist regime exacted heavy penalties. Over 50,000 people who had actively supported, or were suspected of having supported, the insurrection, were sent to Siberia. The nobility was hit by most severe repression. Many women joined their menfolk by voluntarily going with them into punitive exile into distant parts of Asia. Few of those returned to Poland. On completion of the sentence they were usually confined to the region.

After the January Insurrection sections of Polish lands drew apart, developing separately. The pace of change was increasingly set by the partitioning powers. Economic, political and cultural life in each part was determined by what happened in Berlin, Vienna and St Petersburg, rather than by the increasingly hazy notion of the common heritage. The three powers agreed on the need to suppress national uprisings which, they feared, could affect all Polish lands. They nevertheless had no agreements on how to utilise or govern these lands. Thus by 1914 three distinct patterns of development evolved in partitioned Poland.

From 1866 Congress Poland was fully integrated into the Tsarist Empire. Henceforth it was referred to as the Vistula Land. A rolling programme of destruction of all Polish institutions was initiated, replacing them with Russian ones. However, the Napoleonic Code was retained. From 1879 all teaching in schools was in the Russian language. Schooling in Russian was intended to transform Poles into good citizens of the Tsarist Empire. Since the teaching of Polish was forbidden, and all contacts with the state, on all levels, could only be done in Russian, knowledge of Polish and the teaching of Polish were confined to the private domain of the family and home.

After the January Insurrection, the role of Polish women in society became more emotionally charged. A disproportionately large number of educated men and those of noble rank were killed, went into voluntary exile or were punitively sent into the Russian hinterland. Thus women were left in charge of estates and families. In the deeply patriotic atmosphere which followed the insurrection, upon the shoulders of these women fell the sole duty of bringing up the next generation of Poles. Added to this, the ban on teaching and using the Polish language meant that children could only learn their language if they were taught it at home. The role of Polish mothers thus became critical in the maintenance of national self-consciousness. The myth of a Mother Pole (Matka Polka) became particularly strong during this period. Her role was not merely that of provider and carer. She had a sacred responsibility to maintain Polishness and to transmit the knowledge of its history, culture and language to the next generation. It became no less than a woman's national duty.

The Catholic Church, having played a leading role in the insurrection, was subordinated to the Catholic College in St Petersburg. In a concerted attack on the Church, which the Russian Orthodox establishment opposed not only on theological grounds but also because of its close association with Polish nationalism, the Russian authorities did all in their power to limit contacts between the Polish Catholic hierarchy and the Vatican and to control its influence in society. The Russian authorities did not wish to destroy the Church as godlessness was seen as a worse evil. In the circumstances the Catholic Church's moral and spiritual leadership in society was preferable to none. The appointment of priests was nevertheless strictly limited and kept to the minimum required. The authorities had no influence over the liturgy thus the use of Polish in services could not be forbidden. The result was that the Church was the only public place where the Polish language could be used legally. The spiritual bond between Poles and the Catholic Church was made particularly strong during this time and continued to be reaffirmed during the period which followed.

The response of the community to developments following the insurrection was initially muted. Exhausted, cowed and in some cases even irritated by the national preoccupation with uprisings, Poles appeared to accept the inevitability of what had followed. Only slowly did new ideas emerge. Initially the search for accommodation with the Tsarist regime appeared to be the only way forward. Ideas earlier put forward by the Whites persisted. This was the hope that the regime would grant some concessions if only it was assured of loyalty. Briefly it looked as if these modest hopes were to be realised. Gradually permission was granted for associations to be formed and for a limited number of newspapers to be published, even though censorship remained very tight. In 1898 Tsar Nicolas II visited Warsaw and granted permission for the establishment of a scientific university. The symbolic culmination of these efforts was the unveiling in 1898 of the monument to Adam Mickiewicz, arguably the most nationalist of the poets of the Romantic period. The conservative groups, which favoured the conciliatory approach to the Tsarist regime, were able to focus on the economic benefits of Poland being part of the Russian Empire. Disappointingly, Nicholas refused to grant Poland autonomy within the Russian Empire. The Tsarist regime could ignore the representations of Polish leaders since it remained confident that the emancipation of the serfs had separated the nobility from the peasants, thus destroying any likelihood of a successful national uprising.

The disastrous consequences of the insurrection led to a debate on whether and how independence could be secured. Building on the existing trends, which had sought to concentrate on modernisation and improvement of the standard of living, critics of the insurrectionist ideas once more drew attention to the need for industrialisation and economic progress. Closely associated with those groups were liberals, who believed that the way forward was through the evolution of democratic institutions in Russia. They hoped these would, in due course, lead to Poland regaining its independence. Strongly opposed to the gentry's values, and sceptical of the likelihood of successful uprisings, they chose to concentrate on what they saw as socially useful professions and activities. Hence their preoccupation with education, sciences, engineering and medicine. This current in Polish political thinking, which rejected the Romantic and Messianic ideas of the early nineteenth century, came to be known as Positivism. In due course writers and artists who were drawn to these ideas defined their works as Positivist. Eliza Orzeszkowa, Bolesław Prus and Aleksander Świętochowski are the most prominent representatives of this movement.

The rapid development of industry in the Polish part of the Russian Empire led to the emergence of an urban working class and inevitably to contacts with Socialist ideas. Poles first came across the works of Socialist thinkers and with Marxism through their association with Russian Socialists. In 1878–79 a number of conspiratorial Socialist leaders were arrested in Warsaw. Arrests led the remaining leaders to flee abroad and to concentrate their activities in Switzerland, Paris and London where the debates were continued with Socialist exiles from other countries. Basing themselves on their readings of Bakunin, Proudhon and Blanqui, and impressed by the ideas of the Russian Populists, they came to believe that an international working class would stage the future revolution. In 1892 Polish Socialists emerged from a formative stage in which they had been preoccupied primarily with terror and propaganda, and formed a Socialist Party which was to espouse West European Socialist doctrines of mass organisation of the working class. The newly formed Polska Partia Socialistyczna (Polish Socialist Party, PPS) became a member of the Second International. A Marxist programme became the ideology of the PPS. But the exiled Socialists returned to the primacy of the national question, stressing the importance of Poland regaining independence before the rights of the Polish working class could be secured. Within the Second International the PPS took a reformist line, rejecting the revolutionary path and instead concentrating on reforms through the establishment of democratic and representative institutions. One of the leading lights of the newly emerged Polish Socialist movement was Józef Piłsudski.

Not all Socialists agreed with the PPS's gradualist programme. Within the Polish territories a different Socialist Party, the Socjal Demokracja Królestwa Polskiego (Social Democracy of the Kingdom of Poland, SDKP) emerged. In 1900 it broadened its base to include Lithuania, thus becoming the Socjal Demokracja Królestwa Polskiego i Litwy (Social Democracy of the Kingdom of Poland and Lithuania, SDKPiL). They believed that the overthrow of the Tsarist system should be the Socialists' most important short-term objective. In the long term the Socialist revolution was the party's aim. The SDKP did not agree with the PPS's preoccupation with the nationalist question, pointing out that this in itself would not benefit the working class. Rosa Luxemburg was the internationally known leader of the SDKPiL. The national question remained the single most divisive issue within the Polish Socialist movement as it was within the Second International. In 1897 a Jewish Socialist Party, the Bund, was created. At the end of the nineteenth century the Bund was the best established of the Social Democratic parties in the Russian Empire. Its membership exceeded that of other conspiratorial organisations. This was a reflection of the growing political awareness of the Jewish community.

The Jewish communities had been affected by the political and economic changes which had occurred in the Polish territories. In the Russian Empire, Jews, unlike any other national group, were the object of special legislation, which constrained their right to reside in parts of the Empire, limited access to education and confined them to designated professions. Jews from the Polish areas were particularly affected by the arbitrariness of the Tsarist policies. Within their communities, always rich in religious and political ideas, assimilationist trends always had a place. These were encouraged by the successes of some prominent Jews in the economic development of the Polish areas. In Congress Poland Jewish entrepreneurs and bankers had been involved in the process of industrialisation, bringing them close to the debates conducted by the Polish political leaders, who frequently drew attention to the adaptability and resourcefulness of the Jewish communities. In 1882 in Białystok Rabbi Szmuyl Mohilever established what was to become a precursor of the Zionist organisation. But the precarious nature of Jewish life in the Russian Empire was made worse at the beginning of the twentieth century when, with official encouragement, pogroms started taking place in eastern parts of the kingdom territories. This strengthened the desire of the Jewish communities to emigrate either to the United States or to Palestine.

The end of the nineteenth century and the beginning of the twentieth was a time of the growth of nationalist ideologies in Europe. In the Polish areas, nationalism remained the single most important issue in all political debates. But whereas the Positivists and Socialists tried to get away from the waste of successive uprisings, in 1887 a newly formed organisation took nationalism as its main objective. The Polish League established in Switzerland by Zygmunt Miłkowski had one aim only and that was the establishment of an independent Poland. In 1893 Roman Dmowski formed a National League which took Miłkowski's agenda as its programme. Dmowski defined the nation as Christian Poles, though Lithuanians were described as a tribe of the Polish nation. His programme paid particular attention to the peasants, seeing them as the racially purest section of the Polish nation. Although the League's programme advocated economic progress, Dmowski attacked foreign capital for exploiting ethnic Poles. Germans and Jews were identified as the enemies of the Polish nation. In 1897 the League took the name Stronnictwo Narodowo-Demokratyczne. From the initials of its abbreviated name Narodowa Demokracja (National Democracy, ND) it was henceforth known as the Endecja. The Endecja, through its single preoccupation with the nation and its programme of strengthening and invigorating the Polish nation for battle with its enemies, became the most active of political movements in the three sections of partitioned Poland. Its close association with the Catholic faith meant that the Church was generally sympathetic towards its objectives.

In Polish areas incorporated into Prussia and Austria, political developments took a different course. In both, the establishment of constitutional political systems made Poles less inclined to see insurrections as the only way of redressing grievances. In both cases, the Poles enjoyed the same rights as did all other citizens, and as a result became fully active in the political life of both empires.

When Germany was united in 1871 most of the previously Polish territories remained in the Prussian state, and as a result the Prussian Landtag, the state assembly, made decisions relating to the Polish areas. The Reichstag, to which elections were democratic and free, decided matters of state. Poles had the right to vote in both and indeed sent their representatives to both assemblies. At the turn of the century the Endecja became the strongest Polish force in the two assemblies. Polish Social Democrats were less successful. Cooperation with their German counterparts, who formed a majority in the Reichstag, were always constrained by national divisions. During the *Kulturkampf* in 1873 when Chancellor Bismarck attempted to limit the influence of the Catholic Church, the Poles felt themselves particularly threatened. His policy was misconceived and in effect only strengthened the bond between the Catholic Church and the Polish parishioners who rallied in defence of their Church against what they saw as a dual onslaught from the German and Protestant state.

From 1876 a policy of Germanisation was initiated when German was declared the official language. Schooling in Polish was dramatically reduced, and all contact between Poles and the state had to be done in German. Poles found themselves on the receiving end of discriminatory legislation, introduced by both the Prussian Landtag and the Reichstag. Personal prejudice harboured by the Prussians against what they saw as the inferior Slavs played an additional role in policies towards the Poles. In 1886 Bismarck established a Colonising Commission, the aim of which was to Germanise the Polish areas. Generously subsidised by the Reichstag and the Prussian Landtag, it increased German ownership of land by funding settlements. Only partially successful, the Commission's activities nevertheless inflamed relations between Poles and Germans, leading to boycotts and ultimately to the separation of the two communities. Polish deputies in both assemblies were able to fight back by taking legal action against the Commission and by establishing a Polish Land Bank with the aim of maintaining farms in Polish hands. This and similar banks established by the Poles prospered and, due to the high dividends offered, they attracted German capital. The formation of peasant cooperatives and associations of Polish landowners further reduced the impact of German land policies.

The creation of the Austro-Hungarian Dual Monarchy in 1867 was a defining moment for the Polish leadership in Galicia. The Austrian monarchy based its rule in the region on cooperation with the nobility. They in turn appreciated that they had a lot to gain from supporting Austrian policies, and even more to lose were they to try to oppose it. Earlier peasant uprisings acted as a warning. Initially Austria had been reluctant to enter into discussions on the granting of autonomy, but by 1867 autonomy had been conceded to the region. Legislative matters had already been handed over to a locally elected Sejm which had its seat in Lwów. Elections to the Sejm were by estates, guaranteeing that legislative matters would remain in the hands of the landed gentry. In addition Poles had the right to send representatives to the Austrian National Council. Unlike the Czechs, who decided to boycott the National Council in protest against their not being granted the same status as that enjoyed by Hungary, the Poles participated in it fully. Some historians have suggested that, due to the Czechs' absence, the Poles were favoured and that proportionally more Poles had attained high offices due to their loyalty to the Emperor. Alfred Potocki and Kazimierz Badeni on two separate occasions acted as Prime Ministers and Agenor Gołuchowski was briefly responsible for the Empire's foreign relations. But those Polish aristocrats who were drawn into Austrian politics did not concentrate on Polish affairs.

Galicia remained one of the most backward regions of the Austrian Empire, suffering overpopulation and industrial backwardness. Landowners were slow to adopt new agricultural methods and, with no political or economic incentives for them to alter their ways, their estates remained as stagnant as those of the local peasants. In its policy of conciliating the landowners, the Austrian authorities allowed them to retain many old monopolies, such as in the production of vodka and beer. This tended to consolidate Galician backwardness by guaranteeing the nobility a certain standard of living without the need to adopt new crops or extend their economic activities. Oil exploration and coal mining were the only major industrial breakthroughs, while steel production remained at a very low level. For the peasants, emigration to the Americas was often the only escape from poverty.

The agrarian character of the Polish areas explains the emergence of the peasant movement. In 1895 a Peasant Alliance was formed, which in 1903 became the Polskie Stronnictwo Ludowe (Polish Peasant Alliance, PSL). Distrusting the patronage of educated politicians, it addressed issues which affected the peasants' lives, taxes and tariff barriers. It was led by a genuine peasant Wincenty Witos.

At the same time nationalist feelings strengthened among the Ukrainian community, which became more articulate and clearly defined. Ukrainians were no longer willing to accept their subordination to either Polish or Russian tutelage and increasingly advocated independence. In the Russian-controlled sections of Ukraine, persecution of the Uniate Church and the closing of Ukrainian schools and associations were widespread. In eastern Galicia, as a result of the Austrian policy towards its minorities, the Ukrainians were allowed to enjoy relative freedom of national self-expression. The Ukrainian language flourished, writing in Ukrainian was allowed and attempts were made to record Ukrainian music. Sporting associations such as the Sokil and Sich fostered national pride. The Shevchenko Societies named after the poet Taras Shevchenko who, in 1840, started writing in the Ukrainian language encouraged the study of Ukrainian culture. The cooperative movement was particularly important among the peasants in allowing them to maintain their farms and develop local economic activity. At the turn of the century Ukrainian parties tended to separate themselves from non-Ukrainian ones and to take a distinctly nationalist line.

By the end of the nineteenth century the issue of the Polish right to self-determination was increasingly connected with that of social, economic and political transformation of the three empires. This was a time of mass politics. Increased participation in politics through the broadening of the electorate meant that in each case the regimes had to take into account the wishes and desires of the voting citizens. In all three empires a degree of accommodation was reached with the Poles, allowing them some autonomy.

The outbreak of the Russo-Japanese War in 1904 once more raised the possibility of gaining freedom through association with Russia's enemy. Dmowski and Piłsudski travelled to Japan to see if agreements could be reached with the Japanese to assist them in return for commitments to the restoration of Poland. Piłsudski took a strongly anti-Russian line while Dmowski developed the theory that Prussia posed a greater danger to Polish nationalism. At the same time the Socialists continued divided on doctrinaire points into the two movements, the PPS and the SDKPiL. The Socialists were also divided by their diverse experiences in each of the empires. The outbreak of the First World War created just the sort of opportunity for which Polish nationalists had been waiting.

8
. . . .
War and Independence: 1914–1939

On the eve of the outbreak of the First World War political life in the Polish lands was diverse, dependent upon developments in the partitioning power in which the lands found themselves. Nevertheless these differences did not stand in the way of the emergence of a national identity and a national culture, which transcended these differences, creating preconditions for joint action, were opportunities to arise. Independence was an aspiration nursed by all Poles and that objective continued to be the main and eventual aim of political activities. In spite of living in areas which were ruled very differently, Poles everywhere were acutely aware that they had a language in common, and could refer to a recent past when there had been a Polish kingdom. Frontiers between the empires were porous, and literature, newspapers and politicians were able to travel between the three. Whereas political experiences divided Poles in the three occupation zones, a strong sense of national identity continued and indeed grew with time.

The sense of national belonging was in particular fostered during the period after the 1905 uprisings in Russia. In German and Austrian-dominated parts of Poland, governments, fearful of the upsurge of nationalist and revolutionary agitation, made concessions. They allowed the use of the Polish language, tolerated displays of national sentiments and finally granted a degree of political freedom. In Russia in 1906 for the first time the Tsar agreed to elections and a national assembly, the so-called Duma. Polish people within the Tsarist Empire were divided on the relevance of this concession to the national question. Whereas the PPS decided to boycott it, the National Democrats, led by Dmowski, welcomed it and secured a majority of the total of 55

Polish seats. Poles in the Duma, initially with good reason, had pinned their hopes on obtaining autonomy. By the time of the elections to the Third Duma in 1907 these hopes proved illusory and disappointment set in. Nevertheless as a result of the reforms which followed the 1905 revolutions, teaching in the national language was once more permitted in areas incorporated into the Tsarist Empire. As Polish culture flourished, so did Lithuanian, Byelorussian and Ukrainian, encouraging the emergence of national self-awareness within those communities. None of these national groups would henceforth look to the Poles for leadership and increasingly campaigned for their own right to self-determination. But the political freedoms granted by the Tsar to his subjects after 1906 encouraged the development of what is nowadays termed civil society, namely local associations and initiatives that were independent of the state. These in due course increased the communities' self-confidence and desire for the right to self-rule.

In territories incorporated into Prussia, Poles had in the mean time come to appreciate the benefits of a well-run system in which the state respected its citizens. Thus Poles in Prussia and Poznania laid great stress on respect for law and orderliness, all of which had benefited them. Dissent, on the other hand, had been severely punished. Germanisation drives, attempts at increased colonisation of Polish lands and finally introduction of teaching of religion in German, all met with opposition. The Poles' response was no longer to plan insurgencies but to fight back with strikes and by legal means. Recourse to law suggested a degree of confidence in the working of the state and legislative system as a means of protecting the community's economic and cultural interests. The National Democrats became the biggest Polish party in the Reichstag.

Within Austria-Hungary the PPS was the dominant party of the Polish community. Led by Piłsudski, the party established paramilitary organisations, most notably the Riflemen's Association. The Austrian authorities were willing to tolerate these associations, hoping that they could be of use in the event of a war with Russia. A network of similar associations developed after 1911 and spread across the Russian border to Congress Poland. The Peasant Alliance continued as the second largest Polish party in the Austrian Empire. It effectiveness was nevertheless decreased by internal splits.

The First World War opened with Germany declaring war on Russia on 1 August 1914. When Austria followed by declaring war on Russia, the three partitioning powers found themselves at war. The First World

War lasted four years. By the time hostilities ended the economies, political systems and military capacity of the European states had collapsed, not being able to withstand the long and economically draining war. All fighting in the East ceased when on 3 March 1918 Germany and Bolshevik Russia signed the Brest-Litovsk Peace Treaty. By November fighting in the West ended. On 3 November Austria-Hungary completed armistice talks with the Western powers. Germany signed an armistice ending fighting in the West on 11 November. On the same day the German authorities handed over power in the Polish lands to General Piłsudski, thus allowing for the establishment of a provisional authority and with that an independent Poland.

The response of Polish nationals to the outbreak of the war had depended very much on where they lived and how the area was treated by the occupying power. In the first months of the conflict most politically active Poles hoped that in the confusion of changing military fortunes, they might be able to demand independence in return for support for the war effort. In Paris, Washington and London, Polish committees sprang up to campaign for an independent Poland. At the same time, in Moscow, Vienna and Berlin, governments and military leaders were lobbied by Poles to extract promises that Polish territories would be granted autonomy or at least special status within the empires. These negotiations were conducted by prominent community leaders, or simply famous Poles, as was the case of the pianist Ignacy Paderewski, who toured the US to draw attention to the Polish cause. In the mean time developments in Polish-inhabited areas took their own course.

Before the outbreak of the war Austrian rule had been the least oppressive. During the summer months of 1914 Poles in the Austro-Hungarian Empire still thought in terms of Polish autonomy within the Empire, rather than independence. While it was generally noted that the Polish peasant population of Galicia was unmoved by nationalist slogans, the intellectual and political elite took the initiative in negotiating with the Austrian authorities. The basis for cooperation between the Austrian authorities and the Polish community leaders was a shared desire to defeat the Russian Empire. Thus Poles willingly took up arms and rarely avoided mobilisation. Polish nationalist movements, united in a Confederation, declared that Poles should be 'an active force' in the forthcoming war, thus indicating that military cooperation should be rewarded by the granting of increased rights within the Empire. The Austrian authorities were not in a hurry to

respond, as the war was their sole priority. Only when the military situation dictated the need to be conciliatory towards the national minorities was it possible for the Poles to extract vague promises that their
demand for the same status as that enjoyed by the Hungarians would
be considered favourably in the future.

At the beginning of August 1914 Piłsudski marched with a detachment of Riflemen from Austrian Galicia into the Russian territories.
The anticipated uprising did not take place and the enterprise was
abandoned. Henceforth Polish leaders in Austria concentrated their
efforts on diplomatic negotiations in anticipation of either the Entente
or the Central Powers winning the war.

At the time of the outbreak of the war, Poles in the Tsarist Empire
wanted to see Germany defeated. Only the revolutionary section of the
PPS opposed the war effort and pinned its hopes on a future revolution. Nevertheless, attempts to extract from the Tsar concessions in
return for loyal support were only limited. While Nicholas II accepted
the need for the establishment of town and local councils, he was
unwilling to allow for the creation of a Polish central administrative
authority. During the course of the war the Russian authorities tried to
minimise the loss and destruction of industrial capacity by evacuating
whole factories and enterprises into the Russian interior. As the industrial plant was moved, workers and their families were obliged to
follow. In the wake of the German military successes in 1915 approximately 130 major plants were thus moved from the territories of
Congress Poland. This in turn caused panic. When withdrawing, the
military high command also ordered the destruction of all property
which could be of use to the enemy. Tens of thousands of Poles were
thus uprooted and sent into the Russian interior, frequently beyond the
Ural Mountains.

In the spring of 1915 Austrian and German military units prevented
the Russian army from breaking through the Carpathian Mountains.
By the summer of that year German and Austrian troops entered into
the territories of Congress Poland and German troops occupied
Warsaw. Henceforth, as the Central Powers assumed control of all
territories of the one-time Polish kingdom, the Polish Question would
depend on German and Austrian decisions. The issue arose in all talks
concerning war aims and as a military factor in plans for the continu-
ation of war against Russia. Nevertheless, both sides tried to postpone
making any promises until the end of the war. In any case Germany did
not want to allow Austria to assume responsibility for the Polish

Question, as this would give Austria a strong card to play in future negotiations with the Russians. Thus occupied Polish territories were divided into German and Austrian spheres and the military were given full authority to determine policies in relation to the civilian population. Since the Germans were willing to cooperate with local initiatives, citizens' councils sprang up in all major cities. The fact that the use of Polish in public life was allowed and Russian was replaced with Polish as the language of instruction in all schools, raised hopes for an amicable agreement with the German authorities. But Germany continued to be militarily pressed and economic policies towards the Polish territories raised doubts about long-term plans. German military victories had ended the evacuation and flight of population eastwards, but harsh economic exploitation of the occupied areas caused extreme hardship. By the autumn of 1915 most stocks of industrial raw materials and products had been confiscated. This led to the reduction of local manufacture and as a result also to unemployment and shortages in the local economies.

German economic policies towards occupied Polish territories went beyond exploitation for military purposes. The German military administration authorised the selective destruction of certain branches of industry in the areas of Congress Poland so that it would not compete with German industry after the war. In the mean time coal and timber were fully exploited for the benefit of the German war effort. Indifference to the hardship experienced by the civilian population was widespread and, during the winter of 1915–16, Poles were reduced to starvation. In 1916 the German authorities forcefully conscripted manpower for work in German industries. These policies resulted in the growth of hostility towards Germany and raised doubts about plans for an independent Poland based on German support. Nor were the German authorities themselves clear how to proceed with occupied Polish territories. Continuing German military victories in the East, and the collapse of the Eastern Front, inevitably led to discussions on Germany's future Eastern policies. Since a high proportion of the German officers were Prussian landed gentry, their minds turned towards plans for consolidating the German sphere of influence in the Polish territories and along the Baltic coast. They were less willing to plan for the emergence of an independent Polish state.

By mid-1915 the military stalemate led the Entente and Central Powers to look at means of securing the support of various national groups to destabilise the enemy. On 5 November 1916 a Two

Emperors' Manifesto was issued on behalf of the German and Austrian monarchs. Far-reaching in its implications, it appeared to promise the creation of a self-governing Poland. But this was to be in the future and within boundaries still to be determined. For all its shortcomings, the Poles took this to be a formal commitment, whereas in reality the need for Polish recruits had led the Central Powers to avoid long and, as yet, inconclusive debates on the future of the Eastern territories. This initiative, in turn, forced the Entente Powers to come up with matching promises. To date only the Russians had made a gesture of conciliation towards the Poles when on 14 August 1914 Grand Duke Nikolai Nikolaevich promised that Poles would be allowed a greater degree of autonomy within the Empire. In May 1915 the Russian front collapsed. Still the Russians refused to extend the scope of any commitments to the Poles. This caused Dmowski, who up till then had maintained that the future Poland would be part of the Great Slav Federation led by the Russian Empire, to conclude that the diplomatic fight for a future independent Poland would be best pursued in the West.

In Western capitals Poles had been active throughout the war trying to obtain promises of support. They had not been successful, mainly because France and Britain hoped that Austria could be induced to sign a separate peace, and therefore thought it impolitic to make commitments to support the aspirations of national minorities within the Austrian Empire. By 1917, when it became clear that Austria could not be induced to abandon Germany, Paris and London were obliged to consider the issue more extensively. This gave various prominent and vocal Poles an opportunity to put forward their programmes. The French saw Dmowski, who had moved to Paris in the autumn of 1916, as the most likely leader of a future Polish administration. In August 1917 he formed a Polish National Committee in Switzerland. Gradually he extended the Committee's influence both in the West and in occupied Polish territories. The French then took the initiative, largely inspired by what happened in Russia in February 1917. The Russian Provisional Government seemed to be sympathetic to the Poles' aspirations and allowed the creation of separate Polish military units from among the Austrian prisoners of war. The French hoped that these, once formed, could then be transported to the Western Front to assist in fighting there where the French were experiencing shortage of manpower. Naturally Polish troops would fight most willingly under orders from a Polish authority. In order to gain control of the Polish units, the French government needed to concede to Dmowki's demands, and accept the authority of his Committee. Dmowski's Committee also assumed control over Polish units in France. In November 1918 the Polish National Committee was recognised by the French as the de facto government of Poland.

A great moral victory was secured by the Poles in January 1918 when Woodrow Wilson, the US President, listed the creation of an independent Poland as one of the US war aims, the so-called Fourteen Points. This in itself was not a guarantee that the US could or even would do anything to secure the emergence of a free Polish state, but it was an important statement of intent, which encouraged the Poles. After the war, the authority of the US was very high, due to its military assistance and because most European states hoped for US economic aid. In the circumstances, any pronouncements made by the US President carried great weight.

In reality independent Poland emerged from the collapse of the three partitioning powers at the end of the First World War. The first administration was formed when the German war effort failed and troops were withdrawn from Polish territories. As German troops hastily left Poland, authority naturally fell into the hands of Józef Piłsudski who had, at the beginning of the war, hoped that independence could be secured through military cooperation with the Central Powers. In 1916 and 1917 it looked as if he had not only been wrong but that his political career had come to an end. As Germany and Austria made commitments to restore an independent Poland, and called for volunteers, Piłsudski refused to allow them to use the legions unless genuine independence was granted first. For this he was imprisoned and a Regency Council consisting of more compliant Poles was established in Warsaw in October 1917. When the German defeat seemed imminent the Regency Council sought a reconciliation with Piłsudski who was released from imprisonment. As he arrived in Warsaw, Piłsudski's authority was high. He commanded the loyalty of Polish units and both the Left and Right viewed him as a patriot. On 11 November 1918 the Regency Council transferred authority to Piłsudski and the army pledged its support. The uneasy situation whereby Dmowski had gained recognition in Paris, and Piłsudski had actually created a first provisional administration in Polish territories was uneasily resolved with Dmowski accepting Piłsudski's authority. Dmowski in turn was appointed head of the Polish delegation to the Paris Peace Talks. They left unresolved their differences as to the future of Poland. Piłsudski hoped for a federated structure which would include Lithuania and areas previously in the Commonwealth. Dmowski, however, had plans for a national state. The two never agreed on the way forward. Although the Polish Question figured extensively at the Paris talks, in reality the final details of Poland's borders were defined through conflict with neighbouring states and other national groups. The Great Powers used their authority to adjudicate between them, but had no other means of forcing the Poles to heed their advice.

After 123 years Poland had re-emerged, but the road ahead was bound to be difficult. Years of foreign domination left an imprint on Polish lands, which had developed along distinct economic and political paths. Independence required a national economy and political consensus to be built from scratch. In view of the burden of high expectations, based more on nostalgia than reality, it was inevitable that independence would prove a disappointment to most Poles. Romantic notions that self-determination would result in political and material stability were confronted by the realities of post-war reconstruction. At the same time, Poles who had been so determined to fight for an independent Poland were not so willing to tolerate the wishes of other national groups to self-determination. In the process of building the new state, the wishes of the Ukrainians, Ruthenians, Byelorussians and Jews were deemed to be of less importance, as the new Polish state fought to establish its borders in the fluid situation which prevailed in Eastern Europe during the years 1918–21.

While the government faced the formidable task of building consensus in war-ravaged Poland, the first big diplomatic battles were fought in Paris where the winners met to decide the fate of defeated Germany. France, preoccupied with her own security, viewed the newly emerging states east of Germany as possible future allies. During the course of the Paris Peace Talks, the fate of Russia still seemed unclear. Therefore France was torn between, on the one hand, building up Poland and Czechoslovakia and, on the other, intervening in the Russian Civil War in the hope that a democratic government could be established there. France still preferred to have a strong Russian ally east of Germany, rather than weak client states. Since the anti-Bolshevik forces refused to commit themselves to respecting the integrity of the new Polish state, France faced contradictory alternatives. Throughout the inter-war period these were never conclusively resolved. Britain had little interest in Eastern Europe. To the British

Prime Minister Lloyd George, French attempts to build a *cordon sanitaire* in Eastern Europe smacked of French aggrandisement. He therefore stood against France's policy of supporting Poland and Czechoslovakia. In any case Poland had little influence on the course of talks concerning the future of Germany. Squabbles and quarrels between Piłsudski and Dmowski diminished the authority of the Polish delegation. The British and French both warily observed developments in Poland, fearing future instability.

During the early 1920s the settlement of Poland's borders was complicated because the western frontier was dependent on decisions relating to the future of Germany. In the south the border with Czechoslovakia led to conflicts due to a number of territorial disputes between the newly emerging administrations in Poland and Czechoslovakia. In the east and south-east the Russian Civil War raged. The Poles were to find out that the Baltic peoples, Ukrainians and Byelorussians had no desire to be part of a Polish-dominated Commonwealth.

During 1919 Piłsudski, as Commander-in-Chief of the Polish army, led a number of military campaigns aimed at consolidating Poland's eastern border and implicitly subjugating the eastern national groups to Polish domination. In April the Poles occupied the town of Vilnius, held by the Lithuanians. The campaign inspired a lasting hatred of the Poles in Lithuania. Simultaneously war was waged against the Ukrainian People's Republic of Semen Petlura. At issue was Ukrainian East Galicia with its Polish-inhabited town of Lwów. While this conflict was to end in a truce, relations between the Poles and the Ukrainians would fester throughout the inter-war years, leading to instability in the region.

On 25 April 1920 the Polish army started a campaign against the Red Army. Initially the Russians were successful in pushing the Poles back and by August they approached Warsaw. The Poles then appealed to the Western Powers to arbitrate. Their military counter-offensive was successful. In what came to be known, with characteristic Polish piety, as the 'Miracle of the Vistula', the Russians were repulsed. It is debatable whether Piłsudski's military tactics or the Red Army's overstretched supply lines played a decisive role in the final victory. To the Poles this was a seminal point in the defence of Poland against the Russian onslaught. Quickly the myth became greater than the truth and contributed to the overestimation of Poland's military capacity and the underestimation of Soviet strength during the inter-war period. The presence of the French military mission in Warsaw, with de Gaulle as one of its members, further underlined the symbolism of the victory, for it seemed to signify Western commitment and appreciation of Poland's importance. When military supplies from Britain did not arrive due to a strike by British dockers, Poles generally concluded that the 'Red Menace' had spread to the West and that only they had stood up to it and furthermore that they had defeated it. Crude Soviet attempts to justify entry into ethnically Polish territories, by setting up peasant and workers' councils, convinced no one. Polish peasants and workers fought in defence of their land and steadfastly viewed the Red Army as an invasion force. The Communist Party of Poland (KPP) would always be viewed as a Soviet agency and did not succeed in gaining more than a foothold in the working-class movement. Amidst the fighting the town of Vilnius, earlier relinquished to the Lithuanians, was retaken by a supposedly renegade Polish General Lucjan Żeligowski. When the Polish Sejm confirmed the conquest and the General was treated as a national hero, the nature of Polish aggression was obvious. On 18 March 1921 by the Treaty of Riga, brokered by the Western Powers, Poland and the Soviet Union concluded a peace agreement. Britain was furious with the Poles who had flouted earlier requests to confine Poland's territories to ethnically Polish areas, the so-called Curzon Line. These early adventures left a bad impression in Britain and would be used to justify a policy of lack of interest in Polish affairs throughout the following years.

The manner in which the Polish borders had been finally settled left a lasting impression on the national psychology. The prevailing attitude was of distrust of the Great Powers and an overestimation of Poland's military capacities. The army in particular basked in the groundswell of patriotic euphoria. Diplomacy was only too easily dismissed as a weak and unnecessary tool in resolving international conflicts. What the Polish leaders failed to learn was that Poland had only emerged due to German and Russian weaknesses and disunity between the former partitioning powers. Nor were they willing to consider that were Germany or Russia to emerge as powers, Poland's security would once more be threatened.

A bullish approach to diplomacy combined with strong nationalism were the two most important characteristic features of Poland's relations with its neighbours. Initially it was inevitable that Germany was Poland's biggest enemy. The incorporation of the Poznań and Pomeranian districts into Poland, conflict over Silesia and the creation of the corridor cutting through German-inhabited Western Prussia to give Poland access to the Baltic coast, made sure that Germany would be committed to the revision of her borders with Poland. Added to that was the disingenuous solution of the Gdańsk issue. On Lloyd George's insistence the German city, which contained a majority German population but which economically was entirely dependent on trade with Poland, became a Free City. This meant that its security and status were guaranteed by the League of Nations while all internal matters were decided by an elected Senate, which by the early 1930s was dominated by the Nazis. Port facilities, customs and the postal service were placed in Polish hands. Separated by a strip of land from Western Prussia, Gdańsk Germans did all in their power to undermine Polish rights in the city. The League's authority was represented by a High Commissioner, whom the Poles resented as much as the Germans did. Irritated by the League's presence in Gdańsk, the Poles tended to sideline it, preferring to deal directly with Berlin. In addition, approximately 1 million Germans lived in the western parts of Poland, never accepting their incorporation into the Slav state.

Poland's eastern borders had been forged through direct conflict. Approximately one-third of Poland's population belonged to different national groups. These were mainly concentrated in the east. The Ukrainian community, comprising approximately 4 million people, had been thwarted in its hope for a national state. It had little commitment to the Polish state, which was insensitive to their aspirations and ensured that they did not benefit from land redistribution. This favoured Polish ex-combatants who were settled on land made available by the land reform. In the late 1920s and early 1930s a state of near civil war prevailed in the Ukrainian regions. Repression by the army had the result of increasing the militancy of the Ukrainian community. In due course the Czechs and later the Germans financed and trained Ukrainians in order to destabilise the Polish state.

With Czechoslovakia Poland had a territorial dispute over the Teschen region, which was rich in coal deposits. The Czechs captured this territory at the time when the Poles were preoccupied with war with the Soviet Union. The unresolved territorial dispute underlined the absence of any goodwill between the two states. Poland was resentful of France's support for Czechoslovakia and jealous of Czech influence in Eastern and South-eastern Europe. The Poles developed good relations with Hungary, Czechoslovakia's enemy. The rivalry went deeper. In the 1930s Colonel Jósef Beck, Poland's Minister for

Foreign Affairs, tried to establish for Poland an independent role in the region. Misguidedly, he believed that Germany's growing economic and political influence could be stemmed by the creation of a regional bloc. Czechoslovakia with its strong links with the West was seen as an obstacle to this policy.

Successive governments sought to build a consensus within their community on the basis of Poland being a nation state. The result was that the rights of the national minorities were threatened. The Jewish community, which made up approximately 10 per cent of Poland's population, was predominantly not assimilated. The majority of Jews lived in the small towns of the eastern borderland. Yiddish speaking, and with a diversity of Orthodox observance, the Jews of eastern Poland were mainly involved in small-scale retail trade. In the bigger cities of central Poland, the Jewish community was more assimilated and fully involved in the economic, political and cultural life of Poland. In the professions, it was noticeable that a higher than average proportion of lawyers and doctors were Jewish. When the Depression hit Poland's economy in the early 1930s, Jews became the focal point of attacks and boycotts fanned and instigated by the National Democrats. Attacks on Jews increased in the late 1930s. The Polish Fascist Party the 'Falanga' organised classroom ghettos in universities, and intimidated and beat up Jewish students. In 1937 in response to the crisis the Minister of Education Wojciech Świętosławski made it obligatory for the universities to provide separate seating for Jewish students. Thus under the guise of making seating available for all, he effectively gave the government's approval to anti-Semitic policies of marginalising Jewish students. As white-collar unemployment affected graduates, so the government restricted the number of licences granted to lawyers, making it more difficult for Jews to enter the profession. A boycott of Jewish shops was promoted by the Endecja as a national duty. In 1938 the government introduced laws which stripped Jews living abroad of Polish passports, effectively rendering them stateless. Plans for the removal of the Jewish population from Poland were extensively discussed in the press. Madagascar, then a French colony, was mentioned as a possible destination for Polish Jews.

The Catholic Church's response was muted. On an official level it disapproved of attacks on Jews, but at the same time it welcomed legislation which separated the Christian communities from the Jewish one. Under the guise of there being a need to protect the young from being influenced by Jews, the Church called for the removal of Jewish teachers and the isolation of the Jews. The government was only too willing to become drawn into trivial debates on the merits of various types of abattoir methods, supposedly on grounds of these being cruel to animals, in effect to prevent Jews from having their own slaughter houses. It was notable that pig slaughter, traumatic as it is to the slaughtered animal, was never the subject of these public debates. The proliferation of local and governmental legislation on various aspects of daily life, such as bans on cycling without a licence, was introduced and implemented to harass Jews. Although initially Poland subscribed to the League of Nations charter on the protection of national minorities, it became irritated by complaints made against it and finally decided to withdraw from that commitment. Poland's international reputation suffered as it substantiated an earlier comment made by the eminent British economist John Maynard Keynes that Poland was 'an economic impossibility whose only industry is Jew-baiting'.

The 123-year period of foreign domination and the battle for independence had created a burden of expectations which would have been very difficult to fulfil. The post-war depression and the Great Depression of the early 1930s made it even more difficult for Poland to obtain foreign aid. The hope that Poland would break with poverty by introducing an ambitious programme of industrialisation, which in turn would consolidate Poland's strategic and political role in the region, proved too difficult to realise. Successive governments were not able to build a strong industrial infrastructure. The international situation was not favourable and the Poles faced objective difficulties when pre-war trading patterns collapsed. The Russian markets remained closed to foreign goods. Germany waged a tariff war against Polish coal and steel as part of the attempt to destroy the new state. One of the biggest obstacles to a rapid industrialisation was the shortage of indigenous capital. To succeed, industrial development in independent Poland needed the state to support it with capital and protective legislation. Foreign capital was an absolute precondition for economic growth. Neither was easily available. Thus economic development was slow and difficult. Polish industry could not compete with Western production. Foreign capital was not forthcoming and anxiety about a possible German–Polish conflict discouraged foreign banks from becoming involved in Poland. Local entrepreneurial talent was slow to emerge, in particular because the landed gentry continued to dominate politics. This was made worse by the tendency of indigenous capital to mirror foreign investors' reluctance to commit long-term finance to projects in Poland. In the mid-1930s French government loans allowed the Polish government to embark on an ambitious programme of developing industry in central Poland. This was motivated as much by the desire to modernise obsolete industrial capacity as by the anxiety that older enterprises were sited close to the borders and thus vulnerable to attack in the event of a war. Hydroelectric dams, steel production, rubber and chemical industries were established as part of this ambitious undertaking. Unfortunately the outbreak of the war in September 1939 destroyed that achievement.

Land reform, introduced in 1925, was also a disappointment, when it proved not bold enough to succeed. Too little land was released to satisfy peasant land hunger. Small-scale farming remained the norm in Poland, with villages continuing to experience overpopulation. The fact that the Ukrainian population was not allowed to benefit from this land redistribution exacerbated relations between the two communities which would have dire consequences during the wartime and post-war period. Emigration from villages to America was gradually halted by restrictive US policies. In the early 1920s French and Belgian mining attracted thousands of Poles. When the Depression affected European industry, these opportunities came to an end though large Polish communities continued to thrive in the mining areas of the Pas-de-Calais, Toulouse, Clermont-Ferrand and Dijon.

During the immediate post-war period the National Democrats tried to capture power, but the moderate peasant party led by Witos stood in the way. On 12 December 1922 a National Democrat fanatic assassinated Gabriel Narutowicz, the first President. Civil war was only prevented by political leaders making a decision to pull back from the confrontation. The result was that the National Democrats and the Peasant Alliance reached an accommodation. This collapsed during the economic crisis of 1923. In May 1926, Piłsudski, who had been sidelined earlier by the civilian Constitution, staged a military coup d'état. The government had failed to cope with the economic crisis and there was a general fear among centrist and left-wing parties that the National Democrats would take over the government. With the approval of other parties, including the Communists, and the support from rail unions who would have been able to prevent the government from moving loyal troops to the capital, Piłsudski personally led the army into Warsaw and after three days of fighting, took power.

Piłsudski was seen as acting as a patriotic and nationalist alternative to the self-serving actions of the political parties in the Sejm. Or that is the view which he and his supporters cultivated. Piłsudski was a man of modest tastes, blunt in his style and verging on vulgar in his speech. He was prone to making cryptic pronouncements, which at times left foreign visitors bewildered as to their meaning. In principle he claimed to have no interest in politics which of course was not the case. Although initially he only retained the post of Minister of War he made sure that most of the key government posts were held by his own nominees, who usually turned out to be his comrades from the wartime period. The renewal programme (Sanacja) introduced after the coup, included strengthening the Presidency and rooting out corruption and waste. When economic stability returned, the population overlooked the increasing marginalisation of the Sejm. But by 1929 the military regime decided to build a ruling party. Piłsudski made his peace with the wealthy landowners, which inevitably ended any hopes for further land reform. When the centre-left politicians within the Sejm blocked attempts to rewrite the Constitution the military regime took action which to all intents destroyed democracy in Poland. Officers were deployed in the Sejm to intimidate deputies, who were physically threatened and then roughed up. Piłsudski became Prime Minister, and on the eve of general elections, had prominent politicians of the centre and left-wing parties imprisoned under emergency laws. The fortress of Brześć and the camp at Bereza Kartuska became notorious places of internment run by brutal officers. The government party was thus able to destroy the opposition and win the elections.

A process of militarisation of all ministries followed. In April 1935 the Constitution was altered to give the Presidency and the government extensive powers while decreasing the role of the Sejm. Although Piłsudski died a month later, power remained firmly in the hands of the military men. The period that followed is known as the 'Rule of the Colonels'. A military clique divided ministries among themselves, creating fiefdoms over which they had absolute control. Marshal Rydz-Śmigły, the Commander in Chief, was designated as Piłsudski's successor. Colonel Jósef Beck, Minister for Foreign Affairs, was equally powerful and immune to challenge. Both steered Poland along a disastrous path of close political collaboration with Hitler while failing to build up Poland's military strength.

In the early 1920s Poland appeared to be firmly in the French camp. But this was a relationship which made the Poles uneasy. Poland's international standing was very weak from the outset. In 1919 all the

European powers were unwilling to make commitments to the new state. This left Poland exposed, in particular because of the multiplicity of real and potential conflicts with neighbouring states. Polish politicians suspected that France and Britain were more anxious about relations with Germany than with supporting the new states against future aggression. But in 1919 the Poles assumed that their shared anxiety about Germany would lead France to commit itself to the military and economic build-up of Poland. This did not happen. In 1921 France and Poland signed a Political Agreement. The accompanying Military Convention provided for joint action in the event of a German attack on either of the signatories. But the Poles had hoped for more. They had anticipated that France would finance military and economic developments in Poland in order to assure itself of a strong Eastern ally. As it turned out, France wanted to broaden her alliances, tying Poland into a regional bloc including Czechoslovakia, Romania, Hungary and even possibly the Soviet Union. The Poles would have nothing to do with these plans which in turn alienated them from France. Poland came to distrust the French and, when Hitler came to power in Germany in 1933, Colonel Beck decided to try and improve relations with Germany instead. In 1934 Germany and Poland signed a Pact of Non-Aggression. Gdańsk, the biggest obstacle to better relations between the two states, was put on ice, a state of affairs confirmed when the Gdańsk Nazis were instructed by Berlin to stop attacking Polish property. Although Poland signed a treaty with the Soviet Union, and continued to be bound by its agreement with France, relations with Germany determined the pace of Poland's foreign relations during the 1930s.

In 1938 when Germany decided to press Czechoslovakia over its alleged mistreatment of the German minority, the Polish Ministry for Foreign Relations coordinated its attack on Czechoslovakia with Germany. Beck wanted Czechoslovakia broken up and sought the return of Teschen to Poland. Unfortunately for the Poles, during the course of the spring and summer of 1938 the British Prime Minister Neville Chamberlain took the initiative in defusing the European crisis caused by Czechoslovak–German difficulties. The result was the Munich Agreement signed by Germany, Italy, France and Britain, which allowed Hitler to take over the German inhabited regions of Czechoslovakia. Once the process of break-up was initiated it led directly to Hitler marching into Prague in March in 1939. The Poles did manage in the mean time to intimidate the Czechs and to take over disputed territories. What they had not counted on was the growth of Germany's influence in the region, which rendered Poland, the previously valued partner of Hungary and Romania, irrelevant. Poland not only lost influence among the East European and Balkan states; it became the next object of German aggression.

In October 1938 and then again in March 1939 the Poles were warned by Joachim Ribbentrop the Nazi Minister for Foreign Affairs that Gdańsk would have to return to the Reich. Somewhat belatedly, a Polish military mission was sent to Paris to seek confirmation of French commitment to Poland. But the French had no intention of deploying their much needed troops in defence of Poland. An unexpected British guarantee to defend Polish integrity made by the Prime Minister on 31 March 1939 lacked credibility. Chamberlain had reacted to rumours of an impending German attack on Gdańsk and attempts to take over Romanian oil production. When the emergencies proved not to threaten European peace, the commitment remained no more than a political gesture, a warning to Germany not to alter the balance of power in Europe. As transpired in the course of military talks that followed, Britain had no plans to aid Poland directly or indirectly. During the course of summer Colonel Beck desperately tried to reopen talks with the Germans, but to no avail. The German–Soviet Pact of Non-Aggression signed on 24 August sealed Poland's fate. The Secret Annex, which detailed spheres of interest in anticipation of the German attack on Poland, was not made public. Nevertheless experienced politicians had no difficulty in guessing that Poland was the subject of agreement between the two. On the beautiful morning of 1 September, as Polish children prepared to start the first day of school, German bombers struck main towns, railway junctions and military installations.

The Gdańsk issue, which, throughout the inter-war period constantly threatened to blow up into a German–Polish conflict, was dealt with earlier. After weeks of growing tension in the city, on 23 August the Gdańsk Senate declared its decision to revert to the Reich. German units attacked the main Post Office, the symbol of Polish authority in the city. After a siege the Poles surrendered and after a summary trial were shot. The League Commissioner was requested to leave the city, which he did. The League, in spite of its legal obligation to uphold the status of the city, made no reference to the incident.

During the course of the next three weeks, in the full-scale aerial and ground attack on Polish territory, Polish troops were outmanoeuvred and finally defeated. Soviet entry into the eastern regions then completed the rout. The Polish military leaders waited for France and Britain to take action on Germany's western borders. They pinned their hopes on the Franco-Polish Agreement recently augmented by military talks in May 1939 and also the full-blown Polish–British Agreement of Mutual Assistance signed on 25 August. In both, commitments to the defence of Polish sovereignty were solemnly made. What the Poles did not know was that in Paris the desire to keep France out of conflict for as long as possible, had become the top priority. General Gamelin, the French Commander-in-Chief, used the ruse that the political protocol of the Franco-Polish talks had not been ratified by the National Assembly, to persuade himself that undertakings to defend Poland were not binding. On the eve of the outbreak of the war France had no military plans to assist Poland directly, nor were there any plans to attack Germany during the German–Polish War.

The British government had likewise not prepared for any action during the Polish–German conflict. In any case the flight range of British planes in 1939 was too limited for them to reach vital German installations and they most certainly were not able to land in Poland without forward bases being prepared beforehand. More importantly, Britain would not provide the Poles with military equipment. The tacit understanding within the British military circles was that Poland would be unlikely to hold out for longer than three months, in which case it was deemed imprudent to lose materials vital for the pursuit of a long-drawn-out war. In effect both Western powers calculated that they would have to accept Poland's defeat, as they preferred to concentrate on their own preparations for the inevitable conflict with Germany. Neither the French nor British commitments adequately analysed the likely Soviet response to the growth of German belligerence throughout the 1930s. When on 3 September first the British and then the French governments declared war on Germany, no military action followed this declaration.

The Polish military command had overestimated their own military strength and underestimated Germany's. Their air force, in the 1920s capable of impressing the world with its engineering and inventiveness, in the 1930s had been neglected and was not capable of fighting the German onslaught. The supply dumps, anticipating a more likely war with the Soviet Union, were on the wrong side on the Vistula and the call-up had not been completed. Military plans had been prepared on the assumption that the war would be fought during the autumn rains, in which the light cavalry used by the Poles would be at an advantage against the motorised German units. As it turned out September 1939 was dry and sunny. The government and the military command withdrew from Warsaw, with most ministers neglecting their civilian obligations and assuming military duties. The diplomatic corps was left to disconsolately trail eastwards, escaping German bombing raids, but out of touch with the government. When the Red Army crossed into Poland's eastern territories on 17 September, the government, the Catholic Primate of All Poland and the High Command led by Marshal Rydz-Śmigły crossed the border into Romania. The aim was to continue, undefeated, the fight from exile. The population was abandoned by its political and spiritual leaders. The haste of the departure suggested an equal preoccupation with getting to Paris before the opposition regrouped and formed a government in exile. The conviction that Poland had not been truly defeated was only too easily maintained by the pre-war regime. The government's departure caused a flight of the elite. As fighting drew to a close, streams of people headed south-east to the Romanian border and from there proceeded into exile, in the first place to France.

The outbreak of the war cut short a brief period when a concerted effort was made to establish not merely a national state, but also to modernise its social structure. Educational reforms were meant to be the starting point of the transformation of what was no more than a state of national consciousness. In 1919 all three educational systems inherited by the Poles differed widely and had in all cases represented the political and cultural aims of the partitioning powers. In the German section the standard of education had been highest, in the Russian lowest, though in the Austrian part the peasantry had been the most neglected section. Average levels of illiteracy in Poland were 30 per cent. Among women these rates were even higher. The task was thus not only to create a uniform educational system but in essence to create a Polish curriculum and an educated social stratum which would serve the state and national institutions. In spite of the economic difficulties experienced by Poland during the inter-war period the results were impressive. Although not always successfully, consistent attempts were made to make sure that all children received a minimum of seven years' primary schooling. More radical solutions were also introduced, with special schooling for peasants and a workers' university (Towarzystwo Uniwersytetu Robotniczego, TUR). In 1921 a Catholic University was opened in Lublin, where enlightened and progressive Catholic teaching became the norm. Its aim was not to teach theology but to produce a Catholic intellectual community, which the Church believed Poland lacked. Progressive educational ideas emerged at the same time. Child focused and liberal, these were based on a new understanding of how children developed. They rejected the idea that children should be treated as a blank sheet upon which should be imprinted the correct social values in favour of encouraging the creative and social instincts of the child. The best-known exponent of this approach to children was Janusz Korczak, a Jewish educationist who ran children's homes in Warsaw. During the war Korczak perished in Treblinka together with his charges, whom he refused to abandon.

From the outset the Catholic Church enjoyed a privileged position in independent Poland. Its identification with the Polish cause during the partitions created a solid bond between the new state and the Church. With few exceptions, nationalities were identified by their religion, thus explaining the simple equation between being Polish and worshipping as a Catholic. The extreme right and nationalist movements demanded that the Catholic Church should enjoy an unchallenged position within the Polish state. Thus the 1921 and the redrafted 1935 Constitutions stated clearly that 'The Roman-Catholic denomination, being a religion of the prevailing majority of the nation, occupies a central position in the state, while other denominations have equal rights.' Other denominations had to seek, through negotiation, confirmation of their rights. The Concordat signed by the Polish state with the Vatican confirmed this state of affairs. The Papacy was particularly keen to show its approval of the new Polish state, recognising its borders and accepting the state's right to be a party to appointments to the bishoprics. The Catholic Church continued to hold large landed estates which it successfully defended against inclusion in the land reform. The existence of two Catholic trade unions and an extensive network of social organisations confirmed the Church's dominant role in Polish society. But the Church's prominent position in Poland caused a reaction in particular among the intellectual and left-wing political groups. The Church tended to overstate the influence of secular movements within Polish society. Catholic criticism of all who advocated the separation of state and Church contributed to a polarisation of Polish society between the nationalist Catholics versus the secular left. Non-Catholic Christians found that the Catholic Church was hostile to their activities. They benefited little from the dominant position of the Catholics. On the contrary, they had to fight for their parishioners' rights. The Uniate Church, due to its association with Ukrainian nationalism, suffered extensively during this period.

Polish cultural developments had always been part of the West European intellectual trends. In that respect the re-emergence of the independent state did not initiate any new thinking. It merely enriched and added to those which had manifested themselves earlier. Ideas that emerged from among left-wing and socially engaged writers and painters were perhaps the most interesting. Bruno Jasieński represented the Futurist rebellion, which saw the future in terms of 'the machine, democracy and the mob'. In philosophy Witkiewicz wrote of the death of art as an artificial form. Many authors addressed issues of poverty and deprivation. Stefan Żeromski and Maria Dąbrowska wrote of the disappointment that independence had not brought with it economic well-being. Unusual and interesting were attempts to create new literary forms. Bruno Schulz and Witold Gombrowicz both experimented with different styles. Reflections and soul searching remained the norm and were the driving force for many works. This existential approach is apparent in the writings of Jarosław Iwaszkiewicz and the paintings of Felicjan Kowarski.

Mass culture developed during this period in the form of cinema and radio. Polish cinema initially tried to visualise aural forms of great literary works and only at the end of the 1920s did writers start writing entirely for the screen. Since Yiddish continued to be the dominant language of the Jewish community in eastern Poland, Yiddish publishing thrived as did film production in that language. Few examples of the latter survived war destruction. In 1926 radio broadcasting was inaugurated, but only in 1930, with the building of a network of radio stations, did it spread through Poland. Writers were only too happy to use radio as a means of communicating with a new audience but also to produce works specifically intended for that medium.

The Second World War marked a watershed in the development of Polish culture. The high casualty rate among the intellectuals meant that new people and new forms emerged once war ended. The trauma of the war inevitably created new forms of expression and new themes.

9

The Second World War and the Establishment of Communism in Poland

The German attack on 1 September opened the most tragic chapter in recent Polish history. During the occupation Soviet and German policies towards Poles were driven by political objectives rather than human considerations. Displacement and genocide decreased Poland's population by one-fourth in relation to its pre-war levels. Hundreds of thousands of Poles ended in exile, mainly in the West, unwilling or afraid to return to their country. The war destroyed most of Poland's industrial infrastructure so painfully developed during the inter-war period.

The fate of occupied Polish territories after 1939 was entirely dependent on the whim and policies of the occupying powers. In spite of the fact that Nazi Germany and the Soviet Union were allies until June 1941, their agreements concerning Poland went no further than to define spheres of occupation. Since that was accomplished at the end of September 1939 each government proceeded as it chose. In the mean time, in Paris an exile Polish government was established. General Władysław Sikorski became the Prime Minister and also Commander-in-Chief. He had been one of Piłsudski's most bitter critics and that meant that his relations with the army officers and members of the pre-war government who had made their way to Paris, were always fraught. Most European powers and the US nevertheless recognised it as a legitimate government in exile. The diplomatic battle for the restoration of Poland to its pre-war borders was henceforth fought in the West by that government. The fact that from the outset the Poles decided to form military units, initially in France and after its fall in Britain, meant that they fully participated militarily in joint action against Germany. The Poles were determined to fight for their liberation.

When in the summer of 1941 Germany attacked the Soviet Union, the exile government's situation became difficult. To the Poles the Soviet Union remained as much an enemy as was Nazi Germany. Britain and the US nevertheless needed Soviet assistance and put pressure on the Sikorski government to re-establish diplomatic relations with the Soviet Union. This was always a deeply contentious issue within the exile Polish community and in Poland. In 1943, relations between the exile government and the Soviet Union broke down. In the spring of that year German troops discovered mass graves of Polish officers in the forests of Katyń, territories held by the Red Army during the period 1939–41. The natural suspicion was that these were murders perpetrated by the Soviet Union. When the Polish government asked the Red Cross to investigate the matter, Stalin responded by breaking off diplomatic relations. After that the Soviet authorities, in cooperation with a small group of Polish Communists and left-wing Socialists, proceeded to make plans for a pro-Soviet administration in liberated Poland. Those plans were accepted by Britain and the US and the exile government was sidelined. On 4 July 1943 Sikorski died in a plane accident off Gibraltar. His successors never managed to establish Poland's place in international relations with the same degree of authority. Thus, due to the war, the nature of relations between the countries of the anti-German coalition, and Poland's liberation by the entry of Soviet troops on Polish territories, the fate and political future of Poland were determined not by the Poles themselves but, in varying degrees, by developments beyond their control.

In accordance with the agreement signed by Germany and the Soviet Union on 28 September, the two divided Polish territories with the rivers San, Bug and Narva acting as a frontier. On 12 October 1939 Hitler issued an order designating Poland as occupied territory. Whereas western Poland was incorporated into the Third Reich, the remaining central areas, approximately one-third of pre-war territory, including Warsaw and Kraków, became the *Generalgouvernement* (GG), separated from the Third Reich. Poles were displaced from the western areas to the GG. Hans Frank was nominated as the Governor General. The economy of the GG was to cover the cost of occupation and its residents were seen as slave labour. In addition this was an area where 'undesirable elements' from the Third Reich and other occupied areas were to be dumped. Initially, some attempts were made by the Germans to identify potential collaborators. Wincenty Witos, the leader of the Peasant Alliance, was briefly considered, but he refused to consider this role. Although the leader of the Polish Fascist movement, Bolesław Piasecki, offered himself as leader of a collaborationist administration, he was rejected. By April 1940 Hitler forbade his military commanders to make further plans. Henceforth all talk on the subject of a Polish administration and a nominally independent state was finished. Thus, the reason why Poland never had a collaborationist administration was because the German authorities had no interest in granting the Poles any autonomy. In view of the impending attack on the Soviet Union, Poland remained a militarily sensitive area.

German occupation led to major resettlement of population. By 1942 half a million people had been removed from their homes and settled elsewhere. Poles and Jews were forced out of western Poland, which was incorporated in Germany. In their place ethnic Germans from the Baltic States, Romania, Czechoslovakia and other areas in Eastern Europe were transported and settled on farms vacated under duress, where their presence was to consolidate German control. In areas incorporated into Germany, Polish state property, factories and most industrial stockpiles were confiscated. In the GG area, industry, state property and the property of political parties and trade unions, including most Church property, were taken over by the German administration.

Approximately 1.5 million Poles were forced or induced to go to work in German industry and agriculture. Their treatment was brutal and arbitrary; in effect, they were slave labour with no right to leave their place of employment. By 1941 the German need for food led to the imposition of strict quotas for agricultural deliveries. After 1942 food delivery quotas were raised. The fact that the Poles were starving was not considered relevant to the Nazis. The gradual extermination of the Polish 'race' through hard work was the ultimate objective of the racially motivated economic policies.

German brutality in occupied territories manifested itself from the very moment the Wehrmacht entered Polish towns and villages. This was not merely the by-product of military activities but had been part of earlier prepared plans. Poles who had been associated with the nationalist movement were immediately arrested. Public executions were a method of intimidating the local population even before any organised opposition manifested itself.

All aspects of civilian life were affected by German occupation. Poles aged 14 and upwards were obliged to work; thus all secondary and higher education ceased. Some teaching continued in conspiratorial groups, although this was always precarious and dangerous. The Germans targeted the intellectual elite, and most university lecturers and professors were arrested and incarcerated in concentration camps. Parish priests and the Catholic hierarchy were also arrested. Those arrested were transported to concentration or labour camps where life expectancy was very brief. In addition life in occupied Poland created preconditions for corruption, exploitation and fratricidal conflict.

Notwithstanding the degree of demoralisation in civilian life, Poles created one of the most successful underground movements in occupied Europe. The fact that the German authorities did not depend on a collaborationist administration and that Poland was brutally exploited throughout the war meant that the population forged a high degree of unity of purpose. When the government and high command left Poland in September 1939, those officers who stayed in Poland undertook to organise the underground movement. In due course it assumed the name of Armia Krajowa (Home Army, AK). Impressively, the AK leadership reached agreements with most pre-war parties, uniting them behind a common programme of fighting for liberation. Inevitably discussions of the post-war political system had to be set aside in order that unity prevail. The AK was loyal to the government in exile but for operational purposes it had freedom of action. In addition to creating an underground army, a skeleton of the post-war administration was prepared in the occupied territories. The AK embarked on only a limited campaign against the occupiers, the severity of German retaliations discouraging all but the most vital acts of terror. Instead the AK concentrated on preparing for a national uprising which would enable it to capture power when the Nazis were defeated and before the Red Army entered onto Polish territories. It was hoped that as the Nazis eventually retreated the AK would be able to hold its own for long enough to agree with the incoming Red Army the conditions on which it could continue military action against the Germans in Poland. In this way, it was hoped that an independent Polish government could exercise authority before the Russians could install their own administration.

But the Russians had no intention of allowing a potentially hostile administration to dictate anything to them. In July 1944 the Red Army established a provisional Polish administration in the liberated city of Lublin. In August the AK decided to stage an uprising in Warsaw. The apparent withdrawal of the German units led to hopes that Warsaw could be captured before the Russians arrived. But the uprising failed. After extensive fighting, caused by the German units regrouping and returning to Warsaw, the town was reduced to rubble and its population forcefully removed. The fact that the Soviet units, already on the opposite bank of the Vistula, passively waited for the uprising to be quelled by the Germans has led to the conclusion that the Russians welcomed the destruction of the AK. The failure of the Warsaw uprising, and the inability and unwillingness of the Western Allies to assume responsibility for liberating Poland, as the AK had planned, destroyed the underground structures, so painfully built up during the course of the war.

Other forms of opposition, in particular based on revolutionary and progressive ideas, emerged at the same time in occupied Poland. These were connected with the pre-war left-wing sections of the Socialist Party and with the trade unions. The village-based partisan units, styling themselves the Bataliony Chłopskie (Peasant Battalions, BCh), were committed to the government in exile, but wanted a commitment to land reform after the war. But the AK did not want to discuss future reforms. Cooperation between the two tended to vary depending on the region. The Gestapo's response to all forms of opposition was extremely brutal and the policy of collective responsibility, whereby civilians were shot in reprisal for attacks by the underground, discouraged badly thought out actions.

A Communist-organised partisan movement emerged at the end of 1942, after the Soviet authorities parachuted into Poland a number of leading Communists who had been in Russia. On instructions from the Comintern, the Soviet-controlled association of all Communist parties, they embarked on the policy of building a broad anti-fascist block with a generally progressive, though not revolutionary, programme. Although the Communist-led Armia Ludowa (People's Army, AL) partisan units were active in attacking and sabotaging German communication lines during the crucial years from 1942 onwards, the Soviet Union never supplied them with enough arms to make them into a force of any consequence in occupied Poland. In reality the Communists had no standing in Polish society and never managed to supplant the AK underground organisations. When the Red Army units entered Poland all partisan units were disarmed. The military units of the extreme nationalist movements styling themselves the Narodowe Siły Zbrojne (National Armed Units, NSZ) were suspected of killing Jews who fled from the ghettos and were known to assassinate members of the Communist underground movement.

The German policy of applying different laws to Jews and to non-Jews, combined with a residual Polish anti-Semitism, divided Christian Poles from Jews, assigning each to a distinct tragic fate. Until the German attack on the Soviet Union in the summer of 1941, German laws towards Jews appeared to have evolved progressively. In the GG local military administrators instigated laws restricting the Jews' right of movement, and the Jewish population was forced to wear distinctive markings on their clothes, usually a star of David, and to observe curfews. Those in state employment were summarily dismissed. Jewish property was confiscated, bank accounts blocked, and all Jewish religious and charitable organisations forfeited their property. Approximately 40 ghettos were created in Polish areas, variously organised and separate from the outside world. The Warsaw ghetto was consolidated in September 1940, while the Łódź ghetto, which was to become the largest in the Third Reich, was established in April 1940. The German administration again used collective responsibility as a means of both controlling and exploiting the Jewish population in occupied Poland. The *Judenrat* councils, usually headed by community elders, became responsible for the delivery of work, distribution of food and allocation of accommodation within the ghettos.

When Germany attacked the Soviet Union in the summer of 1941 the Nazis entered territories that had been occupied by the Russians in September 1939. These were areas inhabited by a high proportion of unassimilated Jews. Many of the small towns, *stetels*, were frequently inhabited by more than 60 per cent Jewish population. Recent investigations have revealed that in some cases, after the Russians fled and before the German administration was fully established, Poles took brutal action against the Jews. A recent publication by Jan Gross entitled *Neighbours* has attracted a great deal of attention. In it the author proves conclusively that local Poles massacred the Jewish population of the town of Jedwabne. The relevance of this information is that until recently Poles have maintained that both Christian and Jewish Poles were equally victims of Nazi policies. Jan Gross's book shows that where the opportunity allowed, Christians were capable of murdering their Jewish neighbours. This suggests that the Jedwabne issue might be but the tip of an iceberg, and that, with or without German encouragement, Poles instigated and led pogroms in occupied Polish territories.

German policies towards the Jews of eastern Poland were more precise. As the Werhmacht entered, extermination units moved in to murder the Jewish inhabitants immediately. At the same time preparations were made for the mass extermination of all remaining Jews in Poland, in particular in the large ghettos to which German and Austrian Jews had been deported. In March 1942 a first group of Jews was sent from Chełmn to a purpose-built extermination camp in Bełżec. At the end of May inhabitants of the Kraków ghetto were deported to their deaths in Majdanek. In June the first stage of exterminating Jews in the Warsaw ghetto was under way. By September 1942, 254,000 Warsaw Jews had been murdered in Treblinka. In some ghettos, morally freed from the oppressive principle of collective responsibility, the young surviving Jews staged uprisings. On 19 April 1943 a planned military uprising took place in the Warsaw ghetto where fighting continued until 16 May; similar uprisings took place in Białystok and Będzin. The last large ghetto to survive was in Łódź, where the head of the *Judenrat*, Rumkowski, had succeeded in postponing its liquidation until June 1944, mainly because of the Germans' economic dependence on the work done within the ghetto.

The question of Christian–Jewish relations during the occupation remains a very painful issue. The AK took a long-term view of the need to prepare for the liberation of Poland and was loath to sanction actions which would cause reprisals. It made no commitments to the defence of Jews. During the uprising in the Warsaw ghetto it was reluctant to give the Jews guns since it was known that the resistance would soon collapse and thus valuable resources would be lost. But at the same time, there is no doubt that residual anti-Semitism made it easier for the leadership to view the Jewish tragedy as one which did not involve them. The extreme right made it clear that it welcomed the destruction of the Jewish community. Although no organisational collaboration was established between the nationalist organisations and the German administration, it was known that they made it difficult for Christians to harbour Jews and might have killed Jews in hiding. German decrees specified that anyone hiding Jews would be instantly executed. Inhabitants of any block of flats or house where Jews were found to be hiding would suffer the same fate. This meant that while some Poles who refused to aid Jews were motivated by anti-Semitism, many were simply fearful of the consequences of any

attempt to help them. Nevertheless, individual Jews were hidden by
Christians and children were given shelter in orphanages run by nuns.
Due to the practice of circumcision being nearly entirely confined to
the Jewish community, the Germans found it easier to identify male
Jews and therefore a larger proportion of survivors were women. It is
difficult to ascertain how many Jews survived the war. Some left
Poland immediately after the war, due to continuing anti-Semitism and
violence, which took place after the war. But the number of survivors
might have been no more than 30,000.

In the eastern territories, incorporated into the Soviet Union in
September 1939 and maintained until the German attack in June 1941,
complex and at times contradictory policies were implemented. As the
Poles were defeated in September, the Byelorussian and Ukrainian
populations had reasons to rejoice at the defeat of the army that had,
in the 1930s, been used to pacify Ukrainian villages. Initially the Red
Army arrested all Polish soldiers and after a screening process, officers
were transported into the interior of Russia. They were kept in camps
and attempts were made to identify those who were willing to collaborate with the Soviet authorities in forming a Polish unit. Only one,
Zygmunt Berling, agreed. Approximately 40,000 Polish officers were
then massacred, possibly in 1940 in the forests of Katyń, only to be
discovered by the Germans in 1943. The Polish civilian population in
Soviet-occupied territories experienced great hardship. Community
leaders, including priests and landowners, were arrested; most died. In
October 1939 elections were conducted which, not surprisingly,
resulted in a majority decision for the territories to be incorporated into
the Soviet Union. In the winter of 1940 Poles were forcefully removed
to the interior. Approximately a million Poles were then dispersed
throughout the Soviet Union.

Relief only came in July 1941 when the government in exile signed
an agreement with the Soviet authorities for the creation of Polish
military units. Poles from all over the Soviet Union flocked to
Tashkent where the army was being formed. Families and dependants
congregated around the bases and were taken care of by the Polish
military organisation. By the summer of 1942 Stalin decided he did not
want to keep the Polish units in the Soviet Union and allowed them
to depart for Iran where they came under the command of the
Commonwealth and British Forces in the Middle East. General
Władysław Anders, Commander of the Polish units in the Soviet
Union, had never trusted the Soviet authorities. He did not want the

Polish units to fight with the Red Army and felt that after the defeat of Nazi Germany, the Western Powers would turn against the Soviet Union. Stalin's desire to rid himself of potentially troublesome Poles coincided with Anders's desire to fight with the British. As the Polish solders were evacuated, approximately 40,000 civilians went with them. The British acquired valuable manpower, but in the process had to make provisions for the children, women and the infirm. These were dispersed throughout the Commonwealth, where during the remaining years of the war, to the bewilderment of the local population, colonies of Polish women and children were established. Approximately 100,000 men, now under British command, went into battle in the Italian campaign and distinguished themselves in particular during fighting around the monastery of Monte Cassino. Poles who had not been able to join Anders's units were left in the Soviet Union. After the diplomatic break between Stalin and the Polish government in exile the Soviet Union established a new Polish authority. Związek Patritów Polskich (The Union of Polish Patriots, ZPP), in effect a Communist-led organisation, was initially only given authority to look after the welfare of Poles. In due course, and possibly as a result of a request put to Stalin by one of the most prominent members of the ZPP, Wanda Wasilewska, the Russians agreed to form a new Polish army, this time to fight alongside the Red Army. The Kościuszko Division was led by Berling, by then promoted by Stalin to the rank of general.

It would appear that the Soviet leadership was not entirely clear how it proposed to proceed on the Polish Question. In diplomatic contacts with the Western Powers Stalin always stated that he would not relinquish territories taken in September 1939. Because of British and US dependence on the Soviet military contribution to the defeat of Nazi Germany, the allies were in no position to press the Polish case. Instead, the matter was set aside with a view to discussing it later. In his contacts with Western statesmen, Stalin always maintained that he had no intention of incorporating Poland in the Soviet Union and merely asked for a Polish government that was friendly towards the Soviet Union. The latter phrase was telling, as only the Communists could be relied upon to be friendly to the Soviet Union. But even the Communists were not entirely reliable. In 1938 the Polish Communist Party had been disbanded on Soviet instructions and its leaders in Moscow were shot. The pre-war Komunistyczna Polska Partia (Communist Party of Poland, KPP) was seen as ideologically unreliable and infected with Trotskyism. Therefore when a Communist movement was rebuilt at the Comintern's behest, an entirely new organisation was established and named the Polska Partia Robotnicza (Polish Workers Party, PPR). When the Red Army entered ethnically Polish territories in June 1944 it decided on the future administration. In the first place a Polski Komitet Wyzwolenia Narodowego (Polish Committee of National Liberation, PKWN) was established in the town of Lublin. Hand-picked Communists who had spent the wartime in Russia were appointed to head it. A number of Communists from within occupied Poland, a breakaway section of the Peasant Alliance and members of the Revolutionary wing of the Socialist Party joined it. To all intents the matter of Poland's future was fixed from that point onwards, but neither Churchill nor Roosevelt was willing to be outmanoeuvered in so obvious a way. Churchill in particular had to consider the impact of these decisions on the Polish units under British command. In January the PKWN was recognised by the Soviet Union as the Polish provisional government. Churchill could only insist that Stalin broaden its composition.

Poland's contribution to fighting in the West started when in October 1939 an exile government was formed in Paris. The French had used their influence to assist Sikorski, who they believed would be more pro-French than the old Piłsudski coterie was. But even though representatives of all the main political parties who managed to flee Poland and make their way to Paris supported Sikorski, the military units formed in France, dominated by the officer caste, resented him. Sikorski was unique among the exile leadership for accepting that, notwithstanding the Soviet attack on Poland, diplomatic relations with the Soviet Union would have to be re-established. Nevertheless until the Soviet Union itself became a victim of German aggression this contentious proposal could not be considered. When Germany attacked France, Polish units fought bravely. During the evacuation of British troops from the French coast, approximately 25,000 Polish men were also brought to Britain. One Polish unit left behind, rather than accept surrender, fled to Switzerland. Sikorski and his government came to London, where it formed a turbulent group. Units evacuated from France were sent to Scotland and, in 1944, took part in fighting in Normandy. A Polish Air Force was also formed. The fighter squadrons distinguished themselves during the Battle of Britain, while the bombers crewed by Poles participated in major raids over Germany. Polish naval units fought with the Royal Navy. In Britain Polish servicemen were appreciated for their bravery and commitment. Together with the French, other Commonwealth troops and US they were part of the great war effort on the Western Front.

General Sikorski, uniquely among the exile administrations in London at the time, established very good personal relations with Churchill. The British appreciated his diplomatic skills, his commitment to fighting Germany and above all his determination not to make too many difficulties over the Soviet issue. Sikorski early on accepted that Britain would not wage war against the Soviet Union; on the contrary, he saw that there was a military reason to set aside past ideological differences. Thus when Britain made a commitment to aid the Soviet Union in June 1941 Sikorski followed suit by opening talks with the Soviet ambassador to London. The resulting Sikorski–Maisky agreement allowed for the formation of Polish units in the Soviet Union. Sikorski's policies caused anger within the Polish government and the army in Scotland opposed him. The government was riven with intrigues and conflict, which decreased its authority within the allied community. On 4 July 1943 Sikorski died in a still unexplained plane accident in Gibraltar. The Poles generally suspect the Soviet Union's involvement, as the accident followed the diplomatic break between the two governments. The Gibraltar accident has never been explained to the Poles' satisfaction. Speculation continues to be fuelled by the suspicion that the British government has not disclosed all documents relating to the incident. It has become the subject of numerous publications, some more speculative than others, in which Stalin, Churchill or Roosevelt alternate as the evil force behind the tragic event. Most of them overlook the fact that during his lifetime, Sikorski faced the full brunt of the Polish leadership in exile's suspicions for his alleged excessive subordination to British whims. Only after his death did his reputation grow. Few Poles like to dwell on the painful compromises which he made out of necessity and which, during his lifetime, incurred the enmity of his own community.

After Sikorski's death, while Britain continued to make full use of Polish manpower, there was a growing reluctance to support Poland's cause in dealings with the Soviet Union. The new Polish Prime Minister, Stanisław Mikołajczyk, lacked the diplomatic skills and determination which allowed Sikorski to hold the divided Polish community together. In any case, for Britain and the US, the Soviet ally was too important both in European fighting and in the forthcoming final conflict with Japan, to risk a rupture over Poland. The incorporation of the Polish eastern territories into the Soviet Union was a foregone conclusion. The debate now shifted towards the question of Poland's western border at Germany's expense. The principle of the extension of Poland's western border to the line of the river Oder was accepted at the Yalta Conference and finally approved at Potsdam.

The final composition of the Polish Provisional Government was hammered out between Churchill and Stalin. At Churchill's insistence the already existing administration in Poland was broadened by the addition of representatives of the government in exile. Unfortunately, while Mikołajczyk was browbeaten by Churchill into accepting this compromise, the exile government and its military leadership would have nothing to do with it. Thus Mikołajczyk left for Poland after resigning from the government in exile. As leader of the Peasant Alliance he hoped to exercise considerable authority in Poland and to stem the growth of Communist control. In London, in the mean time, recognition was withdrawn from the government in exile, which was forced to hand all official buildings over to the Warsaw government. The exile government continued in existence, though its relevance was increasingly confined to representing the interests of the approximately 250,000 Polish soldiers and their families in the West. Their dependants were allowed to join them in Britain. As the war came to an end, the welcome which had been previously extended to the Poles diminished. Trade unions came to fear that the Poles would compete with the demobilised British servicemen for jobs. Churchill's initial idea to use the Poles as a policing force in Germany was abandoned. Their forceful return to Poland was thankfully not considered, and they were allowed to remain in Britain where, through a Polish Resettlement Corps, soldiers who were brought to Britain from various operational theatres in Western Europe were dispersed to areas of potential employment. There exists fragmentary evidence that, during the Cold War, some Poles were trained by the British and US authorities to pursue subversive activities in Communist Poland, though the exact scope of these plans is still difficult to ascertain.

From 1945 to 1948, Soviet relations with the wartime allies underwent a change, leading to a near total rupture by 1948. The unresolved German issue, which had security implications for the Soviet Union, and the growing distrust of Soviet objectives in the West, decreased the scope for negotiations between the wartime allies. This state of affairs had a profound impact on Poland's situation. The country was now entirely within the Soviet sphere of influence and the West had little leverage on Soviet decisions. The new administration in the US had no desire to be conciliatory towards the Soviet Union. With the new-found confidence gained through the possession of atomic weapons, the US was less willing to use diplomacy in its dealings with the Soviet Union. The collapse of relations between the West and the Soviet Union led to the division of Europe into two antagonistic camps. The Soviet Union and areas under its direct control were thus cut off from the Western world by an invisible, but impregnable, iron curtain.

At the end of the war Poland's borders had once more changed. The new borders were determined by the course of aggression in September 1939 and subsequent agreements between the allies. Neither the London-based exile government nor the Communist-led first administration after 1944 had any genuine input into deciding the new frontiers. The result was that the Soviet Union retained its 1939 gains, which meant that Poland lost Ukrainian and Byelorussian areas. In the north it gained from Germany Western Prussia, Gdańsk and most of Eastern Prussia, while the Soviet Union retained Konigsberg. In the west the Polish new border was based on the Oder–Neisse line which brought into Poland ethnically German territories. Lost were Lwów and Vilnius, two cities with strong historic links with the old Polish kingdom, whereas Gdańsk, Szczecin and Breslau, now renamed Wrocław, were incorporated into Poland.

From the outset it was assumed that the new state would be more ethnically homogeneous than it had been before. The expulsion of the German population was a foregone conclusion, whereas the Soviet authorities only allowed ethnic Poles to move from the eastern areas to the new Polish state. Ukrainians and Byelorussians in the former Polish territories were compulsorily given Soviet citizenship. The fate of the Germans trapped in Polish territories is not a well-researched subject. After the war there was little sympathy for them; the Poles' tragic fate during the war made them unwilling to dwell on the injustice perpetrated on the German community. The Communist authorities, in search of some popular support and in order to present themselves as a patriotic alternative to the bourgeois pre-war government, did little to air these issues. Only recently, after the fall of Communism and with the passage of time, have Polish historians been able to dispassionately analyse what happened to approximately 4 million ethnic Germans who were resident in the spring of 1945 in territories which were to be incorporated into Poland. Many fled ahead of the Red Army's advances, but the first administration still had to deal with the remaining 3 million people who were German nationals. What was meant to be a planned deportation turned out to be everything but that. The relative weakness of state administration meant that the authorities lost control over the situation very quickly. Poles flooded into the newly acquired territories, in search of goods to pilfer and to acquire farms. Germans, and indigenous people, who had been forced in 1939 to take German citizenship, were terrorised and forced to flee. The latter were mainly the Kasubians and Silesians. When it became apparent that the issue of the Oder–Neisse border was still the subject of international negotiations, the Poles tried to create a fait accompli. In the rush to clear the Germans off areas which they insisted would be incorporated into Poland, they summarily expelled as many Germans as possible. In the winter of 1947 many deportees died as a result of badly organised transports. The phrase 'ethnic cleansing' which has been coined in relation to the Yugoslav crisis of the 1990s should retrospectively be applied to the removal of Germans from Poland and the simultaneous removal of Sudeten Germans from Czechoslovakia. In Germany, the deportees formed strong political pressure groups, which kept alive the memory of the injustice of their removal from ethnically German territories granted to Poland.

The desire to establish an ethnically homogeneous Poland required the authorities to deal with the Ukrainian population in the south-eastern corner of new Poland. Initially the PKWN and the Soviet authorities agreed that they would be resettled to the Soviet Union. Polish military units were used to forcibly remove the Ukrainians from their villages and to send them to the Soviet Ukrainian Republic. As in the case of the treatment of the German communities, the fate of the Ukrainians could not be discussed openly during the Communist period. The willingness of some Ukrainians to collaborate with the Nazis, in the hope of securing an independent state, and the cruelties perpetrated during the war by the Ukrainian units under German command, most notably the SS Galizien, meant that there was little public sympathy for them after the war. Recent research suggests that the Soviet and Polish authorities were arbitrary and punitive towards the Ukrainian communities. In conditions that could best be described as a civil war, whole villages were uprooted. The Ukrainians fought back and the Ukraińska Powstańcza Armia (Ukrainian Partisan Army, UPA), responded by massacring Polish villagers. The Poles wanted to rid themselves of the problem and did not pause to reflect as to why the Ukrainian communities hated the Polish state and cooperated with the Nazis. In 1946, 200,000 Ukrainians still remained in Poland. When the Soviet authorities refused to accept them, the Polish army, in an operation code-named 'Wisła', dispersed them throughout the newly acquired territories. Ukrainian nationals were henceforth forbidden to live in areas which had historically been theirs.

It is difficult to ascertain how many Jews survived the war. Nevertheless, the Polish population showed little sympathy for those few survivors who returned to their towns and villages. Continuing anti-Semitism, lawlessness, anxiety about Jews reclaiming property which had since been appropriated by the Poles or the administration, and simple disregard for Jewish life, all account for the frequency with which individual Jews were killed by Poles. The most notorious was a pogrom which took place in the town of Kielce on 23 July 1946. In a spontaneous attack on a Jewish hostel, 43 Jews were massacred by Poles. Until recently it had been presumed that the Communists organised the pogrom. More recent research suggests that a general state of lawlessness, encouraged by the underground nationalist opposition, combined to create an atmosphere where rumours of Jewish ritual murder of Christian children escalated into a full-scale pogrom. Similar incidents, though on a smaller scale, took place throughout Poland in 1945 and 1946. This accelerated the departure of Jews from Poland. Although a number of prominent personalities in the Communist Party, notably the Minister of Public Safety Radkiewicz, were either known or were suspected to be Jewish, they had no commitment to either the Jewish faith or community. The surviving Jews combined to recreate some form of political representation, but in reality Jewish life in Poland had been destroyed by the Holocaust. Entrenched anti-Semitism and the Communists' unwillingness to risk the little appeal they had on so unpopular a cause ensured that the Jewish heritage would henceforth become a matter of official indifference. More recently the need to attract tourists to Poland has forced official organisations to be more welcoming towards Jews who either seek to visit the country of their origin or to pay their respects to monuments of Jewish martyrdom.

The first government formed a coalition which included the Communists (PPR), left-wing Socialists (PPS) and the Peasant Alliance (PSL). Mikołajczyk's return to Poland and his inclusion in the Provisional Government encouraged hopes that Poland would maintain political pluralism. In reality the Communists retained control of key posts, thus allowing them to make the most important decisions. Until the general elections were to take place, it was intended that national unity should facilitate economic reconstruction. But the continuing presence of the Red Army on Polish territories meant that the PPR, the electorally weakest of the three, had most power. The Russian NKVD in the mean time sought out ex-AK commanders and those deemed to be hostile to the new order. Under sweeping security laws, military courts handed down harsh punishment to those accused of having collaborated with the Nazis or of endangering the security of the present regime. The PPR in the mean time tried to prepare the ground for an electoral victory. The tactic was to form broad coalition groupings, which would go to the elections on a joint list. The PSL, with its continuing strong presence in the villages, hoped to win the majority vote, therefore the PPR tried to tie it into agreements. When this did not work, intimidation and violence were used to destroy the party. In factories and workplaces the PPS dominated trade unions had retained their pre-war popularity. On 30 June 1946, with a strong hold on internal security and the Ministries of Justice and Interior, the Communists staged a national referendum. Its aim was to divide the non-Communist parties. Voters were asked whether they agreed with the abolition of the Senate, with the incorporation of the ex-German lands, now named the Recovered Territories, into Poland and with the government's policies of nationalisation of industry and land reform. While the obvious answer to all three was 'Yes', the PPR declared a three times 'Yes' vote to be a vote of confidence for their policies. The PSL was left without a clear alternative platform. In an obviously rigged vote the PPR secured an endorsement for its policies. In the general elections on 19 January 1947 the Communists made sure they won a majority. As a result of blatant intimidation the PSL was destroyed. In October Mikołajczyk fled the country. Within the coming year all independent organisations were either integrated into the Communist umbrella organisations or were destroyed. The PPS, after an agonising series of conferences, accepted the demand for organisational unity of the working class and in December was absorbed into the PPR-dominated Polska Zjednoczona Partia Robotnicza (United Polish Workers' Party, PZPR), which would rule Poland until the fall of Communism in 1989.

As the borders of Poland changed and the composition of the population altered, creating a near absolute Polish majority, so the Catholic Church gained in importance. In the north-east in particular around the town of Białystok the Orthodox Christian Church still had a foothold. Within the Silesian regions the Lutheran Church remained dominant.

The Uniate Church, because of the destruction of the Ukrainian communities, suffered likewise. Thus the Catholic Church gained in importance as the single largest faith in modern Poland. It emerged from the war with enhanced authority and this increased during the difficult period of reconstruction and Communist oppression. The Communists initially tried to reach an accommodation with the Church and talks were conducted to ascertain whether a Catholic Party could be established. The Catholic hierarchy opposed this. As a result Pax, a small splinter organisation with representation in the Sejm, emerged. Pax was allowed to run its own publishing house and conduct small-scale charitable works. The fact that Church properties were not nationalised until 1950 is indicative of the Communists' unwillingness to seek a confrontation with an organisation which was still the focal point of Polish spiritual life. The Papacy's aggressive policy towards the Communist regimes did cause the Polish episcopate some difficulties, in particular because the Vatican refused to accept the incorporation of the Recovered Territories into Poland. This came from an anxiety not to upset the German Federal Republic, which did not recognise the loss of Germany's eastern territories to Poland. Before Polish bishops could be appointed, delicate negotiations had to be conducted with the German Catholic Church. It was a foregone conclusion that Poles would not attend churches served by German priests, so initially the Recovered Territories became part of the Polish episcopate for administrative reasons. Only when the German bishops were induced to resign, could Polish bishops be appointed.

During the Stalinist period, Poland in common with all other satellite states experienced the full measure of Soviet domination. Whereas during the earlier period a veneer of pluralism was maintained, in 1948 the Communists assumed control over all aspects of civilian, economic and political life. In the process, the Communist movement was transformed into a totally obedient tool of Soviet policies. In September 1948 Władysław Gomułka, Secretary of the PZPR, was dismissed from his party post and relieved of all his governmental duties as deputy Prime Minister and Minister with special responsibilities for the Recovered Territories. Unlike his successor Bierut, Gomułka had never been a Moscow man, his political experiences were confined to Poland and he spent the wartime period building up the underground Communist movement. After 1945 he was an outspoken supporter of the 'Polish road to socialism' which accepted Poland's commitment to the Soviet model, but

insisted on national variations, notably a slower pace of industrialisation and no collectivisation.

But in 1948, with the onset of the Cold War, Soviet policies
changed. Communist parties in the Soviet bloc were instructed to take
power. The break with Yugoslavia led to witch-hunts. Whereas earlier
there were some debates on just what route Communists were to take
to power, from 1948 these were viewed as treasonable. In 1951
Gomułka was arrested and accused of 'titoist deviation'. Although
never tried, he was kept under house arrest until 1955. Many of his
party colleagues and collaborators were not so lucky. In 1950 Deputy
Chief of Staff Marian Spychalski, a veteran of the Spanish Civil War,
was arrested, tortured and accused of contact with the AK. As the
circle of arrests widened, those who had fought in the Spanish Civil
War were identified as possible deviationists from the Stalinist line.
Although the purges were not as bloody as those conducted by the
Hungarian and Czechoslovak parties, victims were tortured and some
committed suicide. The whole process was led by a triumvirate of
Moscow-trained Communist ideologues, Bolesław Bierut, Hilary
Minc and Jakub Berman. The nature of the purges and the manner in
which confessions were extracted from the accused became known in
the West when one of the key agents of the Security Service Józef
Światło defected to the West in December 1953 and revealed details in
broadcasts beamed over Poland by Radio Free Europe, a station
financed by the US Central Intelligence Agency.

The imposition of the Stalinist system on Polish society affected all
aspects of daily life. All Poles who had had any contact with the West
were suspect. Those who had fought with the British forces and returned
to Poland were arrested. Participation in wartime resistance movements,
other than the Communist one, was deemed to have been an act of
betrayal and many ex-AK members suffered imprisonment. In factories,
mines and enterprises, where standards of pay fell and production quotas
were increased, workers realised that any attempt to negotiate better
work conditions was treated with extreme harshness. The power of trade
unions and factory committees was reduced to organising workers' holidays and entertainment. The educational system was modelled on the
Soviet one, and army reform based on the Soviet army. Soviet officers
were appointed to the Polish army, most notably Marshal Rokossovsky
who, although of Polish descent, was Russian.

Relations between the Communist state and the Catholic Church,
precariously balanced since 1945, deteriorated in 1950. Individual

priests were arrested, accused variously of spying, having collaborated with the Nazis during the war and of supporting the underground opposition. When in 1948 Primate Hlond died, he was succeeded by Stefan Wyszyński. During the following two years the state proceeded to limit further the Church's prerogatives by taking over the Caritas charitable foundation and stripping the Church of its rights to register births, deaths and marriages. Church properties continued to be confiscated. The Communists were particularly intent on splitting the Church, which they did by interfering in the question of nomination of bishops. In 1953 Wyszyński was prevented from travelling to Rome where the Pope was to confer on him the rank of Cardinal. In September he was arrested. At the Church's request he was not imprisoned but placed under house arrest in a convent.

The transformation of Polish society was driven by the great economic changes which were initiated in 1950 by the Six-Year Plan. As the world divided into two hostile camps, so the Soviet Union both financed and determined the pace of economic investments in the satellite states. Trade and economic exchanges with the industrial capitalist states became very limited. The Soviet Union aimed at creating an independent economic base for its own and the satellite states' economic development. With the stress on heavy industry, mainly steel and coal production, consumer and light industries were severely neglected. Machine production, chemicals and electrification were prioritised. All forms of private production and retail trade ceased. Cooperatives, which had developed extensively in Poland during the inter-war period, lost their independence. The great showcase of the Stalinist exertion was the building of the Nowa Huta steelworks outside Kraków and the new town which was to house workers brought in from the countryside to work in it. The centre of the town was dominated by an enormous opera house, but the absence of churches was telling.

The Stalinist period did at the same time create new opportunities. The great emphasis on education led to investment in primary education, which allowed a larger proportion of children than ever before to have access to free education. In admission to secondary schools and universities children from peasant and working-class families were favoured. Scholarships and student accommodation were offered to children from poor backgrounds, thus making it possible for them to gain an education. Technical schools, evening schools and correspondence courses were established to enable the workforce to improve its

qualifications. Adult illiteracy was rapidly eliminated. The composition of the professional classes was thus altered in future years.
Foreign visitors and the old elites frequently scoffed at these people's
uncouth manners and lack of grooming; nevertheless investment in
education provided opportunities for those who sought them. The
teaching of Marxism was compulsory at degree level, and from the age
of 12 all children had to learn Russian. The first was not as oppressive
as it seems. Few university teachers understood Marxism and a degree
of complicity existed between the teachers and the students few of
whom treated the matter seriously. Not much could be done about
Russian language teaching though, since most teachers of Russian
were Poles displaced from the east who hated the Russians. The task
tended to be discharged with ill grace, and with no threat of the children being indoctrinated. For the first time in their lives, workers were
given subsidised holidays, and were encouraged to enjoy some leisure
activities. A standard sight was that of factory trucks and tractors being
used to ferry workers to lakesides for picnics. Children of factory
workers benefited from subsidised summer holidays. The health
system, destroyed during the war period, was rebuilt at great expense.
A point of pride for the Poles was the fact that tuberculosis among children was eradicated.

On 5 March 1953 Stalin died. In the ensuing year, as the battle for
succession was fought out in the Kremlin, East European Communist
leaders, so used to being given instructions as how to proceed, floundered. By September Nikita Khrushchev established his authority in
the Soviet Communist Party and in the following years, after a
cautious start, changes took place in Poland. Światło's revelations
made a great impact on Polish society. He confirmed what was
generally known about the purges and persecutions even if their full
extent was hitherto unknown. He also revealed that Communist leaders enjoyed a privileged lifestyle and access to scarce goods. The
PZPR was horrified by these revelations. The scope of arrests was
scaled down and gradually political prisoners were granted am-
nesties. Censorship was reduced and, in 1954, the Writers' Union
was for the first time allowed to debate the impact of Stalinism. In
1955 through the process of testing of boundaries of what would be
tolerated, it became apparent that a more robust criticism would be
allowed. The weekly publication *Po Prostu* led the way. Adam
Ważyk and Marek Hłasko are two writers closely connected with this
period.

In 1956 demands for change grew more vocal. Khrushchev's denunciation of Stalinist excesses at the Twentieth Party Congress on 25 February followed by Bierut's death in March forced the party to consider its future role. The party hierarchy, which had for too long lived in isolation from the population, faced widespread discontent. On 28 June strikers in Poznań took to the streets. The army was sent in and in the ensuing battles 56 were killed. State media tried to prevent the information from leaking out, but Radio Free Europe publicised the facts. Throughout the summer the party leadership debated its options. Although the hardliners still held sway, the leadership prudently decided to accept that Gomułka, recently released from house arrest, was their best option. A sense of euphoria and hope inspired Poles once more. They were sufficiently realistic to accept that the Soviet Union would not allow Poland to leave the Soviet bloc. What most wanted was better provisions, decent pay, a larger degree of accountability and a modicum of religious and political freedom. In October in a speech to a full meeting of the Central Committee of the PZPR Gomułka called for democratisation. But before this could be implemented Soviet approval was necessary. When Khrushchev accompanied by his military leaders flew to Poland the situation looked set for a crisis. But the Polish leadership rerouted their plane to a smaller airport, avoiding popular mobilisation, and then in negotiations with the Soviet leaders persuaded them that the party was in control of the pace of change. They were given the chance to prove this and in the coming months Gomułka was able to pacify the disaffected by promising reforms, the scaling down of the industrial plans, decollectivisation and the scrapping of agricultural delivery quotas. By proving to the Soviet leadership that the party would remain in control of the changes and prevent any challenge to Soviet supremacy and military interests, the Poles were able to prevent a Soviet invasion.

In the years to follow Gomułka disappointed many of his supporters. After a brief period of freedom, censorship was reimposed. He did disband the Security Service and Cardinal Wyszyński was released from house arrest. The Soviet Union reviewed its unequal trade agreements with Poland. Soviet military and economic advisers were recalled to the Soviet Union. Nevertheless Poland continued as a Communist regime. The Hungarian experience, in particular, reinforced the need for caution and moderation, something the Poles had learned to do.

During the 1960s Poland was a country in which appearances conflicted with realities in a paradoxical way. It was ruled by a

Communist Party which came to appreciate the need for some public consensus. Economic well-being and security from the still nagging fear of German frontier claims were a way of securing a degree of public support. The regime tried to provide a moderately satisfactory standard of living for all. A massive building programme and the development of educational opportunities were part of this aim. Censorship remained in place, but authors and journalists learned to live with it and to deal with contentious issues in an oblique way. There was also a greater openness in dealing with the capitalist world. Books written by foreign authors were translated into Polish, even if this was done with no regard for the authors' rights. Foreign films, including those from the US, were regularly shown in Poland. Travel to Western Europe was permitted, even though whole families were never allowed to go together for fear that they would defect. Behind the scenes a special mixed commission was established by the Church and state to discuss contentious issues and to arrive at a mutually acceptable state of affairs.

The early 1960s were a time of moderate optimism and hope of better things to come. Poles felt that politically and culturally they were allowed to become part of the developments affecting Europe. Acceptance of Soviet domination was the price to be paid for this optimism, but at least for the time being, this seemed bearable.

10

From Solidarity to the European Union

During the 1960s Poles experienced a degree of stability and economic well-being which made life under Communism bearable. The state policy of maintaining full employment meant that, irrespective of the economic consequences to enterprises, workers could always find work. They generally had no experience of the debilitating consequences of unemployment. Expansion in coal mining, steel production and the chemical industry combined to guarantee economic progress. During the mid-1960s Poles started to enjoy access to consumer goods, better clothes, household and electrical goods, usually items imported from other Communist countries. Political links between the Soviet bloc and newly independent countries of the Third World brought to Poland exotic goods, even if these were at times neither required nor sought. During the Cuban crisis, Poland, a producer of sugar beet, was flooded with sugar cane, while the Suez crisis resulted in a similar bounty of sesame seed, sesame halva and leather goods on the Polish markets.

Nor was Poland closed off from the Western world. Radio Free Europe informed Poles of most important international events, and frequently of developments taking place in Poland. A successful network of informers kept the Munich-based radio up to date with what was happening in Poland, and this guaranteed the broadcasts a loyal audience. Poles learned to ignore most political pronouncements made by their own government, instead gleaning information from foreign radios and the grapevine. Limited cultural and educational exchanges were developed between Poland, West European states and the US. Poles resumed travelling to the West and the US. Employment in French vineyards, vegetable farms in Britain, and on farms in Germany and Belgium all provided opportunities to bring back foreign currency which when converted into Polish złoty guaranteed a degree of luxury otherwise unattainable. Unfortunately these trips rarely gave the Poles a deeper understanding of life in the West.

In spite of being a Soviet satellite state, Poland managed to maintain a degree of independence. In the West, Poland was identified with interesting cultural trends. Thus in addition to the rather predictable Chopin annual festivals, jazz festivals attracted to Poland enthusiasts from abroad. Witold Lutosławski and Krzysztof Penderecki's compositions appeared to be bold and original. The Western musical world considered them striking. Polish film productions became synonymous with outspoken themes. Andrzej Wajda, Jerzy Skolimowski and Agnieszka Holland made films which attracted international attention. Sławomir Mrożek and Stanisław Lem, once their plays and books were translated into Western languages, acquired a devoted following. Only in a dictatorship, dominated by the constant fear of censorship, could producers develop such skill for addressing controversial issues in a nuanced way. Thus, as long as the regime was not confronted in a direct way and as long as no challenge was posed to Soviet domination, film producers, writers and theatre directors were provided with facilities to create critical works.

The period of political stability ended with economic stagnation from the mid-1960s. With full employment guaranteed, the economic stagnation appeared as shortages of consumer goods. 'Meat crises' aroused suspicions that scarce consumption goods were being diverted to the Soviet Union, or to satisfy the appetites of party functionaries. Political discontent culminated in the events of 1968. Earlier the University of Warsaw already had become a centre of debate on the shortcomings of the Communist regime and its policies. A number of prominent Marxists had expressed disagreement with economic and social policies. Leszek Kołakowski, Włodzimierz Brus and Zygmunt Bauman were well known for their vocal disagreements with the course and pace of developments. They were also known in West European academic circles, which might explain why the government decided to silence them. Younger dissidents were just as vocal. Jacek Kuroń, Adam Michnik and Karol Modzelewski came to prominence as student activists. In March 1968 simmering discontent with censorship, political restrictions and stagnation led first to protests at the University of Warsaw and then at universities elsewhere in the country. The government's heavy-handed response made things worse. Police units and civilian militias were bussed into the university campuses and proceeded to break up the protests and to beat up students. The explanation that these were worker activists, disgusted by the students' abuse of the intellectual freedom granted them by the regime, fooled no one. In the purges that followed, prominent academics were stripped of their posts and students were expelled.

But closely connected with these demonstrations was an ongoing internal party conflict. Party infighting overlapped with the purges which followed the student demonstrations. In the mid-1960s a nationalist group led by a wartime partisan Mieczysław Moczar, came out against Gomułka's faction. The Arab–Israeli conflict acted as a background to conflicts within the party. When the Soviet Union took up the Arab cause, Jews came under suspicion for their alleged divided loyalties. A high proportion of Jews who after the war had decided to stay in Poland, were either in the party or active in the creative arts and media. Moczar could not attack Gomułka directly, without being accused of the ultimate crime in intra-party politics, that of 'factionalism'. Instead he concentrated on the 'Zionist' menace. Under the guise of exposing Zionists, who were supposed to have an unquestioning loyalty to Israel, Moczar and his clique proceeded to expose 'disloyal' Jews. The remnants of the Jewish community in Poland, numbering no more than 20,000, found themselves squeezed out of their jobs, thrown out of schools and universities and finally forced out of Poland. As they left, in a final gesture of humiliation, they were stripped of Polish citizenship. Gomułka was not able to stem the anti-Semitic purges, though he himself had no record of anti-Semitism. Within the party leadership Moczar's nationalist group, which adopted the name Grunwald, remained active, stirring up anti-Semitic feelings.

In the coming years, positive discrimination in favour of students from peasant and worker backgrounds was increased. Male students were also obliged to do a longer period of military training while all had a duty to do stints of community work during the summer vacation, the aim of which was to bring them closer to the toiling masses. The regime moved against the intellectuals, fearful that they would find unity with the increasingly frustrated and economically thwarted workers. The Catholic Church, which always strove to balance its own interests against that of acting as spiritual leader to the community, found itself increasingly thrust into the forefront of the debates. The Catholic weekly *Tygodnik Powszechny* continued to voice criticism of the regime, though it too always had to be careful not to provoke too much anger, which would have led to its closing, as had happened during the Stalinist period. Two Sejm Catholic clubs Pax and the genuinely independent Znak continued to function, the latter tentatively criticising the government and addressing controversial issues.

During the period 1968–70 the economic situation worsened. The sense of well-being which was the bedrock upon which the Communists built the regime crumbled. Food shortages and irregular supplies to shops became widespread. In the winter of 1970 an attempt was made to balance the situation in the consumption goods markets by increasing prices of basic foods. Riots broke out in the Gdynia and other coastal towns. The authorities responded with brutality and workers were shot. While the government tried to hide the facts, Radio Free Europe informed the Poles of the events. Gomułka resigned and was replaced by Edward Gierek.

The Gomułka period was one of hope followed by disappointment. After the 1956 riots, Poles were generally willing to work with the regime, on the condition that it provided them with the basics of daily life. When the government failed to deliver the goods, disaffection with economic difficulties quickly turned to anger with the repressive political system, as the government continued to maintain that nothing was amiss. Housing shortages became one of the most pressing problems in the mid-1960s. The post-war demographic bulge was the cause of these difficulties, but bad planning and increasingly shoddy building compounded it. Housing programmes lagged behind growing demand, and most young people continued to live in cramped conditions with their parents, even after marriage. Standards of living stagnated. Central planning failed to resolve continuing problems of production and supply. What Poles had been forced to suffer, in the period of post-war recovery, they were no longer willing to tolerate as permanent features of an allegedly superior socialist system at the end of the 1960s.

Although a member of the Warsaw Pact and Comecon, Poland had managed to retain a degree of independent standing in world politics. The German problem continued to be the single most important issue as the Federal German Republic refused to recognise frontier changes after the Second World War. In 1957, as part of an attempt to review the German issue, Poland, under Soviet tutelage, put forward a plan for the demilitarisation of Central Europe. The so-called Rapacki Plan, named after the Polish Minister for Foreign Affairs, would have resulted in both German republics, Poland and Czechoslovakia making commitments not to station nuclear weapons on their territories. Unfortunately, with the collapse of the German talks, this initiative was lost. Only in December 1970 did Poland and the Federal Republic of Germany sign a treaty, which recognised the Oder–Neisse frontier. As a result of the normalisation of relations between the two states, German nationals who remained after 1945 were allowed to leave Poland.

Throughout the late 1960s and the 1970s relations between state and Church continued to be characterised by tension. The most obvious conflicts had ended, but the state was determined that the Church's role in society was kept to a minimum and that all symbols of religious observance were removed from public areas. An earlier Church initiative to seek reconciliation with the German Catholics by declaring that 'We forgive and seek forgiveness', was met with an attack on alleged Church meddling in foreign policy. Few Poles, however observant, accepted that they had anything to apologise for in relation to the war and post-war period. In 1966 all celebrations of the millennium of Polish Christianity were kept to a minimum by the state. Instead the Communists proclaimed an initiative of building an additional thousand schools to commemorate the millennium. The state's obvious attempts to induce young people not to participate in Church activities usually took the form of state television screening rare and exciting American films, at times of worship.

Unlike Gomułka who was an austere and reclusive person, Gierek was an outgoing and forthright man. While Party Secretary of the Katowice mining district he was well liked for looking after his fiefdom and securing for the miners a high standard of living. A miner by profession, he had worked in French and Belgian mines in the 1930s. He spoke fluent French. During the workers' strikes in 1970 and 1971 he made the unusual gesture, for a party leader, of going directly to the striking workers and asking them what was needed to improve their working and living conditions. His general attitude that, after a hard day's struggle building socialism, the workers deserved to relax in comfort, was welcomed by Poles, tired of shortages and queuing.

The Gierek regime started optimistically. Unfortunately by 1975 economic problems overwhelmed Poland. Gierek had tried to acquire West European advanced technology to accelerate production and improve the quality of goods. It was presumed that this would be paid for through exports to the West. Unfortunately the growth of exports proved insufficient. State enterprises had overextended themselves and foreign debt spiralled out of control. Investments made were badly thought out and were too ambitious. In many cases the central authorities authorised too many badly conceived and unviable projects. The oil crisis of 1974 undermined the West's willingness and capacity to buy from Poland. Further loans proved necessary to finish projects and, disastrously, to service the existing debt. Poland's indebtedness rose alarmingly.

By the mid-1970s Gierek tried to rein in the economy. But this proved impossible. In any case, Poles had come to expect a higher standard of living, and attempts to introduce new pricing schemes caused dangerous backlashes. Price increases, in particular of meat, which the Poles consumed in large quantities, caused strikes. While the government pulled back from a confrontation, it was obvious that there was a need for a major reassessment of the way the economy was regulated.

To Western visitors Poland presented a bewildering picture of inconsistencies. Shops were empty; most grocery shelves appeared to be stacked with bottles of vinegar. At the same time Poles were better dressed than ever before and in the major cities the quality of life seemed to compare well with any West European state even though it was impossible to buy any food or proper clothes in state-run shops. In reality what had happened was that the black market supplied most needs. It had replaced the official state-run and controlled retail system. Fewer goods were distributed through the official outlets, frequently going directly from factory gates into the black market. Enterprises, factories and institutions employed special provisioning agents, who undertook to obtain items of daily need and to distribute them to employees. To Western academics visiting the Polish Academy of Sciences, the sight of respected academicians queuing in the canteen to obtain cheese, tea or even socks which the provisioning agent might have laid his hands on, presented a very odd sight. As the shortage became worse, charitable organisations started sending goods to Poland. Though grateful for this help, Poles found it very humiliating to be placed in such a situation.

Disaffection and anger caused by the economic situation were fuelled by repressive measures taken by the police against those who dared to criticise it. The corruption and venality among provincial party leaders, the police and managers of state enterprises were impossible to overlook. In the mid-1970s political demands were added to the list of grievances voiced by the striking workers. In 1976 the Komitet Obrony Robotników (Committee for the Defence of Workers, KOR) was established. The unusual feature of this organisation was that it was entirely self-effacing. Consisting mainly of intellectuals and professional people, its aim was to assist and aid the workers in their demands, but not to assume the leadership of the opposition. In addition to the known young dissidents from the University of Warsaw, KOR consisted of a number of well-known Catholic intellectuals gathered around the parliamentary group Znak.

During the late 1970s the party faced its own crisis. Young and bolder members were no longer prepared to accept party discipline unquestioningly. Attempts were made to force a greater degree of consultation and to allow the grass roots to have a say in policy making. But the staid and increasingly anxious party leadership was not willing even to trust its younger membership. In any case the party had become a route to promotion and a means of securing posts. Ideology had long ceased to play a role in its policies. Two factors tipped the balance in favour of the disaffected. The first was the election of a Polish Pope in 1978 and the second the outbreak of workers' strikes in the Gdańsk shipyard in 1980.

On 16 October 1978 an announcement from the Vatican that the Polish Cardinal Karol Wojtyła was elected to become the next Pope electrified Poland. Before his elevation he had been the Archbishop of Kraków. Wojtyła assumed the title of John Paul II. Traditionally the Italian and occasionally Spanish Church had monopolised the Papacy. For Polish Catholics this seemed a recognition of the nation's commitment to Christianity and, in many ways also, a reward for their piety and suffering through the years. Apart from the profound international implications of the selection of a Pole to the Papacy, in Poland the Church's authority was confirmed and henceforth grew. Whereas the Eastern Orthodox Christian churches had reached an accommodation with the Communists, the Catholic Church had consistently refused to compromise publicly. The Polish Church had the added advantage that it had been untainted by collaboration during the Nazi occupation. Polish priests had been victims of Nazi policies of destroying the national elite. The association of the Hungarian and Croat Catholic churches with pro-Nazi wartime dictatorships had stripped those churches of moral authority. In Poland the leadership arrived at a degree of accommodation with the Communist regime, but avoided creating the impression of complicity. Furthermore, unlike the

Hungarian anti-Communist Primate Cardinal Mindszenty, whose combative style led the Vatican to silence him after his release from the US
embassy in 1971, Cardinal Wyszyński sought to defend the Church's
prerogatives, without challenging the Communists. In that he was
successful and Pope John Paul was able to build on those achievements.

By all accounts, Wojtyła had been a genuinely popular archbishop.
Lacking guile and modest in his lifestyle, he shared many of his
parishioners' interests and leisure activities, namely skiing and mountain walking. In a community which still identified Jews in hostile
terms, Wojtyła was unusual for showing respect for the Jewish faith.
His return visit to Poland in June 1979 marked a watershed. The
Communist state and its apparatus could not ignore the arrival of a
Pole of such prominence in world affairs and the Poles joyously celebrated their faith and their Pope.

However, continuing economic difficulties rather than political
objectives stimulated workers to take matters into their hands. It is
doubtful whether in August 1980, when strikers in the Gdańsk ship-
yards took action, they aimed to break the power of the state. The
immediate background to the events in Gdańsk were the price
increases of meat. Throughout the summer anger simmered in most
large enterprises. Workers started forming free trade unions, since they
had no confidence in the state-approved ones. In the shipyard, the
sacking of a popular, politically active woman crane driver Anna
Walentynowicz sparked the first strikes. Quickly the strike committee
added other grievances to the original one for the reinstatement of
Walentynowicz. Negotiations with the management were taken over
by the male workers, but it was the women who refused to accept
compromises and called the men back from the brink of surrender. On
14 August the workers started an occupation strike. At this point they
were joined by Lech Wałęsa, an electrician who had been earlier
sacked for political activism. Wałęsa was a very popular worker. His
simple but forthright approach to issues galvanised other workers. He
and his colleagues first organised the Gdańsk shipyard occupation and
then coordinated action with other enterprises along the coast. Within
days they successfully brought all production to a standstill. Photos of
the shipyard gates draped in pictures of the Pope, national emblems
and most importantly, Catholic symbols circulated the world, creating
powerful and unforgettable images. The presence among the strikers
of the local parish priest Father Jankowski confirmed the Catholic

character of the protest. The intellectual-led KOR was invited to assist in preparing for negotiations with government representatives, but it was never allowed to take over, nor did it seek to do anything but to offer advice. Thus the workers remained entirely in control of the negotiations. On 31 August the government delegation which had come to the yard conceded the workers' right to set up free trade unions. A number of other demands were agreed on at the same time, mainly relating to social issues. Nevertheless it was the first which had the most important consequences for the future development of Poland.

Until the imposition of martial law on 13 December 1981, the free trade unions, now adopting the name Solidarity, increased their political power and, though never fully accepting that role, became co-rulers with the Communist Party. Gierek was forced to resign, and his successor Stanisław Kania had to accept that, with the membership of the Solidarity movement rising to 10 million, its power could not be overlooked. Surprisingly there was a great degree of willingness on the party's part to co-opt the new trade unions in decision making. Poland's economic situation was becoming increasingly perilous, with international debt spiralling out of control. With production levels collapsing, the state was unable to service the debt and by 1981 the Polish government and state enterprises owed $25 billion to foreign banks. Without some degree of cooperation between the state and the people, the situation could only get worse.

The leadership of Solidarity consciously opted for a federated struc-ture. The founding members of the Solidarity movement believed that this would be a better guarantee of the trade union remaining receptive to workers' demands. There was also the anxiety that the government would find it easier to establish control over the new trade unions if they were centralised. But the biggest dilemma facing the trade union from the outset was that of its role beyond the workplace. As much as some work-ers wanted Solidarity to confine itself to what is perceived to be trade union functions, it was inevitably drawn into state decision making. Its authority was strong and widespread, while the government's prestige had collapsed. Workers would not agree to price restructuring unless Solidarity approved it. At the same time there was an urgent need to address issues such as wages, working conditions, social provisions and food supply. Workers in most cases refused to act without Solidarity's approval. The Catholic Church, led by Cardinal Wyszyński, cautioned against making excessive demands and counselled moderation. Within

the Solidarity movement Wałęsa fought hard to hold back the hotheads
who wanted to challenge the state in various ways or call general strikes.
The Church put its authority behind Wałęsa, seeing in him a moderating
influence. He was known for his piety. His willingness to follow the
Church's guidance made him an obvious choice in Wyszyński's policy of
limiting the consequences of the radicalisation of Polish society. In due
course most of the founding members of the Solidarity movement were
sidelined and Wałęsa's authority as Solidarity's national leader was not
challenged.

The international situation had an important bearing on developments in Poland. President Reagan warned the Soviet Union not to
interfere. Within the Soviet leadership and military high command, the
desire to stem the growth of dissent in Poland was moderated by a real-
isation that, were the Warsaw Pact countries to take action as they
had in Czechoslovakia in 1968, civil war would ensue. Hardline
Communist leaders in Czechoslovakia and the Democratic Republic of
Germany, fearful of the Polish example spreading, advocated intervention. In the end the Soviet Union decided to advise the Polish leadership to take action against the trade union.

The declaration of martial law in December 1981 at a stroke
rendered Solidarity an illegal organisation. Thousands of activists,
including Wałęsa, were detained in specially established camps. The
most striking feature of the period which followed was the fact that it
was not the Communist Party, but the army which was authorised by
the Soviet Union to assume control of Poland. It is still not clear
whether the Soviet leadership deemed the party too weak and demor-
alised to do so, or whether it feared that such action would have
precipitated a backlash. The man who headed the new government was
General Wojciech Jaruzelski. He was not well known before the imposition of martial law, other than that he and his family had been
deported by the Soviet authorities to Siberia during the war. Jaruzelski
has since tried to paint a benign picture of his motives for the imposition of martial law, insisting on a patriotic duty to overcome the crisis.
In reality, political motives must have been foremost in the minds of
the Soviet leadership, when deciding on action in Poland. In addition
to anxiety about the impact of political developments in Poland on the
remaining countries of the Warsaw Pact, irritation about the way the
Polish issue impacted on Soviet relations with the world powers
played a role. Domestically, economic stabilisation remained an urgent
priority.

Initially all forms of social associations were banned, all enterprises came under the control, or at least the scrutiny, of military commissioners, and a curfew was imposed. Poles, weary with strikes and shortages, supported passive opposition, but in reality could do nothing. Some Solidarity leaders managed to elude arrest and formed underground organisations, which published newsletters and periodically broadcast defiant pronouncements on illegal radio stations. Several attempts were made to call general strikes, which aroused widespread sympathy but were increasingly only partly supported by the exhausted population.

By April 1982 Jaruzelski's government had gradually opened up avenues for a dialogue with the opposition. The death of Cardinal Wyszyński and the appointment of Archbishop Józef Glemp as Primate of All Poland, allowed for the scaling down of conflict with the Church. Glemp was less willing to sanction the Church's direct involvement in political affairs. Jaruzelski's policy continued to be that of heavy-handed suppression of all forms of opposition, but at the same time, by scaling down some of the more oppressive measures and stabilising the economy, he created preconditions for some reconciliation. Wałęsa was released from internment in November 1982. In October 1983 he was awarded the Nobel Peace Prize. The Pope visited Poland in June of the same year. Slowly, talks were resumed between the government and the opposition, even if Solidarity still remained a proscribed organisation. Martial law was ended in July.

At the time it looked as if the political achievements of the 1980–81 period had come to nothing. The intellectuals and artists, after a brief period of boycotting all radio, television and publishing, drifted back to work. Young Solidarity activists, mainly students, who fled abroad, found to their surprise that life in the capitalist economy was far from what they had expected on the basis of their viewing of the US TV soaps. More importantly, with Soviet assistance, the regime managed to overcome some of the worst shortages and was able to guarantee supplies of food and household goods which, however, continued to be rationed. The slow process of reconciliation between the people and the regime was rudely broken in October 1984, when a popular priest Father Popiełuszko was murdered, as it transpired subsequently, by the police. During the martial law period the Church provided shelter for political activists and also meeting places where current problems could be freely discussed. A number of young priests played a very active role, providing assistance to families of interned Solidarity members and supporting the workers and the poor. Father Popiełuszko was one of those young priests and his death caused outrage. The regime managed to save itself by allowing an open trial of the policemen. Doubts persisted as to why the accused believed that they had the authority to silence the priest by killing him. But for the time being the regime survived. In the summer of 1986 all those still detained under martial law were amnestied.

By 1987 discussions taking place in Poland were given a new impetus by changes which had taken place in the Soviet Union. In 1985 Mikhail Gorbachev became First Party Secretary. Even before his election it was known that he would seek to reform the Communist Party of the Soviet Union and would re-establish a dialogue with the US. He took measures to make the Communist Party in the Soviet Union more accountable. To leaders of Communist parties in Eastern Europe, who were used to receiving detailed instructions from the Soviet leadership as to how to proceed in relation to their internal opposition, this change was daunting. At the same time, they realised that détente would result in the Soviet Union allowing its satellite states a larger degree of freedom. This in turn meant that the Soviet Union would not be willing to underwrite untenable internal policies. For the Jaruzelski government, struggling to cope with a growing foreign debt, which in 1988 amounted to $45 billion, this meant that social approval for difficult economic reforms would have to be secured. More was to come. The Poles, the Soviet leadership implied, should open a dialogue with the opposition. Although the Polish Communist leadership was still reluctant to draw Solidarity into discussions, it had no choice. Between 6 February and 4 June 1989 the newly legalised Solidarity trade union, led by Wałęsa, in the course of long debates hammered out conditions under which they would support the government's reforms. As a result of the so-called Round Table Talks free trade unions were legalised. The most important achievement of the talks, fully endorsed by Gorbachev, was the setting up of rules for the process of transformation to a fully democratic political system.

Henceforth a bicameral legislature was established. During the first elections after the Round Table Talks, only 35 per cent of deputies to the Sejm were to be elected freely. Solidarity candidates won all these seats. Jaruzelki became the first President, but Tadeusz Mazowiecki, a well-known intellectual with strong connections with the Catholic Church and one-time adviser to the Gdańsk strikers, became Prime

Minister. The Communist Party in due course transformed itself into a Social Democratic Party, modelled on the West European example.

During the 1990s the political scene in Poland was dominated by parties which emerged from the splintering of the Solidarity movement into political parties with distinct political programmes and trade unions. The first genuinely free general elections were inconclusive. Although a centre and right-wing coalition government was formed, it only survived until 1993. Wałęsa became the first freely elected President in 1990. In a symbolic gesture which was to underline the belief that the Communist period lacked legitimacy, he chose to receive the insignia of the office from the President of the government in exile which still existed in London.

Freedom meant that a whole variety of parties and associations, some with more, others with less clear, programmes emerged. Poles were tangibly intoxicated with the freedom to form their own representation. Thus in addition to the standard parties of the Left, Centre and Right, a Beerdrinkers' Party and the Beekeepers' Association put forward candidates in the general elections of 1991. A party representing the interests of pensioners and those receiving invalidity payments was and still is a powerful player in all party coalition talks.

To Poles the process of transformation from single party state to a pluralist democratic system was difficult, but never violent. Few had the political experience to anticipate the problems which emerged. Still, all agree the political transition has been remarkably stable. Poland now has a well-functioning parliamentary system. The Sejm commands the respect of all parties, including the fringe left- and right-wing ones. Trade unions are slowly learning to refocus from national to workplace issues, where their real role lies.

The Social Demokracja Polski (Polish Social Democrats, SDP) dominates the Left. A smaller Unia Pracy (Union of Work, UP), tends to work closely with the SDP, but is more radical in its demands. The SDP has up to date formed two governments. From the outset it has sought to put a distance between its Communist roots and its present programme, even though all its leaders have impeccable Communist CVs. The party has sought to emulate the moderation and image of established Western Social Democratic parties. It fully supports the free economy and is careful in putting forward proposals for government intervention in fiscal matters. The SDP is unambiguously pro-European. It has fully supported Poland joining NATO. In internal policies it would like to see a larger degree of separation between

Church and state, although in power, it is not willing to pursue that point too vigorously, appreciating that this is a sensitive issue to most Poles.

The Centre and Liberal parties have most probably undergone the most dramatic changes during the 1990s. Initially, both floundered in search for their social base and their own political programme. The present-day Unia Wolnosci (Freedom Union, UW) has emerged from the intellectual wing of the Solidarity movement. Having formed a government after the 1991 elections, their popularity has since collapsed. They have always suffered adversely because of the popular perception that they were solely responsible for the hardship caused by the economic reforms introduced by the then Minister of Finance, Leszek Balcerowicz. However, an attempt to build up a Liberal Party modelled on the West European example, made by Jan Krzysztof Bielecki who was briefly Prime Minister after Mazowiecki's resignation in 1991, was not successful.

The right wing failed to build unity in all Presidential and general elections and that continues to be a source of its major weakness. Doctrinaire divisions into those who are followers of General Piłsudski as opposed to those who subscribe to Dmowski's ideology stand in the way of unity. In addition, a combative Konfederacja Polski Niepodległej (Confederation of Independent Poland, KPN) with a strong following among ex-combatants had mopped up a lot of right-wing votes.

Poland's imminent entry into the European Union has allowed nationalist and patriotic associations to occupy a prominent platform. These tended to fall back onto the well-tried anti-Semitic slogans, to rouse opposition to the EU. In addition to loosely organised skinhead groups which have emerged in parts of Poland blighted by the collapse of previously thriving heavy industries, a small Stronnictwo Narodowe (Nationalist Alliance, SN) tried to make its mark. A Monarchist Party has failed to make headway, though it continues to exist. A populist peasant grouping Samoobrona (Self Help) made its appearance in the mid-1990s but only succeeded in winning seats to the Sejm in the 2001 elections. Its leader Andrzej Lepper is committed to direct action and is a thorn in the side of the parliamentary parties, because of his continuous accusations that the Sejm is corrupt.

The Polskie Stronnictwo Ludowe (Polish Peasant Alliance, PSL) has represented the rural vote since the inter-war period, though during the Communist period it had lost its organisational independence.

Although initially very unhappy about Poland joining the EU, it has come round to supporting it. The party has a wide base, but regional concerns tend to weaken its impact on national politics.

While the Catholic Church continues to declare itself not interested in temporal affairs, it is everything but that. Priests have freely used the pulpit to advise and cajole parishioners to vote in favour of approved parties. The Church had been particularly active during all Presidential elections, taking the initiative in bringing together right-wing parties and giving its open approval to Wałęsa's candidacy during the first and second Presidential elections in 1990 and 1995. In the first case the Church preferred Wałęsa to the intellectual Mazowiecki. During the second Presidential election, the Church, anticipating Wałęsa's defeat, took matters in its own hands and tried to reconcile a number of contenders to the Presidency in order to prevent the election of a widely popular ex-Communist Alexander Kwaśniewski. As it turned out, the Communist background proved to be no impediment to his being elected President on two successive occasions. The Church has since recognised that it had been a mistake to associate so strongly with contenders to political positions. The largest Catholic Party in Poland is the Zjednoczenie Chrześcijańsko Narodowe (Christian Nationalist Association, ZChN).

The Church has been uninhibited in its claim to the monopoly of spiritual leadership of the nation. Not only has it been aggressively pursuing the restoration of all properties confiscated during the post-war period, it has also reclaimed what it considers to be its rightful place in everyday life. Thus in addition to restoring the teaching of the Catholic faith in all schools, priests participate fully in a whole variety of social, ceremonial, state and economic events. A full turn-out of priests in lavish vestments seems to accompany events as disparate as the opening of the new metro station to prize-giving days in schools and institutions. The establishment of Radio Maryja, a Catholic radio station run by a combative and openly anti-Semitic Father Rydzyk, has given the fundamentalist sections of the Church a mouthpiece for some of its worst prejudices. To them secularism, Aids and the EU represent the sins which Western Europe is inflicting upon Poland. The present Sejm contains a vocal group of supporters of Radio Maryja. In the community, the Church has fought a successful battle against any form of sex education, against family planning and abortion. In smaller towns, the Church's stranglehold over these matters is total. Defiance of the Church's teaching on those issues can result in public humiliation during sermons or the priest's refusal to officiate at christenings, weddings or burials of the ungodly. At the other end of the spectrum in the Catholic hierarchy, Primate Glemp and the previous Secretary to the Episcopate Father Pieronek have condemned the expression of continuing anti-Semitic views by priests and prominent Catholics, and have come round to expressing approval for Poland's entry into the EU. In that they are echoing the Pope's own declarations that it is Poland's duty to join Europe.

On two occasions insensitive treatment of Jewish demands for the removal of symbols of the Christian faith from the site of the Oświęcim concentration camp attracted adverse international attention and has drawn the Pope into the debate. More recently, revelations concerning the Jedwabne killings during the war has led to an open breach between the Church hierarchy, which led prayers of contrition and reconciliation with the Jewish community, and the priest of the town of Jedwabne, who publicly and vocally maintains that the Jews were fully responsible for the fate which befell them.

The Presidency still remains an important function in present-day politics. Wałęsa, in spite of his invaluable contribution to the establishment and leadership of the Solidarity movement during the Communist period, proved to be a disastrous President from 1991 until 1996. Poles quickly turned against him when it became clear that he lacked the demeanour required by the representative position of the President. He developed a conviction that Poland's transition from Communism to capitalism was entirely due to his efforts. During celebrations commemorating the tenth anniversary of the Gdańsk strikes, he refused to allow any of the other Solidarity leaders to share the limelight. His unwillingness to invite Anna Walentynowicz was seen as particularly mean. He did not work well with the Sejm, and was out of his depth at international gatherings. One of his biggest failings has been an inability to create a Christian Centrist Party, which it was always presumed would have a strong following in Poland. Kwaśniewski was re-elected during the 2001 Presidential elections, and continues to be Poland's most popular politician. In spite of his earlier commitment to the Social Democratic Party, he has worked well with all parties, even during the period when a Solidarity-led coalition, hostile to him, formed a government after the 1996 general elections.

The process of transformation from Communism to parliamentary democracy and from a command to market-oriented economy has created opportunities for some, while destroying the achievements of others. This accounts for the Poles' ambivalence towards Poland joining the European Union (EU), the benefits of which they have still to see. During the 1990s Polish steel, coalmining and shipbuilding, all industries that had been favoured by the Communists, were affected by the world industrial recession. This has created unemployment and insecurity, which has in turn led to bitterness among some earlier supporters of the Solidarity movement. The Polish state farms, which in most cases were very inefficient but which nevertheless provided employment and a basic standard of living for whole communities, have in virtually all cases gone bankrupt. Since most of the ex-employees of the state farms have not been able to move elsewhere in search of employment, they remain stranded in housing settlements deep in the countryside. They support the fringe parties, notably the Samoobrona movement, which is critical of Poland's entry into the EU.

For most Poles, though, freedom has brought benefits. In the first place the freeing of restrictions of economic activities led to stalls, shops and workshops opening everywhere. In the early 1990s all public places were crammed with every sort of small-scale trade. The state has now established control over these activities. The entry into the EU has required Poland to introduce appropriate legislation and to regulate all aspects of economic activities. Surprisingly, considering the Poles' general distrust of central authorities, these have not been opposed.

Poland's entry into the EU will bring it closer to the West European world and with that Poland will be subject to standardisation of economic and social activities. As is already apparent, Poles will be more exposed to all that the West can provide, from fast food outlets to Western music and cinema. Inevitably so much of what was unique to Poland will become less distinct.

Index